Ajax For Dummies®

D0725052

Configuring an XMLHttpRequest object

To configure an XMLHttpRequest object in JavaScript for use with a particular URL:

```
XMLHttpRequestObject.open("GET", url);
```

Fe...

To ma... the browser fetch data from the URL you've configured the XMLHttpRequest object for, use this JavaScript:

```
XMLHttpRequestObject.send(null);
```

Creating an XMLHttpRequest object

To create an XMLHttpRequest object in JavaScript:

```
var XMLHttpRequestObject = false;
if (window.XMLHttpRequest) {
  XMLHttpRequestObject = new XMLHttpRequest();
} else if (window.ActiveXObject) {
  XMLHttpRequestObject = new ActiveXObject("Microsoft.XMLHTTP");
}
```

Setting up the callback function

To create a function that will be called back when your data has been fetched:

```
XMLHttpRequestObject.onreadystatechange = function()

{

  if (XMLHttpRequestObject.readyState == 4 &&
    XMLHttpRequestObject.status == 200) {

      //Handle XMLHttpRequestObject.responseText or

      //Handle XMLHttpRequestObject.responseXML here.

  }

}
```

Important XMLHttpRequest object properties

- ✔ onreadystatechange: Contains the name of the event handler that should be called when the value of the readyState property changes. Read/write.
- ✔ readyState: Contains the current state of the request. Read-only.
- ✔ responseText: Contains the downloaded data as a string. Read-only.
- ✔ responseXML: Contains the downloaded data as XML. Read-only.
- ✔ status: Contains the HTTP status code returned by a request. Read-only.

For Dummies: Bestselling Book Series for Beginners

Ajax For Dummies®

Important XMLHttpRequest object methods

- **abort**: Aborts the request.
- **open**: Opens a request to the server.
- **send**: Sends a request to the server.

The readyState values

The XMLHttpRequest object's readyState property tells you how the download of your data is going. Here are the possible values (note that a value of 4 means your data is all downloaded):

- 0 uninitialized
- 1 loading
- 2 loaded
- 3 interactive
- 4 complete

The Ajax Gold framework functions

Here are the JavaScript functions of the Ajax Gold framework:

- getDataReturnText(url, callback): Uses the GET method to get text from the server.
- getDataReturnXml(url, callback): Uses the GET method to get XML from the server.
- postDataReturnText(url, data, callback): Uses the POST method to send data to the server. It also gets text back from the server.
- postDataReturnXml(url, data, callback): Uses the POST method to send data to the server. It also gets XML back from the server.

Important status values

The XMLHttpRequest object's status property holds the status of the download itself, using the standard HTTP status codes that browsers get from servers. Here are some of the possible values (a value of 200 means everything is okay):

- 200 OK
- 204 No Content
- 400 Bad Request
- 401 Unauthorized
- 403 Forbidden
- 404 Not Found
- 407 Proxy Authentication Required
- 408 Request Timeout
- 411 Length Required
- 413 Requested Data Entity Too Large
- 414 Requested URL Too Long
- 415 Unsupported Media Type
- 500 Internal Server Error
- 503 Service Unavailable
- 504 Gateway Timeout

For Dummies: Bestselling Book Series for Beginners

by Steve Holzner, PhD

WILEY

Wiley Publishing, Inc.

Ajax For Dummies®

Published by
Wiley Publishing, Inc.
111 River Street
Hoboken, NJ 07030-5774
www.wiley.com

Copyright © 2006 by Wiley Publishing, Inc., Indianapolis, Indiana

Published by Wiley Publishing, Inc., Indianapolis, Indiana

Published simultaneously in Canada

For general information on our other products and services, please contact our Customer Care Department within the U.S. at 800-762-2974, outside the U.S. at 317-572-3993, or fax 317-572-4002.

For technical support, please visit www.wiley.com/techsupport.

Wiley also publishes its books in a variety of electronic formats. Some content that appears in print may not be available in electronic books.

Library of Congress Control Number: 2005937352

ISBN-13: 978-0-471-78597-2

ISBN-10: 0-471-78597-0

Manufactured in the United States of America

10 9 8 7 6 5 4 3 2

1B/QY/QS/QW/IN

WILEY

About the Author

Steve Holzner is the award-winning author of nearly 100 computer books. His books have sold more than 2 million copies and have been translated into 18 languages around the world. He specializes in online topics, especially Ajax, and he has long done commercial Ajax programming.

Dedication

To Nancy, of course!

Publisher's Acknowledgments

We're proud of this book; please send us your comments through our online registration form located at www.dummies.com/register/.

Some of the people who helped bring this book to market include the following:

Acquisitions, Editorial, and Media Development

Senior Project Editor: Paul Levesque

Acquisitions Editor: Katie Feltman

Copy Editors: Virginia Sanders, Heidi Unger

Technical Editor: Vanessa Williams

Editorial Manager: Leah Cameron

Media Development Specialists: Angela Denny, Kate Jenkins, Steven Kudirka, Kit Malone, Travis Silvers

Media Development Coordinator: Laura Atkinson

Media Project Supervisor: Laura Moss

Media Development Manager: Laura VanWinkle

Media Development Associate Producer: Richard Graves

Editorial Assistant: Amanda Foxworth

Cartoons: Rich Tennant (www.the5thwave.com)

Composition Services

Project Coordinator: Maridee Ennis

Layout and Graphics: Carl Byers, Andrea Dahl, Barbara Moore, Lynsey Osborn

Proofreaders: Leeann Harney, Jessica Kramer, TECHBOOKS Production Services

Indexer: TECHBOOKS Production Services

Special Help
Becky Huehls, Elizabeth Kuball

Publishing and Editorial for Technology Dummies

Richard Swadley, Vice President and Executive Group Publisher

Andy Cummings, Vice President and Publisher

Mary Bednarek, Executive Acquisitions Director

Mary C. Corder, Editorial Director

Publishing for Consumer Dummies

Diane Graves Steele, Vice President and Publisher

Joyce Pepple, Acquisitions Director

Composition Services

Gerry Fahey, Vice President of Production Services

Debbie Stailey, Director of Composition Services

Contents at a Glance

Table of Contents

Introduction

Making Web applications look and feel like desktop applications is what this book is all about — that's what Ajax does. Although Web development is getting more and more popular, users still experience the nasty part of having to click a button, wait until a new page loads, click another button, wait until a new page loads, and so on.

That's where Ajax comes in. With Ajax, you communicate with the server behind the scenes, grab the data you want and display it instantly in a Web page — no page refreshes needed, no flickering in the browser, no waiting. That's a big deal, because at last it lets Web applications start to look like desktop applications. With today's faster connections, grabbing data from the server is usually a snap, so Web software can have the same look and feel of software on the user's desktop.

And that, in a nutshell, is going to be the future of Web programming — now the applications in your browser can look and work just like the applications installed on your computer. No wonder Ajax is the hottest topic to come along in years.

About This Book

This book gives you the whole Ajax story, from soup to nuts. It starts with a tour of how Ajax is used today, taking a look at some cutting-edge applications (as well as some games). Then, because Ajax is based on using JavaScript in the browser, there's a chapter on how to use JavaScript (if you already know JavaScript, feel free to skip that material).

Then the book plunges into Ajax itself, creating Ajax applications from scratch, from the beginning level to the most advanced. And you'll see how to put many of the free Ajax *frameworks*, which do the programming for you, to work. Because Ajax also often involves using XML, Cascading Style Sheets (CSS), and server-side programming (using PHP in this book), there's also a chapter on each of these topics.

You can also leaf through this book as you like, rather than having to read it from beginning to end. Like other *For Dummies* books, this one has been designed to let you skip around as much as possible. You don't have to read the chapters in order if you don't want to. This is your book, and Ajax is your oyster.

Conventions Used in This Book

Some books have a dozen dizzying conventions that you need to know before you can even start. Not this one. All you need to know is that new terms are given in italics, like *this*, the first time they're discussed. And that when new lines of code are introduced, they're displayed in bold:

```
function getDataReturnText(url, callback)
{
  var XMLHttpRequestObject = false;

  if (window.XMLHttpRequest) {
    XMLHttpRequestObject = new XMLHttpRequest();
  } else if (window.ActiveXObject) {
    XMLHttpRequestObject = new
      ActiveXObject("Microsoft.XMLHTTP");
  }
        .
        .
        .
}
```

Note also that code that's been omitted has been indicated with three vertical dots. That's all there is to the notation in this book.

Foolish Assumptions

I don't assume that you have knowledge of JavaScript when you start to read this book, but you do have to know JavaScript to understand Ajax. Chapter 2 presents all the JavaScript you'll need in this book.

Also, Ajax often involves some server-side programming, and this book, as most books on Ajax do, uses PHP for that. You won't need to know a lot of PHP here, and what PHP there is is pretty self-explanatory, because it's a lot like JavaScript. However, there's a whole chapter on PHP, Chapter 10, and you can always dip into it at any time.

However, you should have some HTML prowess — enough to create and upload to your server basic Web pages. If you feel shaky on that point, take a look at a good book on HTML, such as *HTML 4 For Dummies,* 5th Edition, by Ed Tittel and Mary Burmeister (published by Wiley).

How This Book Is Organized

Here are the various parts that are coming up in this book.

Part I: Getting Started

Chapters 1 and 2 get you started on your tour of Ajax. Here, you get an overview of how Ajax is used today, and what it has to offer. There are many applications available that use Ajax, and you see a good sampling in this part. Then you get a solid grounding in JavaScript, the programming language Ajax is built on. (If you're already a JavaScript Meister, feel free to skip this material.) To use Ajax, you have to use JavaScript, and in this part, you build the foundation that the rest of the book is based on.

Part II: Programming in Ajax

In Chapters 3 and 4, you delve into Ajax programming for real. Here, you see how to grab data from the server — whether that data is plain text or XML — and how to put that data to work. To illustrate how these techniques work, you see plenty of examples using Ajax, Dynamic HTML to update Web pages without needing a page refresh, and even advanced techniques like connecting to Google behind the scenes for real-time same-page Web searches. At last but not least, you find out how to support multiple Ajax requests to your server at the same time.

Part III: Ajax Frameworks

Ajax can involve a lot of programming involved, and Part III takes a look at some of the many shortcuts that are available. Rather than reinventing the wheel yourself, you can use the Ajax *frameworks*. These frameworks are free and do most of the programming for you, so you'll definitely want to check out this part. You can find all kinds of Ajax techniques, such as using Ajax for drag-and-drop operations, pop-up menus, downloading images behind the scenes, and more.

Part IV: In-Depth Ajax Power

Chapters 8 to 10 give you even more of the Ajax story. Chapter 8 is all about working with XML in JavaScript, and that's what you often do in Ajax. In this chapter, you discover how to deal with XML documents that can get pretty complex, extracting the data you want, when you want it.

Chapter 9 gives you the story on Cascading Style Sheets (CSS), which offer all kinds of options (such as creating pop-up menus) to display the data you fetch from the server using Ajax techniques. Because using Ajax means displaying data in a Web page without a page reload, using CSS is a big part of Ajax programming.

Chapter 10 is about another big part of Ajax programming — writing code for the server so that you can send data back from the server to the browser. Like most Ajax books and Ajax samples you can find on the Internet, this book uses PHP on the server. You won't need to know PHP to read this book, but it'll help when you start using Ajax yourself, so Chapter 10 gives you a foundation in writing and working with PHP.

Part V: The Part of Tens

No *For Dummies* is complete without a Part of Tens. Chapter 11 is all about ten Ajax design issues you're going to run into — and what to do about them. For example, working with web pages interactively, as Ajax does, means that the browser's Back button isn't going to work if the user wants to undo a recent update. You'll find some of the solutions that have been attempted discussed in Chapter 11.

Chapter 12 introduces you to ten essential Ajax resources. Knowing where to find these resources, and the Google groups and Ajax discussions on the Internet, will let you join the worldwide Ajax community.

Icons Used in This Book

You'll find a handful of icons in this book, and here's what they mean:

Tips point out a handy shortcut or help you understand something important to Ajax programming.

This icon marks something to remember, such as how you handle a particularly tricky part of Ajax.

 This icon means that what follows is technical, insider stuff. You don't have to read it if you don't want to, but if you want to become an Ajax pro (and who doesn't?), take a look.

 Although the Warning icon appears rarely, when you need to be wary of a problem or common pitfall, this icon lets you know.

 This icon lets you know that there are some pretty cool Web resources out there just waiting for you to peruse. (In fact, one little corner of the Net, www.dummies.com/go/ajax, has the code for this book available for free download.)

Where to Go from Here

Alright, you're all set and ready to jump into Chapter 1. You don't have to start there; you can jump in anywhere you like — the book was written to allow you to do just that. But if you want to get the full story from the beginning, jump into Chapter 1 first — that's where all the action starts. (If you're familiar with what Ajax is and are already quick with JavaScript, you might want to flip to Chapter 3 to start tinkering with the code that makes Ajax go.)

Part I
Getting Started

The 5th Wave   By Rich Tennant

"I can't really explain it, but every time I animate someone swinging a golf club, a little divot of code comes up missing on the home page."

In this part . . .

This part introduces you to Ajax. You get a guided tour of the Ajax world here, and you get a chance to see how Ajax is used today. A good sampling of Ajax applications are on view in Chapter 1, just waiting for you to check them out for yourself so you can see what Ajax has to offer. From autocomplete and live searches to Google Maps, I pack a lot of Ajax in here. Next comes Chapter 2, which provides the JavaScript foundation that the rest of the book relies on. If you already know JavaScript, feel free to skip that material, but otherwise, take a look. Ajax is built on JavaScript, so you want to make sure you've got all the JavaScript you need under your belt before going forward.

Chapter 1

Ajax 101

*W*e aren't getting enough orders on our Web site," storms the CEO. "People just don't like clicking all those buttons and waiting for a new page all the time. It's too distracting."

"How about a simpler solution?" you ask. "What if people could stay on the same page and just drag the items they want to buy to a shopping cart? No page refreshes, no fuss, no muss."

"You mean people wouldn't have to navigate from page to page to add items to a shopping cart and then check out? Customers could do everything on a single Web page?"

"Yep," you say. "And that page would automatically let our software on the server know what items the customer had purchased — all without having to reload the Web page."

"I love it!" the CEO says. "What's it called?"

"Ajax," you say.

Welcome to the world of Ajax, the technology that lets Web software act like desktop software. One of the biggest problems with traditional Web applications is that they have that "Web" feel — you have to keep clicking buttons to move from page to page, and watch the screen flicker as your browser loads a new Web page.

Ajax is here to take care of that issue, because it enables you grab data from the server without reloading new pages into the browser.

How Does Ajax Work?

With Ajax, Web applications finally start feeling like desktop applications to your users. That's because Ajax enables your Web applications to work behind the scenes, getting data as they need it, and displaying that data as you want. And as more and more people get fast Internet connections, working behind the scenes to access data is going to become all the rage. Soon, it'll be impossible to distinguish dedicated desktop software from software that's actually on the Internet, far from the user's machine. To help you understand how Ajax works, the following sections look at Ajax from a user's and a programmer's perspective.

A user's perspective

To show you how Ajax makes Web applications more like desktop applications, I'll use a simple Web search as an example. When you open a typical search engine, you see a text box where you type a search term. So say you type Ajax XML because you're trying to figure out what XML has to do with Ajax. Then, you click a Search the Web button to start the search. After that, the browser flickers, and a new page is loaded with your search results.

That's okay as far as it goes — but now take a look at an Ajax-enabled version of Yahoo! search. To see for yourself, go to `http://openrico.org/rico/yahooSearch.page`. When you enter your search term(s) and click Search Yahoo!, the page doesn't refresh; instead, the search results just appear in the box, as shown in Figure 1-1.

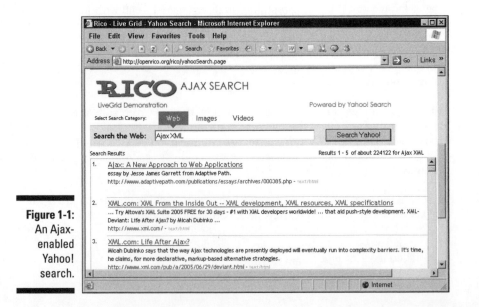

Figure 1-1:
An Ajax-
enabled
Yahoo!
search.

That's the Ajax difference. In the first case, you got a new page with search results, but to see more than ten results, a user has to keep loading pages. In the second case, everything happens on the same page. No page reloads, no fuss, no muss.

You can find plenty of Ajax on the `http://openrico.org` Web site. If you're inclined to, browse around and discover all the good stuff there.

A developer's perspective

In the article "Ajax: A New Approach to Web Applications" (`www.adaptive path.com/publications/essays/archives/000385.php`), Jesse James Garrett, who was the first to call this technology Ajax, made important insights about how it could change the Web. He noted that although innovative new projects are typically online, Web programmers still feel that the rich capabilities of desktop software were out of their reach. But Ajax is closing the gap.

So how does Ajax do its stuff? The name *Ajax* is short for Asynchronous JavaScript and XML, and it's made up of several components:

- ✔ Browser-based presentation using HTML and Cascading Style Sheets (CSS)
- ✔ Data stored in XML format and fetched from the server
- ✔ Behind-the-scenes data fetches using `XMLHttpRequest` objects in the browser
- ✔ JavaScript to make everything happen

JavaScript is the scripting language that nearly all browsers support, which will let you fetch data behind the scenes, and XML is the popular language that lets you store data in an easy format. Here's an overview of how Ajax works:

1. In the browser, you write code in JavaScript that can fetch data from the server as needed.

2. When more data is needed from the server, the JavaScript uses a special item supported by browsers, the `XMLHttpRequest` object, to send a request to the server behind the scenes — without causing a page refresh.

   The JavaScript in the browser doesn't have to stop everything to wait for that data to come back from the server. It can wait for the data in the background and spring into action when the data does appear (that's called *asynchronous* data retrieval).

3. The data that comes back from the server can be XML (more on XML in Chapters 2 and 8), or just plain text if you prefer. The JavaScript code in the browser can read that data and put it to work immediately.

That's how Ajax works — it uses JavaScript in the browser and the `XMLHttpRequest` object to communicate with the server without page refreshes, and handles the XML (or other text) data sent back from the server. In Chapter 3, I explain how all these components work together in more detail.

This also points out what you'll need to develop Web pages with Ajax. You'll add JavaScript code to your Web page to fetch data from the server (I cover JavaScript in Chapter 2), and you'll need to store data and possibly write server-side code to interact with the browser behind the scenes. In other words, you're going to need access to an online server where you can store the data that you will fetch using Ajax. Besides just storing data on the server, you might want to put code on the server that your JavaScript can interact with. For example, a popular server-side language is PHP, and many of the examples in this book show how you can connect to PHP scripts on Web servers by using Ajax. (Chapter 10 is a PHP primer, getting you up to speed on that language if you're interested.) So you're going to need a Web server to store your data on, and if you want to run server-side programs as well, your server has to support server-side coding for the language you want to work with (such as PHP).

What Can You Do with Ajax?

The technology for Ajax has been around since 1998, and a handful of applications (such as Microsoft's Outlook Web Access) have already put it to use. But Ajax didn't really catch on until early 2005, when a couple of high-profile Web applications (such as Google Suggest and Google Maps, both reviewed later in this chapter) put it to work, and Jesse James Garrett wrote his article coining the term Ajax and so putting everything under one roof.

Since then, Ajax has exploded as people have realized that Web software can finally start acting like desktop software. What can you do with Ajax? That's what the rest of this chapter is about.

Searching in real time with live searches

One of the truly cool things you can do with Ajax is live searching, where you get search results instantly, as you enter the term you're searching for. For example, take a look at `http://www.google.com/webhp?complete=1 &hl=en`, the page which appears in Figure 1-2. As you enter a term to search for, Ajax contacts Google behind the scenes, and you see a drop-down menu that displays common search terms from Google that might match what you're typing. If you want to select one of those terms, just click it in the menu. That's all there is to it.

You can also write an Ajax application that connects to Google in this way behind the scenes. Chapter 4 has all the details.

Figure 1-2:
A Google
live search.

Getting the answer with autocomplete

Closely allied to live search applications are autocomplete applications, which try to guess the word you're entering by getting a list of similar words from the server and displaying them. You can see an example at `www.paper mountain.org/demos/live`, which appears in Figure 1-3.

As you enter a word, this example looks up words that might match in a dictionary on the server and displays them, as you see in Figure 1-3. If you see the right one, just click it to enter it in the text field, saving you some typing.

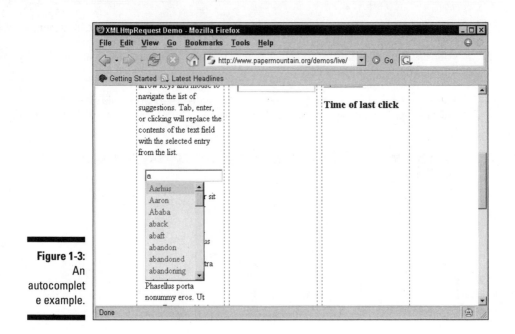

Figure 1-3:
An
autocomplet
e example.

Chatting with friends

Because Ajax excels at updating Web pages without refreshing the displayed
page, it's a great choice for Web-based chat programs, where many users can
chat together at the same time. Take a look at `www.plasticshore.com/
projects/chat`, for example, which you can see in Figure 1-4. Here, you just
enter your text and click the Submit button to send that text to the server. All
the while, you can see everyone else currently chatting — no page refresh
needed.

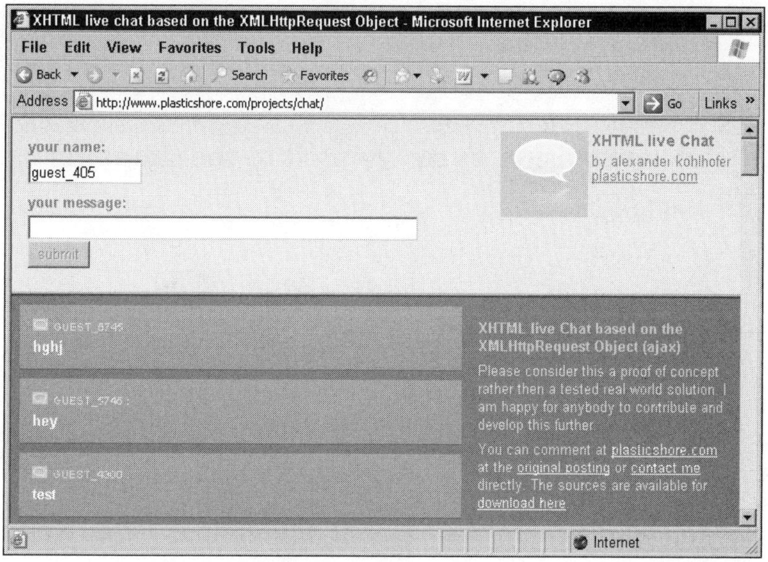

Figure 1-4:
An Ajax-based chat application.

There are plenty of Ajax-based chat rooms around. Take a look at
`http://treehouse.ofb.net/chat/?lang=en` for another example.

Dragging and dropping with Ajax

At the beginning of this chapter, I mention a drag-and-drop shopping cart example. As shown in Figure 1-5, when the user drags the television to the shopping cart in the lower-right, the server is notified that the user bought a television. Then the server sends back the text that appears in the upper left, "You just bought a nice television." You find out how to create this shopping cart in Chapter 6.

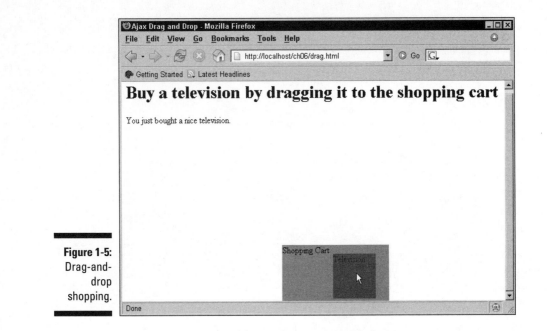

Figure 1-5:
Drag-and-
drop
shopping.

Gaming with Ajax

Here's a cute one — a magic diary that answers you back using Ajax techniques, as shown in Figure 1-6. You can find it at `http://pandorabots.com/`
`pandora/talk?botid=c96f911b3e35f9e1`. When you type something,
such as "Hello," the server is notified and sends back an appropriate
response that then appears in the diary, such as "Hi there!"

Or how about a game of chess, via Ajax? Take a look at `www.jesperolsen.`
`net/PChess`, where you can move the pieces around (and the software on
the server can, too) thanks to Ajax.

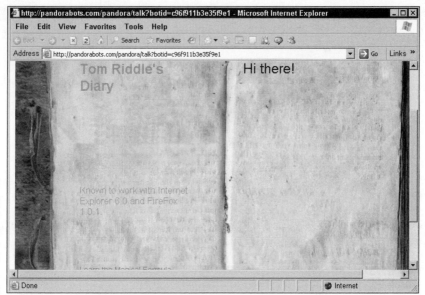

Figure 1-6:
An
interactive
Ajax-
enabled
diary.

Getting instant login feedback

Another Internet task that can involve many annoying page refreshes is log-
ging in to a site. If you type the wrong login name, for example, you get a new
page explaining the problem, have to log in on another page, and so on. How
about getting instant feedback on your login attempt, courtesy of Ajax?
That's possible, too. Take a look at `www.jamesdam.com/ajax_login/`
`login.html`, which appears in Figure 1-7. I've entered an incorrect username
and password, and the application says so immediately. You'll see how to
write a login application like this in Chapter 4.

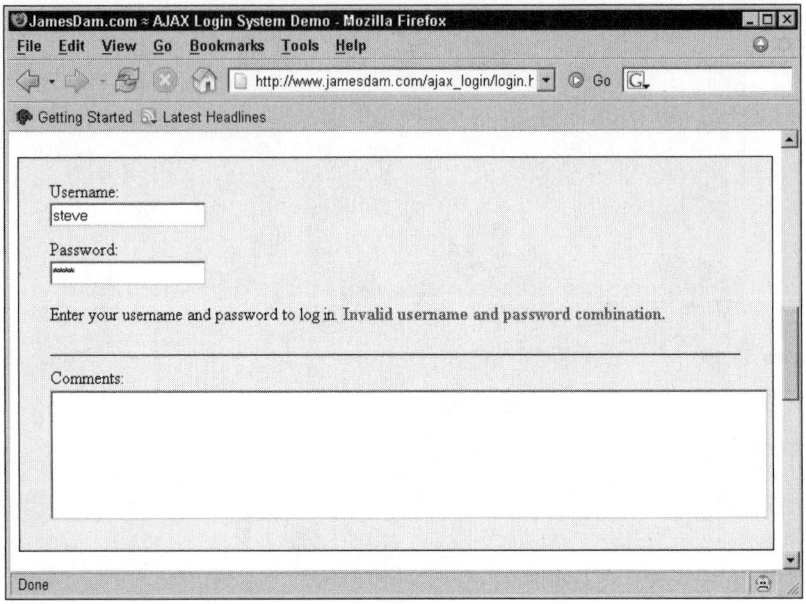

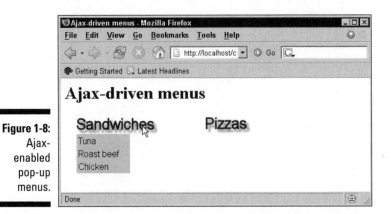

Figure 1-7:
Ajax makes
correcting
login
mistakes
easier.

Ajax-enabled pop-up menus

You can grab data from the server as soon as the user needs it using Ajax. For example, take a look at the application in Figure 1-8, which I explain how to build in Chapter 9. The pop-up menus appear when you move the mouse and display text retrieved from the server using Ajax techniques. By accessing the server, Ajax allows you to set up an interactive menu system that responds to the menu choices the user has already made.

Figure 1-8:
Ajax-
enabled
pop-up
menus.

Modifying Web pages on the fly

Ajax excels at updating Web pages on the fly without page refreshes, and you can find hundreds of Ajax applications doing exactly that. For example, take a look at the Ajax rolodex at `http://openrico.org/rico/demos.page?demo=ricoAjaxInnerHTML.html`, shown in Figure 1-9. When you click someone's name, a "card" appears with their full data.

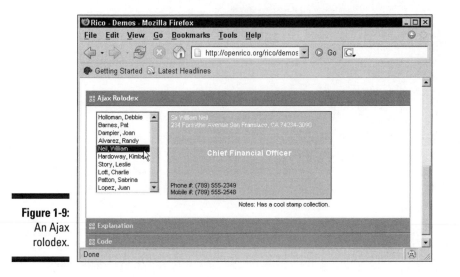

Figure 1-9:
An Ajax
rolodex.

You can see another example at `http://digg.com/spy`. This news Web site uses Ajax techniques to update itself periodically by adding new article titles to the list on the page.

Updating the HTML in a Web page by fetching data is a very popular Ajax technique, and you see a lot of it in Chapters 3 and 4.

Google Maps and Ajax

One of the most famous Ajax application is Google Maps, at `http://maps.google.com`, which you can see at work in Figure 1-10, zooming in on South Market Street in Boston.

Figure 1-10:
Using
Google
maps.

See that marker icon near the center of the map? The location for that marker is passed to the browser from the server using Ajax techniques, and the Ajax code in the browser positions the marker accordingly. Ajax at work again!

When Is Ajax a Good Choice?

The examples I show in the preceding section are just the beginning — dozens more, including those you can write yourself, appear in later chapters. Got a Web application that asks the user to move from page to page and therefore needs to be improved? That's a job for Ajax.

Chapter 2

It's All About JavaScript

So what is this Ajax thing, anyway? You've heard that it's a great way to combine some of the Web languages you're familiar with (such as HTML, XML, CSS, and JavaScript) to create a Web application that looks and works like a seamless desktop application. But you want to know much more, and you've come to the right place.

As you might have heard, Ajax is based on JavaScript. And because you need a good foundation in JavaScript to use Ajax (and to follow many chapters in this book), this chapter is all about working with this scripting language. This book might show you how to do things you've never done before — even if you've been using JavaScript for a while. So get ready for a crash course in JavaScript. If you think you already have a solid grounding in JavaScript, feel free to jump right into working with Ajax in Chapter 3.

Taking a First Look at Ajax in Action

Here's an sample Ajax application that demonstrates what kind of JavaScript you'll be seeing throughout the book. Take a look at Figure 2-1; that Web page displays a message `The fetched data will go here`. That text is going to change when you click the Display Message button, and no new page fetch will be required.

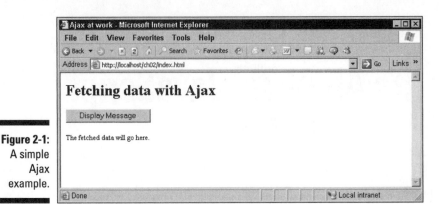

Figure 2-1:
A simple
Ajax
example.

To replace the text by using Ajax methods, just click the button now. The browser won't flicker. All you'll see is the displayed text change to `This text was fetched using Ajax.`, as shown in Figure 2-2.

Figure 2-2:
You can
fetch text
with Ajax.

That kind of a change is nothing unusual in Web development — as long as the text was stored locally in a script built into the Web page, for example. But that text wasn't stored locally; it came from a simple text file named `data.txt`, stored on the server. And the browser fetched that text by using Ajax methods.

When you download the example code for this book from the companion Web site, you'll find the examples stored in folders chapter by chapter. The page you see in Figure 2-1 is `index.html` in the ch02 folder, and the data file that holds the text fetched from the server is stored in the file `data.txt`, which is also in the ch02 folder. To run this example, all you need to do is upload the `index.html` and `data.txt` files to the same directory on your Web server. Then navigate to `index.html` in your browser as you would any other Web page. The URL looks something like this: `http://www.your domain.com/yourname/index.html`. If you already have an `index.html` file, you might want to change the name of this one to something like `ajax example.html` to avoid conflicts — the example will still run as before.

Taking a look at the code

So what does the JavaScript code for this example look like? Listing 2-1 shows you what's in `index.html`. Notice that there's a healthy amount of JavaScript here. As you find out in Chapter 3, you have a number of different ways of making JavaScript do what it has to do. So the code I show in Listing 2-1 is just one way to write it.

Listing 2-1:   Getting Ajax to Work

```html
<html>
  <head>
    <title>Ajax at work</title>

    <script language = "javascript">
      var XMLHttpRequestObject = false;

      if (window.XMLHttpRequest) {
        XMLHttpRequestObject = new XMLHttpRequest();
      } else if (window.ActiveXObject) {
        XMLHttpRequestObject = new ActiveXObject("Microsoft.XMLHTTP");
      }

      function getData(dataSource, divID)
      {
        if(XMLHttpRequestObject) {
          var obj = document.getElementById(divID);
          XMLHttpRequestObject.open("GET", dataSource);

          XMLHttpRequestObject.onreadystatechange = function()
          {
            if (XMLHttpRequestObject.readyState == 4 &&
              XMLHttpRequestObject.status == 200) {
                obj.innerHTML = XMLHttpRequestObject.responseText;
            }
          }
          XMLHttpRequestObject.send(null);
        }
      }
    </script>
  </head>

  <body>
```

(continued)

Listing 2-1 (continued)

```
<H1>Fetching data with Ajax</H1>

<form>
  <input type = "button" value = "Display Message"
    onclick = "getData('http://localhost/ch01/data.txt',
    'targetDiv')">
</form>

<div id="targetDiv">
  <p>The fetched data will go here.</p>
</div>

</body>
</html>
```

The other file is `data.txt`, and here's all the text it contains:

```
This text was fetched using Ajax.
```

That's the code for your first Ajax example. If you want to be an ace number one Ajax programmer (and who doesn't?), you have to have a firm grasp on the JavaScript. Many Web developers coming to Ajax for the first time don't know as much JavaScript as they're going to need, so the rest of this chapter is dedicated to helping you get that essential JavaScript foundation.

Delving deeper into JavaScript

This chapter doesn't try to cover all there is to know about JavaScript, but it does cover what you need to know before you turn to the following chapters on Ajax programming. In this chapter, I explain all the JavaScript you need in order to work your way through this book. For more information on JavaScript, track down some of the tutorials on the Web, such as the one at `www.w3schools.com/js/js_intro.asp`, or take a look at a good JavaScript book, such as *JavaScript For Dummies,* 4th Edition, by Emily A. Vander Veer (Wiley Publishing, Inc.).

Enter JavaScript

Despite its name, JavaScript has little to do with Java. It all began at Netscape Communications Corporation in 1995 when a developer named Brendan Eich was assigned to the task of making Navigator's newly added Java support more accessible to non-Java programmers. He called his creation *LiveScript,* but ultimately renamed it *JavaScript,* even though it really didn't resemble the Java programming language at all.

Examining the standards

So where are all these standards? You can find the JavaScript 1.5 user's guide at `http://web.archive.org/web/20040211195031/devedge.netscape.com/library/manuals/2000/javascript/1.5/guide`. And you can find the documentation for JScript 5.6 online as well at `http://msdn.microsoft.com/library/default.asp?url=/library/en-us/script56/html/js56jsoriJScript.asp`. The ECMAScript specifications are also online:

✔ **ECMAScript Language Specification, 3rd Edition:** `http://www.ecma-international.org/publications/standards/Ecma-262.htm`

✔ **ECMAScript Components Specification:** `http://www.ecma-international.org/publications/standards/Ecma-290.htm`

✔ **ECMAScript 3rd Edition Compact Profile Specification:** `http://www.ecma-international.org/publications/standards/Ecma-327.htm`

JavaScript was fun and allowed all kinds of visual tricks, such as rollover images and text, which change when the viewer rolls the mouse over them. As JavaScript became more popular, Netscape's chief competitor, Microsoft, decided it could no longer ignore this new language. Microsoft decided to create its own version of JavaScript, which it called JScript.

And so began the cross-browser wars that have made life for JavaScript programmers so interesting ever since. Programmers started to find that although JScript looked just like JavaScript, some scripts would run in Netscape and not in Internet Explorer, and vice versa.

Hoping to stave off some of the chaos, Netscape and Sun turned to the European Computer Manufacturers Association (ECMA) to standardize JavaScript, and the standardized version is called ECMAScript.

JavaScript is converging among browsers now, and at least the core part of the language matches ECMAScript version 3.0. Some differences still exist, as you see later in this book, but the situation is far better than it used to be.

Creating a script

It's time to get started slinging JavaScript around. If you want to write JavaScript, you put that JavaScript in a `<script>` element like this:

```
<html>
  <head>
    <title>A First Script</title>
```

```
   <script language="javascript">
       .
       .
       .
   </script>
 </head>

 <body>
   <h1>A First Script</h1>
 </body>
</html>
```

This `<script>` element uses the `language` attribute to indicate that the language of the enclosed script is JavaScript, as you see here.

Accessing the Web page from JavaScript

Suppose you want to write the message `You're using JavaScript` to a Web page by using JavaScript. How do you access the Web page from your script?

In JavaScript, you access the Web page and the browser itself with a variety of built-in objects. The available objects include `document` (which refers to a Web page), `window` (which refers to the browser window), and `history` (which refers to a history list that lets the browser navigate forward and backward).

Each of these objects includes *methods* and *properties*. You can *call* a method to make something happen (like writing to a Web page) and *set* the value of a property to configure those objects (like setting the background color of a Web page). Here are examples of a few useful object methods and the tasks they perform:

✔ `document.write`: Writes text to the current Web page.

✔ `history.go`: Navigates the Web browser to a location in the browser's history.

✔ `window.open`: Opens a new browser window.

Here are a few of the useful properties you can set for these methods:

✔ `document.bgcolor`: Background color of the current page.

✔ `document.fgcolor`: Foreground color of the current page.

✔ `document.lastmodified`: Date the page was last modified.

✔ `document.title`: Title of the current page.

> ✔ `location.hostname`: Name of the Internet service provider (ISP) host.
>
> ✔ `navigator.appName`: Name of the browser, which you can use to determine what browser the visitor is using.

You now have the tools to write that welcome message. You use the `document.write` method and embed your JavaScript in HTML. Here is a first example of writing text to a Web page:

```html
<html>
  <head>
    <title>A First Script</title>
    <script language="javascript">
      document.write("You're using JavaScript");
    </script>
  </head>

  <body>
    <h1>A First Script</h1>
  </body>
</html>
```

In this case, you are passing the text `You're using JavaScript` to the document object's `write` method. The `write` method will display that text on the Web page, no worries.

Type the preceding HTML into a new file and save it as `firstscript.html` or download `firstscript.html` from the ch02 folder on the companion Web site. Open the file in your browser. As shown in Figure 2-3, this page uses JavaScript to write a message to the Web page when that page loads.

Excellent — `firstscript.html` is a complete success, and everything's off to a good start.

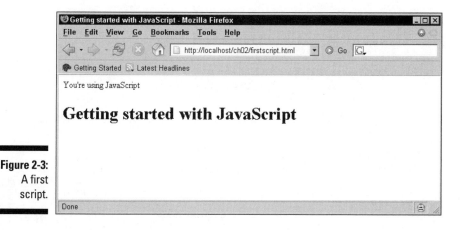

Figure 2-3:
A first
script.

Oh, those semicolons

Technically speaking, each line of JavaScript should end with a semicolon (;) just like in Java if you're at all familiar with that language. Notice the semicolon at the end of the bold line of JavaScript code shown in the following:

```
<html>
  <head>
    <title>A First Script</title>
    <script language="javascript">
    document.write("You're using JavaScript");
    </script>
  </head>

  <body>
    <h1>A First Script</h1>
  </body>
</html>
```

Including the semicolon is the correct way of doing things in JavaScript, and that's the way I do it in this book. However, browsers have become very forgiving on this point. If you omit the semicolons at the end of lines, browsers won't have a problem with it.

Adding comments to your JavaScript

JavaScript supports a one-line comment with the double slash (//) marker, which means that JavaScript doesn't read anything on a line after //. So you can add comments for people to read throughout your code, and they won't interrupt how your JavaScript runs. See the comment line added in bold in the following code:

```
<html>
  <head>
    <title>A First Script</title>
    <script language="javascript">
    //Write the message to the Web page
    document.write("You're using JavaScript");
    </script>
  </head>

  <body>
    <h1>A First Script</h1>
  </body>
</html>
```

In fact, JavaScript also supports a second type of comment, which you can use for multiple lines. This comment starts with /* and ends with */. When JavaScript sees /*, it ignores everything else until it sees */. Here's an example:

```
<html>
  <head>
    <title>A First Script</title>
    <script language="javascript">
      /* Write the message
         to the Web page */
      document.write("You're using JavaScript");
    </script>
  </head>

  <body>
    <h1>A First Script</h1>
  </body>
</html>
```

Using separate script files

Here's a very common practice in Ajax applications: If you want to store your JavaScript code in a file outside the Web page you'll use it in, store it in a file with the extension .js. This can be a good idea when you're dealing with cross-browser issues, for example, because you can load one .js file for one browser and another .js file for another browser.

For example, say that you put this line of JavaScript code into a file named script.js:

```
document.write("You're using JavaScript");
```

Now you can refer to script.js in a new HTML file, usescript.html, by using the <script> element's src attribute, like this:

```
<html>
  <head>
    <title>A First Script</title>
    <script language="javascript" src="script.js">
    </script>
  </head>

  <body>
    <h1>A First Script</h1>
  </body>
</html>
```

That's all there is to it. Now when you load `usescript.html`, `script.js` is loaded automatically as well, and the code from that file is run. Many of the Ajax applications I show you use external scripts, so understanding this aspect of JavaScript is important.

Examining script errors

Believe it or not, sometimes the JavaScript that people write has errors in it (perhaps not your scripts, but errors have been known to crop up in mine). You can view the errors and get a short description of them from various browsers. These errors can help you debug the problem — except, that is, when the error message is so terse that it's no help at all.

The following script has an error in it — can you spot it?

```
<html>
  <head>
    <title>A First Script</title>
    <script language="javascript">
      docment.write("You're using JavaScript");
    </script>
  </head>

  <body>
    <h1>A First Script</h1>
  </body>
</html>
```

Yep, the object `document` is misspelled as `docment`, although that might not be obvious at first reading. This JavaScript isn't going to run. What happens when you open this document, which I've named `error.html`, in a browser such as Internet Explorer? You get the results you see in Figure 2-4. The JavaScript didn't do anything, and you see a small yellow triangle icon in the lower-left corner. JavaScript programmers call this the *yellow triangle of death*.

Double-clicking the yellow triangle of death opens the dialog box you see in Figure 2-5, which explains the problem: Internet Explorer can't understand `docment`. Now that you know what the problem is, you can fix it.

How would Firefox handle the same problem? If you open `error.html` in Firefox, the JavaScript won't run, just as with Internet Explorer. But there's no yellow triangle of death here to click. Instead, you can choose Tools⇨ JavaScript Console to open the Firefox JavaScript Console. This displays the window shown in Figure 2-6.

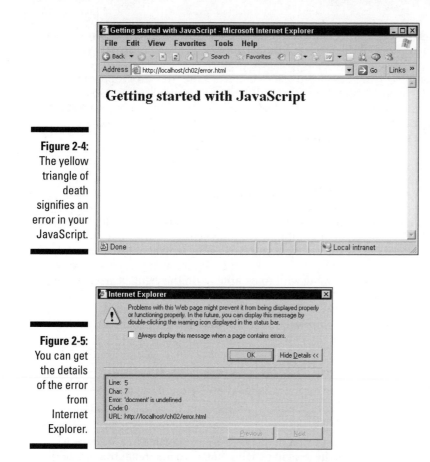

Figure 2-4:
The yellow
triangle of
death
signifies an
error in your
JavaScript.

Figure 2-5:
You can get
the details
of the error
from
Internet
Explorer.

Figure 2-6:
The Firefox
JavaScript
Console.

You can read right away what the error is: `docment` isn't defined. And now that you know what the error is, you can fix it.

Which of these two popular browsers helps out the Ajax programmer the best with the most complete explanation of each error? Firefox. As you develop your own scripts, the Firefox JavaScript console can be an invaluable aid to fixing any bugs that might crop up. The console will give you more details on the errors than Internet Explorer would.

Which browser are you using?

Here's a question that bears some examination: Which browser does the user have? The JavaScript incompatibilities among browsers are small these days, but some still exist — such as how you create the central object you need in Ajax scripts, the `XMLHttpRequest` object. So sometimes you need to know which browser you're dealing with to be able to do the right JavaScript trick.

This is where the `navigator` browser object comes in. This object holds all kinds of details about the browser. Here are the relevant properties of this object:

- ✔ `navigator.AppName`: Provides the name of the browser application.

- ✔ `navigator.AppVersion`: Provides the version of the browser.

- ✔ `navigator.UserAgent`: Provides more details about the browser.

For example, here's a script that displays these properties in a Web page, `browser.html` — note the + sign, which you use to join text strings together in JavaScript:

```html
<html>
    <head>
        <title>
            What's Your Browser?
        </title>
    </head>

    <body>
        <script language="javascript">
            document.write("You're using: " + navigator.appName)
            document.write("<br><br>")
            document.write("Version: " + navigator.appVersion)
            document.write("<br><br>")
            document.write("Browser details: " + navigator.userAgent)
        </script>

        <h1>What's Your Browser?</h1>
    </body>
</html>
```

You can see what this HTML page looks like in Firefox in Figure 2-7, and in the Internet Explorer in Figure 2-8. When you have this information, you can make JavaScript do one thing for one browser and another thing for a different browser. The detailed how-to is coming up in this chapter — watch for the section, "Picking and Choosing with the if Statement."

Figure 2-7:
Determining the browser type in Firefox.

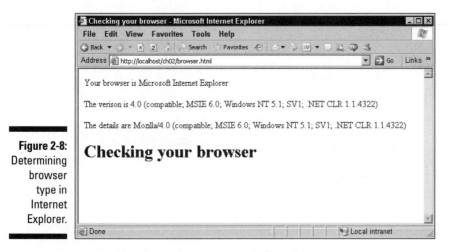

Figure 2-8:
Determining browser type in Internet Explorer.

Making Something Happen: Browser Events

Ajax applications often respond to user actions — button clicks, mouse double clicks, page loads, and so on. How does the script know when to respond to something that has happened? You can use browser *events,* something you're going to see a lot of in this book. When the user performs some action that you can respond to, an event occurs, such as a mouse click.

So what events are available? Table 2-1 lists some common ones that you might see in Ajax applications.

Table 2-1	JavaScript Events Common in Ajax
Event	*Occurs When . . .*
onabort	Occurs when the user aborts an action
onblur	Occurs when an element loses the input focus
onchange	Occurs when data in a control, such as a text field, changes
onclick	Occurs when the user clicks an element
ondblclick	Occurs when the user double-clicks an element
ondragdrop	Occurs when the user drags and drops an element
onerror	Occurs when there's been a JavaScript error
onfocus	Occurs when an element gets the focus
onkeydown	Occurs when the user presses down on a key
onkeypress	Occurs when the user presses a key
onkeyup	Occurs when the user releases a key
onload	Occurs when the page loads
onmousedown	Occurs when the user presses down a mouse button
onmousemove	Occurs when the user moves the mouse
onmouseout	Occurs when the user moves the cursor away from an element
onmouseover	Occurs when the user moves the cursor over an element
onmouseup	Occurs when the user releases a mouse button
onreset	Occurs when the user clicks a Reset button
onresize	Occurs when the user resizes an element or page
onsubmit	Occurs when the user clicks a Submit button
onunload	Occurs when the browser unloads a page and moves to another page

Putting browser events to work

To make any of the browser events in Table 2-1 happen, you need to drop them in a Web page's HTML. For example, what if you want to change the color of a Web page to pink when the user clicks that page? You can use the events in Table 2-1 as attributes in various HTML elements; for example, the Web page itself is represented with the <body> element, so you can use the onmousedown attribute in the <body> tag with a little JavaScript to turn the page pink.

What does all that mean? Here's what that looks like in a page named blusher.html — note that you can execute JavaScript simply by assigning it to an event attribute such as the onmousedown attribute without having to place that JavaScript in a <script> element; such scripts are called *inline scripts* (the text of an inline script must be enclosed in quotes, as here):

```
<html>
    <head>
        <title>
            JavaScript Event Example
        </title>
    </head>

    <body onmousedown="document.bgcolor='pink'">
        <h1>
            Click this page to turn it pink!
        </h1>
    </body>
</html>
```

To turn the page pink with JavaScript, you have to set the Web page's bgcolor property, just as you'd use the <body> element's bgcolor attribute to set the page color in HTML. In JavaScript, you access the page by using the document object, which supports a bgcolor property that will let you set the page color on the fly. (To see which browser objects support which properties, take a look at JavaScript manuals I refer to at the beginning of the chapter.)

In this case, here's the JavaScript executed when the user clicks the Web page:

```
body onmousedown="document.bgcolor='pink'"
```

This sets the document.bgcolor property to the text 'pink'. (Note the single quotation marks, which I elaborate on in the next section.) When you click this page, it turns pink, as you can see in Figure 2-9 (where it appears in glorious black and white). Not bad.

Will the browser understand the word *pink?* Sure will — all modern browsers come with dozens of words standing for colors already built in. You can assign all kinds of colors to `document.bgcolor`, not only *pink* but *blue, green, yellow,* and even *coral* or *cyan.*

If you don't want an event to trigger an inline script but instead want to call JavaScript in a `<script>` element when something happened on the page, such as a mouse click or a button press, you have to use JavaScript *functions.* To find out how, see "Dividing and Conquering: JavaScript Functions," later in this chapter.

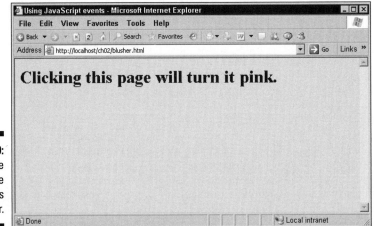

Figure 2-9:
Clicking the page changes its color.

Getting the quotation marks right

You always have to enclose the values that you assign to a property in quotation marks. Note the single quotation marks here! Because the whole inline script is quoted with double quotation marks, you'd confuse JavaScript if you entered

```
body onmousedown="document.bgcolor="pink""
```

When JavaScript comes to the second double quotation mark (at the beginning of `"pink"`), it thinks the inline script is done and it doesn't know how to proceed. To avoid that, you can enclose the text you assign to a property in single quotation marks.

If you want to change the color of the Web page in JavaScript in a `<script>` element, not in an inline script, you wouldn't have to enclose the whole line of JavaScript in quotation marks, so you could use double quotation marks around `"pink"`, like this:

```
document.bgcolor="pink";
```

Or you could use single quotation marks if you like them better:

```
document.bgcolor='pink';
```

Dividing and Conquering: JavaScript Functions

When you use Ajax techniques, you often want to place text in a Web page at a specific location after fetching that text from the server. Making that happen correctly will address a couple of important JavaScript issues.

To make text appear is specific place, you need to make your JavaScript run only when you want it to run. To do that, you can place that code into a JavaScript *function*. In JavaScript, a function is a set of lines of code that are run only when you specifically call that function — just what you want here. (A function is just like the methods you've already seen — like the document object's write method — except that a function isn't connected to an object.)

Functions are important for you as an Ajax programmer because unless you pack your code into a function, it runs immediately when the HTML page loads. And if you've put your `<script>` element into the `<head>` section of the page, it's even worse because your code won't be able to access elements in the `<body>` section because they haven't even loaded yet. To be able to fetch data interactively when you want without reloading the whole page, you need to use functions, so make sure you know how they work. This section breaks down how you put together functions and then how to pass arguments to functions.

You also find more on functions a little later in this chapter — they're very handy when the user clicks a button to make something happen, for example, because button clicks are just other events that you can connect to functions.

Understanding the problem

To know when functions are necessary, it helps to know how inline scripts can create problems. This is the script that you developed earlier in this chapter to display a message:

```
<html>
  <head>
    <title>Getting started with JavaScript</title>
    <script language="javascript">
      document.write("You're using JavaScript");
    </script>
  </head>

  <body>
    <h1>Getting started with JavaScript</h1>
  </body>
</html>
```

When this page loads in a browser, the JavaScript in the `<script>` element in the `<head>` section is executed immediately. In this case, that means this line is executed as soon as the browser reads it:

```
document.write("You're using JavaScript");
```

And that, in turn, means that the text `You're using JavaScript` appears in the browser. After the `<head>` section is loaded, the `<body>` section of the page is loaded, and the `<h1>` header text, `"A First Script"`, then appears on the page (refer to Figure 2-3).

That looks okay, but it's a little upside down. The header needs to appear on top, and the normal text underneath it. How could you make that happen? Wouldn't it be nicer to execute the JavaScript after the header has already appeared?

One way of getting the text under the header is to place the JavaScript in the `<body>` section of the page instead of in the header. That might look like this, for example:

```
<html>
  <head>
    <title>Getting started with JavaScript</title>
  </head>

  <body>
    <h1>Getting started with JavaScript</h1>
    <script language="javascript">
      document.write("You're using JavaScript");
    </script>
  </body>
</html>
```

This works — the text You're using JavaScript appears underneath the header A First Script when you open this page in a browser. In other words, knowing what part of a page loads first can make a difference — for example, if you have JavaScript in the <head> section that refers to elements in the <body> section, and if that JavaScript executes as soon as the page loads, the script will fail because the <body> section hasn't been loaded yet.

Although you can put <script> elements into the <body> section of a page, things aren't usually done that way. The modern JavaScript convention is to put <script> elements only in the <head> section of a page. Okay, so what do you do now? In this case, you don't want your JavaScript executed before the rest of the page loads.

The problem here is that when the page loads, the <head> section gets loaded first, so the code in the <script> section is run immediately. That places the You're using JavaScript text on the Web page first. Then the <body> section is loaded, which puts the A First Script heading on the Web page.

The bottom line is that you simply don't get the control you need by using the inline script. To make the JavaScript run only when you want, you need a function.

Putting together a function

To illustrate how JavaScript functions typically work in Ajax applications, say that you create a function named displayText, which works like this:

```
<html>
  <head>
    <title>Getting started with JavaScript</title>

    <script language="javascript">
    function displayText()
    {
        .
        .
        .
    }
    </script>

  </head>

  <body>

    <h1>Getting started with JavaScript</h1>

    </body>
</html>
```

Note that you use the function keyword, follow the name of the function with parentheses (the parentheses indicate what, if any, data is passed to the function — there will be none here), and enclose the lines of JavaScript you want to execute — called the body of the function — in curly braces, { and }.

Now the JavaScript inside the displayText function will only be run when you want it to be run. But with this extra flexibility comes more work. You need to call the function and place the code that writes the message.

Calling the function

To call this function and run that code, you can use browser events. There's an event that's perfect here — the onload event, which occurs after the page has been loaded.

There's an onload attribute for the <body> element that you can use like this:

```
<html>
  <head>
    <title>Getting started with JavaScript</title>

    <script language="javascript">
      function displayText()
      {
            .
            .
            .
      }
    </script>

  </head>

  <body onload="">

    <h1>Using a div</h1>

    <div id="targetDiv">
    </div>

    </body>
</html>
```

But what do you put into the quotation marks here? What inline script can you use to call the displayText function? All you have to do to call a function is to give its name, followed by a pair of parentheses (if you want to pass data to the function, you put the data between the parentheses, as I show you a little later):

```html
<html>
  <head>
    <title>Getting started with JavaScript</title>

    <script language="javascript">
      function displayText()
      {
          .
          .
          .
      }
    </script>

  </head>

  <body onload="displayText()">

  </body>
</html>
```

Great. If you're familiar with using functions in code, you might intuitively think you can place the code to write the message in the displayText() function, like this:

```javascript
function displayText()
{
  document.write("You're using JavaScript");
}
```

Unfortunately, you can't. The displayText function will be called after the page is loaded, which is fine. But here's the catch — when you call the document.write method, the document is *opened* for writing, which clears any text that's already in the document now — and that means all that will appear in the browser will be the text You're using JavaScript, because the browser will have overwritten the header text, A First Script, as you see in Figure 2-10.

Why doesn't this happen when you place the <script> element inside the <body> element? In that case, the document is still open for writing because the <body> element is still loading when your JavaScript executes. But after the page is loaded, the document is closed and has to be reopened if you want to write to it again — and opening the document clears the text in it.

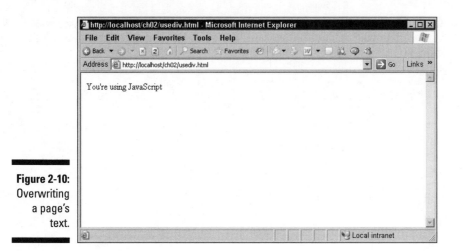

Figure 2-10:
Overwriting
a page's
text.

So what should you do? The solution is to do what a lot of Ajax scripts do — write to a specific part of the page *after* the page has been loaded. In this case, you might do that by adding a `<div>` element to the page.

This `<div>` element will display the text `You're using JavaScript` after the page has loaded (note that I give it the ID `"targetDiv"`):

```html
<html>
  <head>
    <title>Using a div</title>
    <script language="javascript">
      function displayText()
      {
          .
          .
          .
      }
    </script>

  </head>

  <body onload="displayText()">

    <h1>Using a div</h1>

    <div id="targetDiv">
    </div>

    </body>
</html>
```

So far, so good. But how do you access the <div> element from JavaScript? This <div> has the ID "targetDiv", and you can use that ID to reach it. You can reach this <div> by using the document object, which represents the Web page, in JavaScript code. The document object has a very handy method named getElementById, and if you pass the ID of the <div> to this method, it will pass back to you a JavaScript object corresponding to the <div>.

That's how it works in JavaScript — you can get a JavaScript object corresponding to a Web page or any element in the page. After you get an object corresponding to the <div>, you can use that object's built-in methods and properties to work with it. To paste text into the <div>, for example, you can use the innerHTML property. If you want to write new text to the <div> element, you can use the expression document.getElementById ('targetDiv') to get an object that corresponds to the <div> element, and then you can use the innerHTML property of that object (like this: document.getElementById('targetDiv').innerHTML) to be able to access the text inside the <div>.

Whew.

Here's what it looks like in code — after the page loads, the JavaScript here writes the text "You're using JavaScript" to the <div> element:

```html
<html>
  <head>
    <title>Using a div</title>

    <script language="javascript">
      function displayText()
      {
        document.getElementById('targetDiv').innerHTML =
          "You're using JavaScript";
      }
    </script>

  </head>

  <body onload="displayText()">

    <h1>Using a div</h1>

    <div id="targetDiv">
    </div>

    </body>
</html>
```

Is all this going to work? Sure. You can see this page, `usediv.html`, at work in Figure 2-11. Perfect.

REMEMBER

This is a technique that Ajax applications use frequently — after you've used Ajax techniques to fetch data from the server, you can display that data in a `<div>` element.

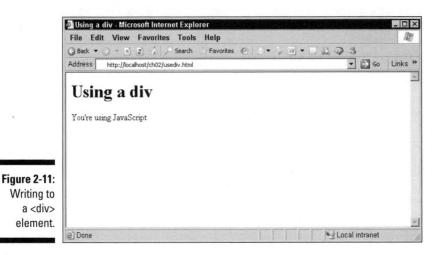

Figure 2-11:
Writing to
a <div>
element.

Passing a single argument to a function

When you use the `document.write` method, you pass the text to write to that method like this: `document.write("You're using JavaScript")`. You can also pass data to the functions you write.

Here's how to do it: Say that you want to pass the text to write to the `displayText` function. It's easy; when you call the function, just pass the text you want to write in the parentheses following the name of the function, like this: `displayText('You're using JavaScript')`. The data you pass to a function this way — in this case, that's just the text `"You're using JavaScript"` — is called an *argument*. So here, you're passing a single argument to the `displayText` function.

Then you set up the function itself by giving a name to the passed data in the parentheses like this, where I name that text simply `text`:

```
function displayText(text)
{
        .

        .

        .

}
```

Now you can refer to the text passed to your function by name like this, where the function is displaying that text in the <div> element:

```
function displayText(text)
{
  document.getElementById("targetDiv").innerHTML = text;
}
```

Here's what it all looks like in place:

```
<html>
  <head>
    <title>Using a div</title>

    <script language="javascript">
      function displayText(text)
      {
        document.getElementById("targetDiv").innerHTML = text;
      }
    </script>

  </head>

  <body onload="displayText('You're using JavaScript')">

    <h1>Using a div</h1>

    <div id="targetDiv">
    </div>

  </body>
</html>
```

This gives you the same results as before, where the text appears under the heading (refer to Figure 2-11). When the page finishes loading, the display Text function is called with the text of the message to write You're using JavaScript, which is promptly sent to the target <div> element.

Not bad.

Using <div> versus <span>

Elements like <div> are *block elements* in HTML (and XHTML), which means they're automatically set off on their own lines (much like a header, such as <h1>). Sometimes, you might not want the data you fetch by using Ajax techniques to appear on its own line — you might want it to appear on the same line as other text, such as text that explains what your data means (for example, "Record number: ", or something similar). To place text inline in real-time, you can use a <span> element instead of a <div>. You can find an example, usespan.html, in the code you can download for this book.

That example inserts text directly inline into the sentence: The new text will appear here: <span id="targetSpan"></span>. Here's what it looks like in the actual code.

```
<html>
  <head>
    <title>Using a span</title>

    <script language="javascript">
      function displayText()
      {
        document.getElementById('targetSpan').innerHTML =
          "You're using JavaScript";
      }
    </script>

  </head>

  <body onload="displayText()">

    <h1>Using a span</h1>

    The new text will appear here: "<span id="targetSpan">
    </span>".

  </body>
</html>
```

You can see this in action in Figure 2-12, where the <span> is doing its thing.

Figure 2-12:
Writing to
a <div>
element by
using a
function.

Using Ajax is all about inserting fresh data into a page without having to reload that page, and using the Dynamic HTML (DHTML) technique of inserting text into a `<div>` or a `<span>` is very popular. Want to display some new data? Fetch it from the server, pop it into a `<div>`, and pow!, there you are. The `<div>` element is the most popular, but don't forget that it's a block element and so takes up its own line(s) in the browser. If you want to place new text inline, consider `<span>`.

Before you start sticking new text into a Web page left and right by using `<div>`, and even more when you use `<span>`, you have to consider how well the user is going to realize you've changed things. That's one of the Ajax topics — and criticisms of Ajax — I discuss in Chapter 4: that the user might not realize that anything's changed. Because you have Dynamic HTML techniques such as popping text into `<div>` and `<span>` elements, the whole page won't change — just the element you're working with. Did the users notice? Should you bring the change to their attention? This is one of the elements of Ajax style coming up in Chapter 4.

So far, so good. But there's more to this story of using JavaScript functions. The `usediv.html` and `usespan.html` examples just passed a single argument to the `displayText` function, but you aren't limited to that — you can pass multiple arguments to a function just as easily.

Passing multiple arguments

To see how you pass multiple arguments, take a look at the `usearguments. html` example in the code available for download from the Web site associated with this book. The inline Javascript code in this example passes not only the text to display, but also the name of the `<div>` to insert text into:

```
<html>
  <head>
    <title>Passing multiple arguments to a function</title>

    <script language="javascript">
      function displayText(text, divName)
      {
        document.getElementById(divName).innerHTML = text;
      }
    </script>

  </head>

  <body onload="displayText('You're using JavaScript', 'targetDiv')">

    <h1>Passing multiple arguments to a function</h1>
```

```
    <div id="targetDiv">
    </div>

    </body>
</html>
```

As you can see, passing multiple arguments to a function is easy — just use commas:

```
displayText('You're using JavaScript', 'targetDiv')
```

And when you set up the function, you give names to the data items you want the function to be passed, separated by commas. And then you can refer to those data items by using those names in the body of the function:

```
function displayText(text, divName)
{
  document.getElementById(divName).innerHTML = text;
}
```

You can see this page in action in Figure 2-13, where both arguments — the text to display and the name of the `<div>` element to write the text to — were successfully passed to the function. Cool.

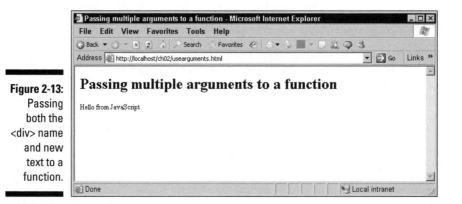

Figure 2-13:
Passing both the `<div>` name and new text to a function.

You Must Remember This: Storing Data

Ajax applications can use JavaScript pretty intensively, and among other things, that means handling data like the current price of music CDs, the number of LCD monitors in stock, the temperature in San Francisco, and so on. And in JavaScript, you can store data using *variables*.

For example, say that you wanted to store that `"You're using Java Script"` message in your script for easy handling. That way, you wouldn't have to pass that message to the `displayText` function each time you want to display that text, as I explain earlier in this chapter. Instead, that text would already be available to the `displayText` function.

Simple data storage with the var statement

To store data like the `"You're using JavaScript"` text by using Java Script, you use the JavaScript `var` (short for variable) statement. For example, to store the message's text in a variable named `text`, you could use this line of JavaScript in your `<script>` element:

```
var text = "You're using JavaScript";
```

Then you could refer to that text by name from then on in your JavaScript code. For example, when you want to display that text, you could do this:

```
<html>
  <head>
    <title>Using variables</title>

    <script language="javascript">

      var text = "You're using JavaScript";

      function displayText()
      {
        document.getElementById('targetDiv').innerHTML = text;
      }
    </script>

  </head>

  <body onload="displayText()">

    <h1>Using variables</h1>

    <div id="targetDiv">
    </div>

  </body>
</html>
```

That's all it takes — you've created a variable named `text` and then made use of that variable like this to display the text you've stored in it:

```
document.getElementById('targetDiv').innerHTML = text;
```

Very nice.

Churning your data with operators

Many programming languages make big distinctions between the type of data you can store in variables, and they give you a different types of variables to store different types of text — for example, one type of variable is for text strings, another is for integers, and so on. But JavaScript isn't that uptight — you can store all kinds of data with the same `var` statement. For example, say that you wanted to store numbers in two variables named, say, `operand1` and `operand2`. You could do that like this:

```
var operand1 = 2;
var operand2 = 3;
```

Then say you wanted to add these two values and store the result in a variable named sum. JavaScript has a bunch of *operators* that will let you perform operations like addition (the + operator) or subtraction (the – operator), and you can see them in Table 2-2. (*Don't* try to memorize what you see there — come back to this table throughout the book as needed.) So here's how you might create a new variable named sum and store the sum of `operand1` and `operand2` in it (note that this code doesn't give the sum variable any initial value when it's first created):

```
var sum;
sum = operand1 + operand2;
```

Listing 2-2 shows what it would all look like on a Web page, `usenumbers.html` in the code for this book, where JavaScript adds together the values in `operand1` and `operand2`, stores them in the variable named `sum`, and displays that result.

Listing 2-2:   Putting JavaScript Operators to Work

```
<html>
  <head>
    <title>Using numeric variables</title>

    <script language="javascript">
```

```
     var operand1 = 2;
     var operand2 = 3;
     var sum = 0;
     function displayText()
     {
       sum = operand1 + operand2;
       document.getElementById('targetDiv').innerHTML =
             operand1 + " + " + operand2 + " = " + sum;
     }
   </script>

</head>

<body onload="displayText()">

  <h1>Using numeric variables</h1>

  <div id="targetDiv">
  </div>

</body>
</html>
```

You can see this page in action in Figure 2-14, where the users learns that
2 + 3 = 5. They might have already have known the math, but they can't help
but be impressed by your use of variables.

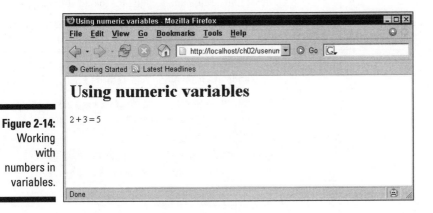

Figure 2-14:
Working
with
numbers in
variables.

Table 2-2	JavaScript Operators
Operator	*Description*
Arithmetic Operators	
+	Addition — Adds two numbers.
++	Increment — Increments by one the value in a variable.
-	Subtraction, negation — Subtracts one number from another. Can also change the sign of its `operand` like this: `-variableName`.
--	Decrement — Decrements by one the value in a variable.
*	Multiplication — Multiplies two numbers.
/	Division — Divides two numbers.
%	Modulus — Returns the remainder left after dividing two numbers using integer division.
String Operators	
+	String addition — Joins two strings.
+=	Joins two strings and assigns the joined string to the first operand.
Logical Operators	
&&	Logical AND — Returns a value of `true` if both operands are true; otherwise, returns `false`.
||	Logical OR — Returns a value of `true` if either operand is true. However, if both operands are false, returns `false`.
!	Logical NOT — Returns a value of `false` if its operand is true; `true` if its operand is false.
Bitwise Operators	
&	Bitwise AND — Returns a 1 in each bit position if both operands' bits are 1s.
^	Bitwise XOR — Returns a 1 in a bit position if the bits of one operand, but not both operands, are 1.
|	Bitwise OR — Returns a 1 in a bit if either operand has a 1 in that position.

Operator	*Description*
Bitwise Operators	
~	Bitwise NOT — Changes 1s to 0s and 0s to 1s in all bit positions — that is, flips each bit.
<<	Left shift — Shifts the bits of its first operand to the left by the number of places given in the second operand.
>>	Sign-propagating right shift — Shifts the bits of the first operand to the right by the number of places given in the second operand.
>>>	Zero-fill right shift — Shifts the bits of the first operand to the right by the number of places given in the second operand, and shifting in 0s from the left.
Assignment Operators	
=	Assigns the value of the second operand to the first operand if the first operand is a variable.
+=	Adds two operands and assigns the result to the first operand if the first operand is a variable.
-=	Subtracts two operands and assigns the result to the first operand, if the first operand is a variable.
*=	Multiplies two operands and assigns the result to the first operand if the first operand is a variable.
/=	Divides two operands and assigns the result to the first operand if the first operand is a variable.
%=	Calculates the modulus of two operands and assigns the result to the first operand if the first operand is a variable.
&=	Executes a bitwise AND operation on two operands and assigns the result to the first operand if the first operand is a variable.
^=	Executes a bitwise exclusive OR operation on two operands and assigns the result to the first operand if the first operand is a variable.
|=	Executes a bitwise OR operation on two operands and assigns the result to the first operand if the first operand is a variable.

(continued)

Table 2-2 *(continued)*

Operator	Description
Assignment Operators	
<<=	Executes a left-shift operation on two operands and assigns the result to the first operand if the first operand is a variable.
>>=	Executes a sign-propagating right-shift operation on two operands and assigns the result to the first operand if the first operand is a variable.
>>>=	Executes a zero-fill right-shift operation on two operands and assigns the result to the first operand if the first operand is a variable.
Comparison Operator	
==	Equality operator — Returns true if the two operands are equal to each other.
!=	Not-equal-to — Returns true if the two operands are not equal to each other.
===	Strict equality — Returns true if the two operands are both equal and of the same type.
!==	Strict not-equal-to — Returns true if the two operands are not equal and/or not of the same type.
>	Greater-than — Returns true if the first operand's value is greater than the second operand's value.
>=	Greater-than-or-equal-to — Returns true if the first operand's value is greater than or equal to the second operand's value.
<	Less-than — Returns true if the first operand's value is less than the second operand's value.
<=	Less-than-or-equal-to operator — Returns true if the first operand's value is less than or equal to the second operand's value.
?:	Conditional operator — Executes an if...else test.

Operator	Description
,	Comma operator — Evaluates two expressions and returns the result of evaluating the second expression.
delete	Deletion — Deletes an object and removes it from memory, or deletes an object's property, or deletes an element in an array.
function	Creates an anonymous function. (Used in Chapter 3.)
in	Returns true if the property you're testing is supported by a specific object.
instanceof	Returns true if the given object is an instance of the specified type.
new	Object-instantiation — Creates an new object form the specified object type.
typeof	Returns the name of the type of the operand.
void	Used to allow evaluation of an expression without returning any value.

Altering a variable's data

You can change the data in a variable simply by assigning a new value to that variable. For example, if you did this:

```
var operand1 = 2;
var operand2 = 3;
        .
        .
        .
```

But then changed the value in operand1 to 12 like this:

```
var operand1 = 2;
var operand2 = 3;
operand1 = 12;
        .
        .
        .
```

Then operand1 would hold 12 and operand2 would hold 3. If you added them together and placed the result in a variable named sum:

```
var operand1 = 2;
var operand2 = 3;
operand1 = 12;
var sum;
sum = operand1 + operand2;
```

then sum would hold 15. Note that you can use the var statement anywhere in a script, but you should use it before you use the variable you're creating with that statement.

Storing JavaScript objects in a variable

Besides text and numbers, you can store JavaScript objects, which support methods and properties, in variables, too. In this book, the most important (and the most famous) object is the XMLHttpRequest object that Ajax uses to communicate with a server behind the scenes.

A detailed explanation of how this works is coming up in the next chapter, but here's a preview. Creating an XMLHttpRequest object works differently in different browsers; here's how you do it in Firefox and Netscape Navigator (note the use of the operator named new here, which is how you create objects in JavaScript):

```
var XMLHttpRequestObject;
XMLHttpRequestObject = new XMLHttpRequest();
        .
        .
        .
```

Now that you have an XMLHttpRequest object in the variable named XMLHttpRequestObject, you can use the methods and properties of that object (which I detail in the next chapter) just as you'd use the built-in JavaScript document object's write method. For example, to use the XMLHttpRequest object's open method to start fetching data from a server, you'd just call that method as XMLHttpRequestObject.open:

```
var XMLHttpRequestObject;
XMLHttpRequestObject = new XMLHttpRequest();
        .
        .
        .
XMLHttpRequestObject.open("GET", dataSource);
```

JavaScript's data type guessing game

Because JavaScript doesn't have different types of variables for different types of data, it has to guess whether the data in a variable should be treated as, say, a number or as text. JavaScript makes that guess based on the context in which you use the variable, and sometimes it guesses wrong. For example, say that instead of storing the sum in a variable named sum, you simply did this to display the result of adding operand1 + operand2 (note the last line of this code):

```
document.getElementById('targetDiv').innerHTML =
  operand1 + " + " + operand2 + " = "
    + operand1 + operand2;
```

The problem here is that everything else in this JavaScript statement treats data like text strings, so JavaScript treats the operand1 and operand2 as strings — which means the + operator here will be used to join those strings ("2" and "3") together instead of adding the values as numbers. So you'll be surprised by the display "2 + 3 = 23" here, which doesn't look too mathematically correct. You need a variable such as sum here to make it clear to JavaScript that you're dealing with numbers:

```
sum = operand1 + operand2;
document.getElementById('targetDiv').innerHTML =
  operand1 + " + " + operand2 + " = "
    + sum;
```

And this gives you the correct result.

Oh, those functions!

When working with variables and functions in JavaScript, one of the most important things to know is this: *Variables created inside a function will be reset to their original values each time the script calls the function.* Not knowing that fact has stymied many JavaScript programmers. If you want to avoid confusion, place the var statement to create the variables you want to use *outside* the function.

Here's an example — a hit page counter that increments each time you click it. There are two counter variables here, one stored outside a function (counter1), and one stored inside a function (counter2). Because this page uses the <body> element's onclick attribute, each time the user clicks the page, the displayText function is called and both counters are incremented by one using the JavaScript ++ operator, which looks like this (see Table 2-2 for the ++ operator):

```
counter1 = counter1++;
counter2 = counter2++;
```

However, `counter1` was created outside the `displayText` function, and `counter2` is inside that function:

```
var counter1 = 0;
function displayText()
{
  var counter2 = 0;
  counter1 = counter1++;
  counter2 = counter2++;
    .
    .
    .
```

This means that each time `displayText` is called, the `counter2` variable is created anew and reset to the value given in the preceding code, 0. Even though it's incremented each time the function is called, it'll never get past a value of 1. The other variable, `counter1`, created outside any function, however, will be able to preserve its value between page clicks, so it'll act as a true counter. You can see all this on the Web page itself, `usevariablesand functions.html` (see Listing 2-3).

Listing 2-3: Using Variables and Functions Together

```
<html>
  <head>
    <title>Using variables</title>

    <script language="javascript">
      var counter1 = 0;
      function displayText()
      {
        var counter2 = 0;
        counter1 = counter1++;
        counter2 = counter2++;
        document.getElementById('targetDiv').innerHTML =
          "First counter equals " + counter1 + "<br>" +
          "But the second counter is still stuck at " + counter2;
      }
    </script>

  </head>

  <body onclick = "displayText()">

    <h1>Using variables (Click Me!)</h1>

    <div id="targetDiv">
    </div>

  </body>
</html>
```

What does it look like at work? You can see that in Figure 2-15, where I've clicked the page six times. The counter variable that was created outside the function holds the correct value — but the counter variable created inside the function was reset to its original value each time the page was clicked, so it always just displays a value of 1.

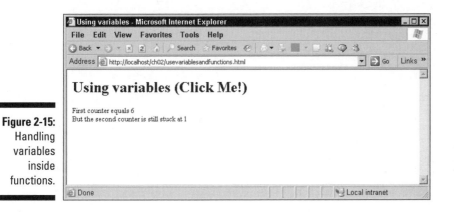

Figure 2-15: Handling variables inside functions.

Picking and Choosing with the if Statement

The JavaScript `if` statement lets you test whether a certain condition is true (is the value in the temperature variable over 65 degrees?) and if so, take appropriate action (picnic time!). The `if` statement also includes an optional `else` clause that holds code to be executed if the test condition is false. Here's what the syntax of this statement looks like, formally speaking — note that the code to execute is between curly braces, { and }, and that the part in standard braces, [and], is optional:

```
if (condition) {
    statements1
}
[else {
    statements2
}]
```

Using the if statement

It's time for an example. Is the value in the temperature variable over 65 degrees? If so, the example in Listing 2-4, `temperature.html`, displays the message `Picnic time!`. To check the temperature, the code uses the > (greater than) operator (see Table 2-2).

Listing 2-4: Working with the if Statement

```html
<html>
  <head>
    <title>Using the if statement</title>

    <script language="javascript">

      function displayText()
      {
        var temperature = 70;
        if(temperature > 65) {
            document.getElementById('targetDiv').innerHTML =
                "Picnic time!";
        }
      }
    </script>

  </head>

  <body onload="displayText()">

    <h1>Using the if statement</h1>

    <div id="targetDiv">
    </div>

    </body>
</html>
```

You can see the results in Figure 2-16, where, as you see, it's picnic time.

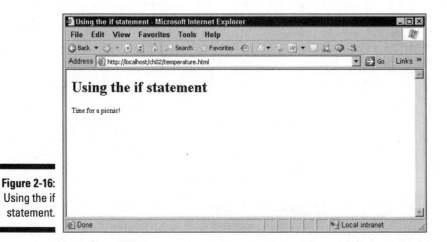

Figure 2-16:
Using the if
statement.

Using the else statement

You can also execute code if a condition is *not* true by using the `if` statement's optional `else` statement. For example, if it isn't picnic time, you might want to say `"Back to work!"` in `temperature.html`, and Listing 2-5 shows what that might look like with an `else` statement — note that I've changed the temperature so the `else` statement will be executed.

Listing 2-5:   Working with the else Statement

```html
<html>
  <head>
    <title>Using the if statement</title>

    <script language="javascript">
      function displayText()
      {
        var temperature = 62;
        if(temperature > 65) {
            document.getElementById('targetDiv').innerHTML =
                "Picnic time!";
        }
        else {
            document.getElementById('targetDiv').innerHTML =
                "Back to work!";
        }
      }
    </script>

  </head>

  <body onload="displayText()">

    <h1>Using the if statement</h1>

    <div id="targetDiv">
    </div>

  </body>
</html>
```

And you can see the results in Figure 2-17, where, regrettably, the temperature is low enough so that it's time to go back to work. Ah well.

Figure 2-17:
Using the
else
statement.

Determining browser type and version

Here's another, more advanced, example that determines which browser the user has and lets you execute code depending on browser type to display the browser version. This example puts to use the if and else statements as well as several built-in JavaScript functions that handle strings. In JavaScript, text strings are considered objects, and they have some built-in properties and methods that make life easier. Here's what this example uses:

- ✔ The length property gives you the length of the string, in characters.

- ✔ The indexOf method searches for the occurrence of a substring and gives you the location of the first match — or –1 if there was no match. (The first character of a string is considered character 0.)

- ✔ The substring method lets you extract a substring from a larger string. You can pass this method the start and end locations of the substring that you want to extract.

This example searches the navigator.userAgent property, which, as I introduce in "Which browser are you using?" earlier in this chapter, holds the browser name and version, extracts that information, and displays it. (You really don't have to memorize the string functions here — I put together this example because it's often important in Ajax programming to know what browser and version the user has.) Listing 2-6 shows what the code, browserversion.html, looks like.

Listing 2-6:   Finding Out What Browser You're Working With

```html
<html>
  <head>
    <title>
      Determining your browser
    </title>

    <script language="javascript">

    var versionBegin, versionEnd

    function checkBrowser()
    {
      if(navigator.appName == "Netscape") {
        if(navigator.userAgent.indexOf("Firefox") > 0) {
          versionBegin = navigator.userAgent.indexOf("Firefox") +
          "Firefox".length + 1;
          versionEnd = navigator.userAgent.length;
          document.getElementById("targetDiv").innerHTML =
            "You have Firefox " +
            navigator.userAgent.substring(versionBegin, versionEnd);
        }
      }

      if (navigator.appName == "Microsoft Internet Explorer") {
        versionBegin = navigator.userAgent.indexOf("MSIE ") +
        "MSIE ".length;
        if(navigator.userAgent.indexOf(";", versionBegin) > 0) {
          versionEnd = navigator.userAgent.indexOf(";", versionBegin);
        } else {
          versionEnd = navigator.userAgent.indexOf(")", versionBegin)
            + 2;
        }
        document.getElementById("targetDiv").innerHTML =
          "You have Internet Explorer " +
          navigator.userAgent.substring(versionBegin, versionEnd);
      }
    }
    </script>
  </head>

  <body onload="checkBrowser()">
    <h1>Determining your browser</h1>
    <div ID="targetDiv"></div>
  </body>
</html>
```

You can see the results in Figure 2-18, where the user is using Firefox 1.0.6. Using code like this, you can figure out what browser the user has — and whether the browser he has doesn't do what you want, put in some kind of workaround.

Figure 2-18:
Determining
browser
type and
version.

One thing computers are good at is doing the same kind of task over and over, and JavaScript helps out here with loops. I take a look at them in the following section to set the stage for working with buttons in Web pages that the user can click.

It Just Gets Better: The for Loop

Say you have the test scores of 600 students in a class you were teaching on Ajax and you want to determine their average test score. How could you do it? You can *loop* over their scores — that is, get the first one, then the next one, then the next one, and so on — by using a `for` loop. This is the most common loop in JavaScript, and it works like this:

```
for ([initial-expression]; [condition]; [increment-expression]) {
    statements
}
```

Programmers usually use the `for` loop with a *loop index* (also called a *loop counter*) which is just a variable that keeps track of the number of times the loop has executed. Here's how it works:

1. In the initial-expression part, you usually set the loop index to a starting value.

2. In the condition part, you test that value to see if you still want to keep on looping.

3. Then, the increment-expression lets you increment the loop counter.

How about an example to make all this clear? Say that you wanted to add the numbers 1 to 100. Listing 2-7 shows how that might look in a an example, `for.html`.

Listing 2-7:   Putting the for Loop to Work

```html
<html>
  <head>
    <title>Using the for statement</title>

    <script language="javascript">

      function displayText()
      {
        var loopIndex;
        var sum = 0;

        for(loopIndex = 1; loopIndex <= 100; loopIndex++) {
          sum += loopIndex;
        }

        document.getElementById('targetDiv').innerHTML =
          "Adding 1 to 100 gives: " + sum;
      }
    </script>

  </head>

  <body onload="displayText()">

    <h1>Using the for statement</h1>

    <div id="targetDiv">
    </div>

  </body>
</html>
```

Note that this code uses two new operators (see Table 2-2 for both of them): <= and +=. The <= operator is the less-than-or-equal operator. The += operator is a shortcut for the + and the = operator; in other words, these two lines do the same thing:

```
sum = sum + loopIndex;
sum += loopIndex;
```

JavaScript lets you combine operators like + (addition) and – (subtraction) with the = operator in handy shortcut versions like this: += and –=. Very neat.

The `for` loop in this example adds all the numbers from 1 to 100 by progressively incrementing the variable `loopIndex` and stopping when that index reaches a value of 100. What's the answer? You can see that in Figure 2-19 — summing 1 to 100 gives you 5050.

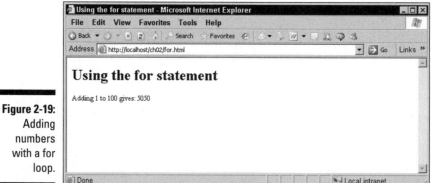

Figure 2-19:
Adding
numbers
with a for
loop.

Over and Over with the while Loop!

Another way of looping involves using the `while` loop. This loop simply keeps going while its condition is true. Here's what it looks like, formally speaking:

```
while (condition) {
    statements
}
```

Here's an example that uses the `while` loop and one other aspect of JavaScript — *arrays* — to push the envelope. In JavaScript, you can use an array to hold data that you can reference by an index number. For example, say that you wanted to store a list of everyday items. You could do that by creating an array of six elements (each element works just like a normal variable, and you can store a string, a number, or an object in each element) like this:

```
var items = new Array(6);
```

That's how you create an array with a particular number of elements (in this case, six) in it. Now you can access each element by using a number inside square braces, [and], like this:

```
items[0] = "Shoe";
items[1] = "Sandwich";
items[2] = "Sand";
items[3] = "Rocks";
items[4] = "Treasure";
items[5] = "Pebbles";
```

Note that the five elements in the items array start at index 0 and go to index 4. Now, items[0] holds "Shoe", items[1] holds "Sandwich", and so on. The reason that arrays are so perfect to use with loops is that an array is just a set of variables that you can access by number — and the number can just be a loop index, which means that a loop can loop over all the data in an array for you.

In this case, say that you want to search for the "Treasure" item in the array. You can do that by looping over the elements in the array until you find "Treasure". In other words, you want to keep looking and incrementing through the array as long as the current array element does not hold "Treasure". In this case, you have to check whether an element in the array holds "Treasure", and you can use the JavaScript == (equal to) or != (not equal to) operators for that. If, for example, items[3] holds "Treasure", then the JavaScript expression items[3] == "Treasure" would be true, and the expression items[3] != "Treasure" would be false. Because you need to keep looping until you find "Treasure" here, you can do it this way:

```
var loopIndex = 0;

while(items[loopIndex] != "Treasure"){
  loopIndex++;
}
```

At the end of this loop, the variable loopIndex will hold the index of the element that holds "Treasure". But there's a problem here — what if no element contains "Treasure"? You should put a cap on the possible number of values to search, saying, for example, that the loop should keep going if the current array element doesn't hold "Treasure" and that the current loop index is less than 6. JavaScript has an operator && that means *and,* so you can check both these conditions like this:

```
while(items[loopIndex] != "Treasure" && loopIndex < 5){
  loopIndex++;
}
```

Whew, ready to go. You can see the code that searches for `"Treasure"` in `while.html`, in Listing 2-8.

Listing 2-8:   Putting the while Loop to Work

```html
<html>
  <head>
    <title>Using the while statement</title>

    <script language="javascript">

      function findTreasure()
      {
        var loopIndex = 0, items = new Array(6);

        items[0] = "Shoe";
        items[1] = "Sandwich";
        items[2] = "Sand";
        items[3] = "Rocks";
        items[4] = "Treasure";
        items[5] = "Pebbles";

        while(items[loopIndex] != "Treasure" && loopIndex < 6){
          loopIndex++;
        }

        if(loopIndex < 6){
          document.getElementById('targetDiv').innerHTML =
          "Found the treasure at index " + loopIndex;
        }
      }
    </script>

  </head>

  <body onload="findTreasure()">

    <h1>Using the while statement</h1>

    <div id="targetDiv">
    </div>

  </body>
</html>
```

Will JavaScript be able to find the treasure? Sure thing, as you can see in Figure 2-20.

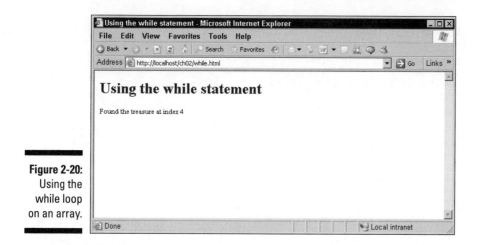

Figure 2-20:
Using the
while loop
on an array.

Pushing Some Buttons

Ajax applications usually wait for the user to do something before fetching data from the server, and doing something means causing an event in the browser, such as clicking a button. Many HTML *controls* can appear on a Web page, such as list boxes, text fields, radio buttons, and so on, and you need to know how to work with them in a general way. This next example shows how to connect a button click to a JavaScript function.

To display an HTML control like a button, you need to use an HTML form. And to connect that button to a JavaScript function, all you need to do is to assign that button's `onclick` attribute the name of that function to call that function like this (the value HTML attribute sets the caption of the button):

```
<form>
  <input type="button" onclick="showAlert()" value="Click Me!">
</form>
```

Displaying a message with a button click

When the user clicks this button, the JavaScript function `showAlert` is called. In that function, you might display a message box called an *alert box* to indicate that the user clicked the button. Listing 2-9 shows what it looks like in JavaScript, in a `button.html` file.

Listing 2-9: Handling Button Clicks

```html
<html>
    <head>
        <title>Using buttons</title>

        <script language="javascript">
            function showAlert()
            {
                alert("Thanks for clicking.")
            }
        </script>

    </head>

    <body>
        <h1>Using buttons</h1>
        <form>
            <input type="button" onclick="showAlert()" value="Click Here">
        </form>
    </body>
</html>
```

You can see this page in a browser in Figure 2-21. When the user clicks a button, the `showAlert` function is called, and it displays an alert box, as you see in Figure 2-22. So this button is indeed connected to the JavaScript. Very cool.

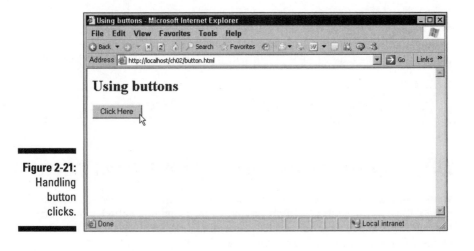

Figure 2-21: Handling button clicks.

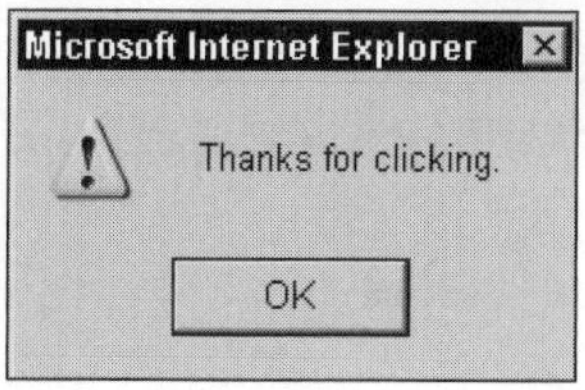

Figure 2-22:
Displaying
an alert box.

```
Microsoft Internet Explorer    [X]

   ⚠    Thanks for clicking.

        [   OK   ]
```

Reading a text field with a button click

In this example, the JavaScript code that's called when a button is clicked reads the text in an HTML text field and then displays that text in a `<div>` element. To do this, you need to add an HTML text field to the form like this — note that the text field is given the ID `"textField"`:

```
<form>
  Enter some text: <input type="text" id="textField">
  <br>
  Then click the button: <input type="button"
    onclick="handleText()" value="Read the text">
</form>
```

To get access to the text in the text field in your code, you can refer to that text like this: `document.getElementById('textField').value`. So you can read the text from the text field when the user clicks the button, and then display that text in a `<div>` element, as you see in Listing 2-10 in the file `textfield.html`.

Listing 2-10: Reading Text from a Text Field

```
<html>
    <head>
        <title>Clicking buttons</title>

        <script language="javascript">
            function handleText()
            {
                document.getElementById('targetDiv').innerHTML =
                "You entered: " +
                document.getElementById('textField').value;
            }
        </script>
    </head>

    <body>
        <h1>Reading text</h1>

    <form>
```

(continued)

Listing 2-10: (continued)

```
        Enter some text: <input type="text" id="textField">
        <br>
        Then click the button: <input type="button"
          onclick="handleText()" value="Read the text">
      </form>

      <div id="targetDiv">
      </div>

    </body>
</html>
```

That's all there is to it. You can see what this page, `textfield.html`, looks like in Figure 2-23, where the user has entered some text into the text field.

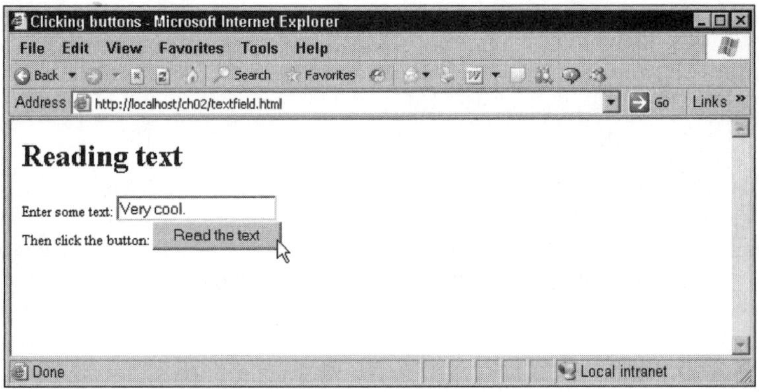

Figure 2-23: Using a text field.

When the user clicks the button, the JavaScript reads that text and displays it in a `<div>` element, as you see in Figure 2-24. Not bad.

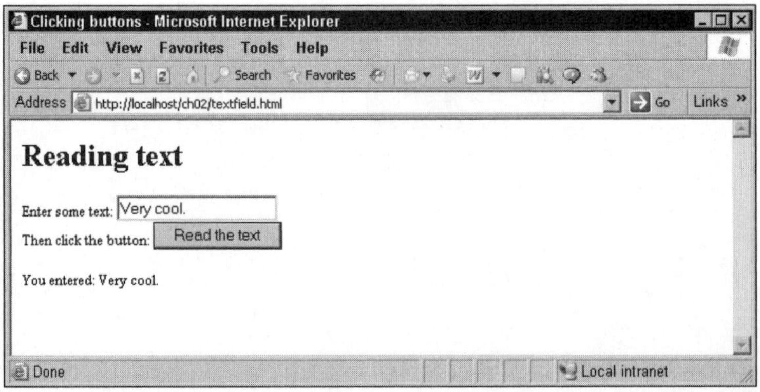

Figure 2-24: Reading text from a text field.

Part II
Programming in Ajax

The 5th Wave   By Rich Tennant

"Great goulash, Stan. That reminds me, are you still scripting your own Web page?"

In this part . . .

Here's where you get to dive into true Ajax programming. All through this part, you use Ajax to grab text and XML data from a server behind the scenes in a browser, and you put that data to work. Dozens of examples are coming up in this part. You use Ajax and Dynamic HTML to update Web pages on the fly — no page refresh from the server need apply! I also show you some advanced techniques at work here, such as connecting to Google behind the scenes for realtime same-page Web searches, or supporting multiple Ajax requests to the same server at the same time.

Chapter 3

Getting to Know Ajax

● ●

In This Chapter

▶ Developing an Ajax application

▶ Getting XML from the server

▶ Working with the `XMLHttpRequest` object

▶ Passing data to the server by using Ajax

▶ Getting data from the server with the `GET` method

▶ Getting data from the server with the `POST` method

● ●

"*L*ook at that!" the CEO hollers. "No wonder users don't like making purchases on our site. The page is always flickering."

"That's because you're refreshing the page each time you get more data," you say calmly, coming out of the shadows.

"Who are *you*?" the CEO cries.

"A master Ajax programmer," you reply. "And my rates are quite reasonable. For a major corporation, anyway."

"Can you solve that perpetual flickering?" asks the CEO.

"Certainly," you say, "for a hefty price."

"Anything!" the design team says.

You sit down at the computer and calmly take over. This, you think, is going to be good. And the money's not half bad either. All it's going to take is a little Ajax in the right places, and the problem is as good as solved.

This chapter is where you start coding some Ajax. You're going to start working with the `XMLHttpRequest` object in depth here and in the next chapter. This chapter gives you a working knowledge of Ajax — from the very beginnings all the way up to sending and receiving data to and from the server.

Writing Some Ajax

To illustrate Ajax, the code in Listing 3-1 asks the user to click a button, fetches data from the server using Ajax techniques, and displays that data in the same Web page as the button — without refreshing the page. Check out the code first, and then check out the explanation that follows it.

Listing 3-1: A First Ajax Application

```
<html>
  <head>
    <title>Ajax at work</title>

    <script language = "javascript">
      var XMLHttpRequestObject = false;

      if (window.XMLHttpRequest) {
        XMLHttpRequestObject = new XMLHttpRequest();
      } else if (window.ActiveXObject) {
        XMLHttpRequestObject = new ActiveXObject("Microsoft.XMLHTTP");
      }

      function getData(dataSource, divID)
      {
        if(XMLHttpRequestObject) {
          var obj = document.getElementById(divID);
          XMLHttpRequestObject.open("GET", dataSource);

          XMLHttpRequestObject.onreadystatechange = function()
          {
            if (XMLHttpRequestObject.readyState == 4 &&
              XMLHttpRequestObject.status == 200) {
                obj.innerHTML = XMLHttpRequestObject.responseText;
            }
          }

          XMLHttpRequestObject.send(null);
        }
      }
    </script>
  </head>

<body>

  <H1>Fetching data with Ajax</H1>

  <form>
    <input type = "button" value = "Display Message"
      onclick = "getData('http://localhost/ch03/data.txt',
      'targetDiv')">
```

```
    </form>

    <div id="targetDiv">
       <p>The fetched data will go here.</p>
    </div>

  </body>
</html>
```

This Ajax application appears in Figure 3-1. (In the code that you can download from the Web site associated with this book, the application is the
`index.html` file in the ch03 folder).

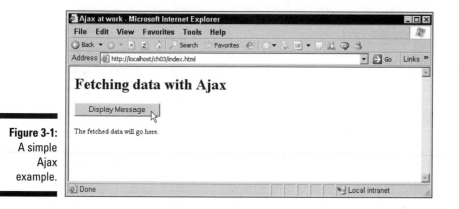

Figure 3-1:
A simple
Ajax
example.

When you click that button, the JavaScript in the page fetches some new text
and replaces the original text in the application with this new version, as you
see in Figure 3-2. No screen flicker, no page fetch, no fuss, no muss. Very nice
Of course, you *can* display data like this using simple JavaScript, but the difference here is that when you use Ajax, you're able to fetch the data from a
Web server.

So how does this page, `index.html`, do what it does? How does it use Ajax
to get that new text? The body of the page starts by displaying the original
text in a `<div>` element. Here is the `<div>` element in bold:

```
  <body>

    <H1>Fetching data with Ajax</H1>

    <form>
      <input type = "button" value = "Display Message"
        onclick = "getData('http://localhost/ch03/data.txt',
        'targetDiv')">
```

```
    </form>

    <div id="targetDiv">
      <p>The fetched data will go here.</p>
    </div>

  </body>
```

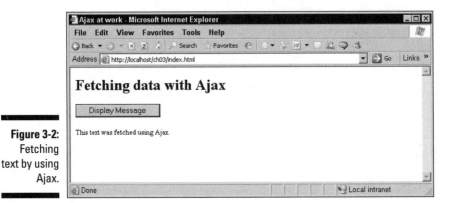

Figure 3-2:
Fetching
text by using
Ajax.

There's also a button on this page, and when the user clicks that button, a JavaScript method named getData is called, as you see here:

```
  <body>

    <H1>Fetching data with Ajax</H1>

    <form>
      <input type = "button" value = "Display Message"
        onclick = "getData('http://localhost/ch03/data.txt',
        'targetDiv')">
    </form>

    <div id="targetDiv">
      <p>The fetched data will go here.</p>
    </div>

  </body>
```

As you see here, the getData function is passed two text strings: the name of a text file, data.txt, to fetch from the server; and the name of the <div> element to display the fetched text in. The data.txt file contains just this text:

```
This text was fetched using Ajax.
```

That's the text you want the browser to download from the server in the background, as the user is working with the rest of the Web page. So what does the JavaScript that does all the work look like? You get to find that out in the following sections.

Creating the XMLHttpRequest object

This example application is going to need an XMLHttpRequest object to start, so it begins with the code that will create that object; this code is outside any function, so it runs immediately as the page loads. You start everything by creating a variable for this object, XMLHttpRequestObject like this:

```
<script language = "javascript">
  var XMLHttpRequestObject = false;
    .
    .
    .
```

This variable is initialized to the value false so that the script can check later whether the variable was indeed created. Besides the false value, JavaScript also supports a value named true — these two are *Boolean* values that you can assign to variables. The Netscape (version 7.0 and later), Apple Safari (version 1.2 and later), and Firefox browsers let you create XMLHttpRequest objects directly with code, like this:

```
XMLHttpRequestObject = new XMLHttpRequest();
```

How can you determine whether you're dealing with a browser where this code will work? The XMLHttpRequest object is usually part of the browser's window object, so to check whether XMLHttpRequest is ready to use, you can use this if statement to check if XMLHttpRequest objects — which, again, you can access as window.XMLHttpRequest — are available this way:

```
<script language = "javascript">
  var XMLHttpRequestObject = false;

  if (window.XMLHttpRequest) {
    .
    .
    .
```

If XMLHttpRequest is there and available, you can create the XMLHttp Request object you'll need this way:

```
<script language = "javascript">
  var XMLHttpRequestObject = false;

  if (window.XMLHttpRequest) {
    XMLHttpRequestObject = new XMLHttpRequest();
        .
        .
        .
```

On the other hand, if you're dealing with the Internet Explorer, you have to work with the different way that browser has of handling this object-creation process. You use an ActiveX object in the Internet Explorer (version 5.0 and later) to create an XMLHttpRequest object, so to check whether you're dealing with that browser, you can check whether ActiveX objects are available, like so:

```
<script language = "javascript">
  var XMLHttpRequestObject = false;

  if (window.XMLHttpRequest) {
    XMLHttpRequestObject = new XMLHttpRequest();
  } else if (window.ActiveXObject) {
        .
        .
        .
```

If you're working with the Internet Explorer, you can create an XMLHttpRequest object this way:

```
<script language = "javascript">
  var XMLHttpRequestObject = false;

  if (window.XMLHttpRequest) {
    XMLHttpRequestObject = new XMLHttpRequest();
  } else if (window.ActiveXObject) {
    XMLHttpRequestObject = new ActiveXObject("Microsoft.XMLHTTP");
  }
        .
        .
        .
```

Now you have an XMLHttpRequest object in the variable named XMLHttp RequestObject From this point on, the differences among the various types of browsers disappear as far as the rest of this chapter goes. But a few differences exist among browsers when it comes to this object, so what properties and methods are available in XMLHttpRequestObject objects in different browsers? You can see the properties of the Internet Explorer XMLHttpRequest object in Table 3-1, and its methods in Table 3-2. The properties of this object for Mozilla, Netscape Navigator, and Firefox appear in Table 3-3, and Table 3-4 shows the methods. Apple hasn't published a full version of the properties and methods for its XMLHttpRequest object yet, but it has published a set of commonly used properties, which appear in Table 3-5, and commonly used methods, which appear in Table 3-6.

Table 3-1   XMLHttpRequest Object Properties for Internet Explorer

Property	Means	Read/write
onreadystatechange	Holds the name of the event handler that should be called when the value of the readyState property changes	Read/write
readyState	Holds the state of the request	Read-only
responseBody	Holds a response body, which is one way HTTP responses can be returned	Read-only
responseStream	Holds a response stream, a binary stream to the server	Read-only
responseText	Holds the response body as a string	Read-only
responseXML	Holds the response body as XML	Read-only
status	Holds the HTTP status code returned by a request	Read-only
statusText	Holds the HTTP response status text	Read-only

Table 3-2   XMLHttpRequest Object Methods for Internet Explorer

Method	Means
abort	Aborts the HTTP request
getAllResponseHeaders	Gets all the HTTP headers
getResponseHeader	Gets the value of an HTTP header
open	Opens a request to the server
send	Sends an HTTP request to the server
setRequestHeader	Sets the name and value of an HTTP header

Table 3-3   **XMLHttpRequest Object Properties for Mozilla, Firefox, and Netscape Navigator**

Property	Means	Read/write
channel	Holds the channel used to perform the request	Read-only
readyState	Holds the state of the request	Read-only
responseText	Holds the response body as a string	Read-only
responseXML	Holds the response body as XML	Read-only
status	Holds the HTTP status code returned by a request	Read-only
statusText	Holds the HTTP response status text	Read-only

Table 3-4   **XMLHttpRequest Object Methods for Mozilla, Firefox, and Netscape Navigator**

Method	Means
abort	Aborts the HTTP request
getAllResponseHeaders	Gets all the HTTP headers
getResponseHeader	Gets the value of an HTTP header
openRequest	Native (non-script) method to open a request
overrideMimeType	Overrides the MIME type the server returns

Table 3-5   **XMLHttpRequest Object Properties for Apple Safari**

Property	Means	Read/write
onreadystatechange	Holds the name of the event handler that should be called when the value of the readyState property changes	Read/write
readyState	Holds the state of the request	Read-only
responseText	Holds the response body as a string	Read-only
responseXML	Holds the response body as XML	Read-only

Property	Means	Read/write
status	Holds the HTTP status code returned by a request	Read-only
statusText	Holds the HTTP response status text	Read-only

Table 3-6   **XMLHttpRequest Object Methods for Apple Safari**

Method	Means
abort	Aborts the HTTP request
getAllResponseHeaders	Gets all the HTTP headers
getResponseHeader	Gets the value of an HTTP header
open	Opens a request to the server
send	Sends an HTTP request to the server
setRequestHeader	Sets the name and value of an HTTP header

Checking to make sure you have a valid XMLHttpRequest object

Now that you've got the needed XMLHttpRequest object stored in the variable XMLHttpRequestObject, how do you actually fetch the text the application wants when the user clicks the button? All that takes place in the getData function in the <script> element, as shown here:

```
<script language = "javascript">
      .
      .
      .
   function getData(dataSource, divID)
   {
      .
      .
      .
   }
</script>
```

In this function, the code starts by checking to make sure that there really is a valid object in the XMLHttpRequestObject variable with an if statement. (Remember, if the object creation didn't work, this variable will hold a value of false — and because JavaScript treats anything that isn't false as true, if the variable contains a real object, the if statement's condition will be true.)

```
<script language = "javascript">
   .
   .
   .
   function getData(dataSource, divID)
   {
     if(XMLHttpRequestObject) {
       .
       .
       .
       .
     }
   }
</script>
```

Opening the XMLHttpRequest object

At this point, you have an XMLHttpRequest object in the XMLHttpRequestObject variable. You can configure the object to use the URL you want by using this object's open method. Here's how you use the open method (keep in mind that items in square braces, [and], are optional):

```
open("method", "URL"[, asyncFlag[, "userName"[, "password"]]])
```

Table 3-7 tells you what these various parameters mean.

Table 3-7	Parameters for the open Method
Parameter	*What It Means*
method	The HTTP method used to open the connection, such as GET, POST, PUT, HEAD, or PROPFIND.
URL	The requested URL.
asyncFlag	A Boolean value indicating whether the call is asynchronous. The default is true.
userName	The user name.
password	The password.

The URL you want to fetch data from is passed to the `getData` function as the `dataSource` argument. To open a URL, you can use the standard HTML techniques like `GET`, `POST`, or `PUT`. (When you create an HTML form, you use these methods to indicate how to send data to the server.) When using Ajax, you usually use `GET` primarily when you want to retrieve data, and `POST` when you want to send a lot of data to the server, so this example uses `GET` to open the `data.txt` file on the server this way:

```
<script language = "javascript">
    .
    .
    .
  function getData(dataSource, divID)
  {
    if(XMLHttpRequestObject) {

      XMLHttpRequestObject.open("GET", dataSource);
      .
      .
      .
    }
  }
</script>
```

This configures the `XMLHttpRequestObject` to use the URL you've specified — `http://localhost/ch03/data.txt` in this example — but doesn't actually connect to that file yet. (If you want to try this example on your own server, be sure to update that URL to point to wherever you've placed `data.txt`.) Make sure that `data.txt` is in the same directory on your server as `index.html` is.

By default, the connection to this URL is made *asynchronously,* which means that this statement doesn't wait until the connection is made and the data is finished downloading. (You can use an optional third argument, `asyncFlag`, in the call to the open method to make the call synchronous, which means that everything would stop until the call to that method finishes, but things aren't done that way in Ajax — after all, Ajax stands for Asynchronous JavaScript and XML.)

So how can you be notified when the data you're downloading is ready? Glad you asked; check out the following section.

When you're ready: Handling asynchronous downloads

The `XMLHttpRequest` object has a property named `onreadystatechange` that lets you handle asynchronous loading operations. If you assign the name of a JavaScript function in your script to this property, that function will be called each time the `XMLHttpRequest` object's status changes — as when it's downloading data.

You can use a shortcut to assign a Javascript function to the `onreadystate change` property, a shortcut which you often see in Ajax scripts — you can create a function on the fly (sometimes called an *anonymous* function because it doesn't have a name). To create a function on the fly, just use the `function` statement and define the body of this new function in curly braces this way:

```
<script language = "javascript">
        .
        .
        .

    function getData(dataSource, divID)
    {
      if(XMLHttpRequestObject) {
        var obj = document.getElementById(divID);
        XMLHttpRequestObject.open("GET", dataSource);

        XMLHttpRequestObject.onreadystatechange = function()
        {
             .
             .
             .
        }

      }
    }
</script>
```

This new, anonymous function will be called when the `XMLHttpRequest Object` undergoes some change, as when it downloads data. You need to watch two properties of this object here — the `readyState` property and the `status` property. The `readyState` property tells you how the data loading is going. Here are the possible values the `readyState` property can take (note that a value of 4 means your data is all downloaded):

- ✔ 0 uninitialized
- ✔ 1 loading
- ✔ 2 loaded
- ✔ 3 interactive
- ✔ 4 complete

The status property holds the status of the download itself. (This is the standard HTTP status code that the browser got for the URL you supplied.) Here are some of the possible values the status property can hold (note that a value of 200 means everything is just fine):

- ✔ 200 OK
- ✔ 201 Created
- ✔ 204 No Content
- ✔ 205 Reset Content
- ✔ 206 Partial Content
- ✔ 400 Bad Request
- ✔ 401 Unauthorized
- ✔ 403 Forbidden
- ✔ 404 Not Found
- ✔ 405 Method Not Allowed
- ✔ 406 Not Acceptable
- ✔ 407 Proxy Authentication Required
- ✔ 408 Request Timeout
- ✔ 411 Length Required
- ✔ 413 Requested Entity Too Large
- ✔ 414 Requested URL Too Long
- ✔ 415 Unsupported Media Type
- ✔ 500 Internal Server Error
- ✔ 501 Not Implemented
- ✔ 502 Bad Gateway
- ✔ 503 Service Unavailable
- ✔ 504 Gateway Timeout
- ✔ 505 HTTP Version Not Supported

To make sure the data you want has been downloaded completely and everything went okay, check to make sure the XMLHttpRequestObject object's readyState property equals 4 and the status property equals 200. Here's how you can do that in JavaScript:

```
<script language = "javascript">
   .
   .
   .

 function getData(dataSource, divID)
 {
   if(XMLHttpRequestObject) {
     var obj = document.getElementById(divID);
     XMLHttpRequestObject.open("GET", dataSource);

     XMLHttpRequestObject.onreadystatechange = function()
     {
       if (XMLHttpRequestObject.readyState == 4 &&
         XMLHttpRequestObject.status == 200) {
         .
         .
         .
       }
     }

   }
 }
</script>
```

Very cool — if all systems are go at this point, the browser got your data from the server (that is, the text inside the data.txt file that you pointed to with the URL you passed to the open method). Now how do you get that data yourself? Find out in the following section.

You got the data!

To get the data with the XMLHttpRequest object, use one of the two usual ways:

  ✔ **If you retrieved data that you want to treat as standard text,** you can use the object's responseText property.

  ✔ **If your data has been formatted as XML,** you can use the responseXML property. In this example, data.txt simply contains text, so you use the responseText property.

To make the downloaded text actually appear on your Web page which is where you wanted it all along — you can assign that text to the <div> element, whose ID is targetDiv in the Web page and whose name was passed to the getData function. Here's how it works:

```
<script language = "javascript">
   .
   .
   .
```

```
function getData(dataSource, divID)
{
  if(XMLHttpRequestObject) {

    var obj = document.getElementById(divID);

    XMLHttpRequestObject.open("GET", dataSource);

    XMLHttpRequestObject.onreadystatechange = function()
    {
      if (XMLHttpRequestObject.readyState == 4 &&
        XMLHttpRequestObject.status == 200) {
          obj.innerHTML = XMLHttpRequestObject.responseText;
      }
    }

  }
}
</script>
```

Okay, you've set up your code to handle the response from the server when that response is sent to you. But now how do you actually connect to the server to get that response? You use the send method. When you're using the GET method, you send a value of null (null is a built-in value in JavaScript — it's a special value that holds zero in JavaScript) as in the following code to connect to the server and request your data using the XMLHttpRequest object that you've already configured:

```
<script language = "javascript">
    .
    .
    .
  function getData(dataSource, divID)
  {
    if(XMLHttpRequestObject) {
      var obj = document.getElementById(divID);
      XMLHttpRequestObject.open("GET", dataSource);

      XMLHttpRequestObject.onreadystatechange = function()
      {
        if (XMLHttpRequestObject.readyState == 4 &&
          XMLHttpRequestObject.status == 200) {
            obj.innerHTML = XMLHttpRequestObject.responseText;
        }
      }

      XMLHttpRequestObject.send(null);
    }
  }
</script>
```

That call to `send` is what actually downloads the data so that the anonymous function can handle that data. Excellent. You've just completed your first, full-fledged, Ajax application. This application fetches data behind the scenes from the server and displays it in the page without any full page refreshes. You can see it at work in Figures 3-1 and 3-2, which are shown earlier in this chapter.

You did all this by creating an `XMLHttpRequest` object and using its open method to configure that object, and the `send` method to connect to the server and get a response. And you recovered text from the server by using the request object's `responseText` property. Not bad for a first try.

Deciding on relative versus absolute URLs

This example fetched text from a file named data.txt, and that file is in the same ch03 folder as `index.html` you'll find available for download from the Web site associated with this book. Here's the URL that `index.html` uses to point to that file, `http://localhost/ch03/data.txt`:

```
<body>

  <H1>Fetching data with Ajax</H1>

  <form>
    <input type = "button" value = "Display Message"
      onclick = "getData('http://localhost/ch03/data.txt',
        'targetDiv')">
  </form>

  <div id="targetDiv">
    <p>The fetched data will go here.</p>
  </div>

</body>
```

However, because `data.txt` is in the same directory as `index.html`, you can refer to `data.txt` simply as `data.txt`, not `http://localhost/ch03/data.txt`:

```
<body>

  <H1>Fetching data with Ajax</H1>

  <form>
    <input type = "button" value = "Display Message"
      onclick = "getData('data.txt', 'targetDiv')">
  </form>

  <div id="targetDiv">
```

```
    <p>The fetched data will go here.</p>
  </div>

</body>
```

When you look at `index.html` in the browser, the directory `index.html` where it is located on the server becomes the default directory as far as the server is concerned. When `index.html` looks for `data.txt`, it isn't necessary to use the full URL, `http://localhost/ch03/data.txt` — instead, you can say simply `data.txt`, and the server will search the same directory where the page you're already looking at (`index.html`) is in for `data.txt`. `http://localhost/ch03/data.txt` is an *absolute URL,* but just the name `data.txt` is a *relative URL* (relative to the location of `index.html` — relative URLs can also include pathnames if appropriate).

Because the examples in this and the next few chapters are made up of HTML files, PHP scripts, and other files that are all supposed to go into the same directory on the server, I use relative URLs from now on. That way, you can run the examples no matter what the URL to your server is — you don't have to rewrite a URL such as `http://localhost/ch03/data.txt` to point to your server instead (such as `http://www.starpowder.com/frank/data.txt`).

Make sure that, when you run the examples in this book, any PHP, text, or other documents needed by a particular HTML file are in the *same directory* on your server as that HTML file. The easiest way to do that is to keep all files in the ch03 folder in the code for this book together in the same directory on your server, all the files in the ch04 folder together in the same directory, and so on.

Other ways of getting XMLHttpRequest objects

The example spelled out in the preceding sections shows one way to get an `XMLHttpRequest` object and work with it. Other ways exist as well, letting you work with more recent `XMLHttpRequest` objects. It's rare that you need to use newer `XMLHttpRequest` objects with Ajax, but if you want to, it's worth knowing how to do it.

For example, Internet Explorer has various versions of its `XMLHttpRequest` object available. You create the standard version of this object with the `Microsoft.XMLHTTP` ActiveX object, but there's a more recent version available: `MSXML2.XMLHTTP`. The `Microsoft.XMLHTTP` ActiveX object offers all the functionality you need for anything in this book, but if you want to work with `MSXML2.XMLHTTP` — or even newer versions, such as `MSXML2.XML-HTTP.3.0`, `MSXML2.XMLHTTP.4.0`, or now `MSXML2.XMLHTTP.5.0` — you can do that.

Here's an example showing how to work with a newer XMLHttpRequest object, using the JavaScript try/catch construct. If you try some code that might fail in a try statement, and it does fail, the code in the associated catch statement will be executed, allowing you to recover from the problem. So you might try to get an MSXML2.XMLHTTP ActiveX object first, and catch any problems that might result this way:

```
var XMLHttpRequestObject = false;

try {
    XMLHttpRequestObject = new ActiveXObject("MSXML2.XMLHTTP");
} catch (exception1) {
    .
    .
    .

}
```

If the browser couldn't create an MSXML2.XMLHTTP ActiveX object, you can try for a standard Microsoft.XMLHTTP ActiveX object by using another try/catch construct, as you see here:

```
var XMLHttpRequestObject = false;

try {
    XMLHttpRequestObject = new ActiveXObject("MSXML2.XMLHTTP");
} catch (exception1) {
    try {
        XMLHttpRequestObject = new ActiveXObject("Microsoft.XMLHTTP");
    } catch (exception2) {
        XMLHttpRequestObject = false;
    }
}
```

And if neither of these work, you can use the Mozilla/Firefox/Netscape Navigator/Safari way of doing things like this (note the use of the JavaScript ! operator here, which means "not," as listed in Chapter 2 — in other words, !XMLHttpRequestObject is true if the XMLHttpRequestObject doesn't exist):

```
var XMLHttpRequestObject = false;

try {
    XMLHttpRequestObject = new ActiveXObject("MSXML2.XMLHTTP");
} catch (exception1) {
    try {
        XMLHttpRequestObject = new ActiveXObject("Microsoft.XMLHTTP");
    } catch (exception2) {
        XMLHttpRequestObject = false;
    }
```

```
    }

    if (!XMLHttpRequestObject && window.XMLHttpRequest) {
        XMLHttpRequestObject = new XMLHttpRequest();
    }
```

Interactive Mouseovers Using Ajax

Here's another Ajax example — one that's a little more impressive visually.
This example, `mouseover.html`, appears in Figure 3-3. When you move the
mouse over one of the images on this page, the application fetches text for
that mouseover by using Ajax. Give it a try — just move the mouse around
and watch the text change to match.

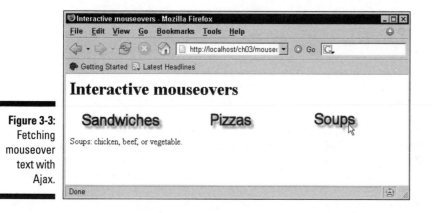

Figure 3-3:
Fetching
mouseover
text with
Ajax.

This one isn't hard to implement. All you really have to do is to connect the
`getData` function (which fetches text data and displays it in the `<div>` element whose name you pass) to the `onmouseover` event of each of the
images you see in Figure 3-3.

The text data for each image is stored in a different file — `sandwiches.txt`,
`pizzas.txt`, and `soups.txt` — so here's how everything works:

```
<body>

    <H1>Interactive mouseovers</H1>

    <img src="Image1.jpg"
        onmouseover="getData('sandwiches.txt',
        'targetDiv')">

    <img src="Image2.jpg"
```

```
    onmouseover="getData('pizzas.txt',
    'targetDiv')">

<img src="Image3.jpg"
    onmouseover="getData('soups.txt',
    'targetDiv')">

<div id="targetDiv">
    <p>Welcome to my restaurant!</p>
</div>

</body>
```

No problem at all. The rest is just the same as in the first example in this chapter. Here's the contents of `sandwiches.txt`:

```
We offer too many sandwiches to list!
```

And `pizzas.txt`:

```
Toppings: pepperoni, sausage, black olives.
```

And `soups.txt`:

```
Soups: chicken, beef, or vegetable.
```

So you can download text to match the image the mouse cursor is over. What about downloading some pictures? Unfortunately, that's no go. Can't do it, because you only have two choices with the `XMLHttpRequest` object — text or XML (which is also just text, although formatted following the XML rules).

There might be a way to download images and other binary data by using the Internet Explorer `XMLHttpRequest` object one day, because it has an interesting property: `responseStream`. The `responseStream` property represents a binary data stream from the server, and that will indeed let you send binary data from server to the browser. The problem is that JavaScript doesn't give you any way to work with such a stream. Other Microsoft Web-enabled languages, such as Visual Basic, can work with this property, but not Internet Explorer's Jscript (yet).

Getting Interactive with Server-Side Scripting

All the preceding examples in this chapter show you how to download static text files behind the scenes by using Ajax methods, but you can also connect to server-side applications. And doing that opens all kinds of possibilities because you can send data to those server-side applications and get their responses behind the scenes.

This is where the real power of Ajax comes in. You can create an application that watches what the user is doing, and the application can get data from the server as needed. Virtually all Ajax applications connect to some kind of server program.

Choosing a server-side scripting language

I'm going to use two different server-side scripting languages in this book — PHP and JavaServer Pages (JSP). The main issue here is Ajax, of course, so you won't have to know how to write PHP or JSP to follow along. However, if you want to put your Ajax expertise to work in the real world, it's useful to have a working knowledge of these two languages because they're probably the easiest type of server-side programming around. Among the Ajax examples you'll see on the Web that connect to server-side scripts, PHP is the most popular choice. I start in this chapter by taking a look at connecting to some PHP scripts using Ajax so that you can handle XML data and send data to the server to configure the response you get back from the server.

Thousands of Web servers support PHP, so if you want to sign up for one, they're easy to find. Your current server might already support PHP, because most do these days — just ask them. For testing purposes, you can also install PHP on your own machine. You can get PHP for free at www.php.net, complete with installation instructions (on Windows, installing can be as easy as running .exe files).

Connecting to a script on a server

To start, how about converting the first example, index.html (Listing 3.1), in this chapter to talk to a PHP script instead of just downloading a text file? Instead of connecting to data.txt on the server, this next example, index2. html, connects to a PHP script, data.php.

The text in data.txt is "This text was fetched using Ajax.", so data.php will return the same text for this first example. Here's what that PHP file looks like (remember, you don't have to know PHP or JSP to read this book):

```php
<?php
    echo 'This text was fetched using Ajax.';
?>
```

If you install `data.php` on your own computer for testing purposes in a folder named ch03, its relative URL is `sample.php`. You can modify `index.html` into `index2.html` by connecting to that URL, like this:

```html
<html>
  <head>
    <title>Ajax and PHP at work</title>

    <script language = "javascript">
      var XMLHttpRequestObject = false;

      if (window.XMLHttpRequest) {
        XMLHttpRequestObject = new XMLHttpRequest();
      } else if (window.ActiveXObject) {
        XMLHttpRequestObject = new ActiveXObject("Microsoft.XMLHTTP");
      }

      function getData(dataSource, divID)
      {
        if(XMLHttpRequestObject) {
          var obj = document.getElementById(divID);
          XMLHttpRequestObject.open("GET", dataSource);

          XMLHttpRequestObject.onreadystatechange = function()
          {
            if (XMLHttpRequestObject.readyState == 4 &&
              XMLHttpRequestObject.status == 200) {
                obj.innerHTML = XMLHttpRequestObject.responseText;
            }
          }

          XMLHttpRequestObject.send(null);
        }
      }
    </script>
  </head>

<body>

  <H1>Fetching data with Ajax and PHP</H1>

  <form>
    <input type = "button" value = "Display Message"
      onclick = "getData('data.php', 'targetDiv')">
  </form>

  <div id="targetDiv">
    <p>The fetched data will go here.</p>
  </div>

</body>
</html>
```

This time, the text the application fetches comes from a PHP script, not a text file. You can see this application at work in Figure 3-4. When the user clicks the button, JavaScript connects to `data.php`, and the returned text appears on the Web page. Cool.

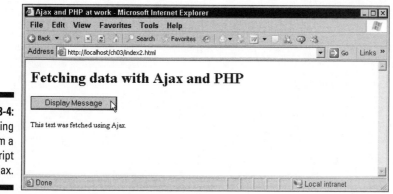

Figure 3-4:
Fetching data from a PHP script with Ajax.

Time for Some XML

Ajax applications can transfer data back and forth by using simple text, but, after all, Ajax stands for Asynchronous JavaScript and XML. How about getting some XML into this equation? Take a look at the new example in Figure 3-5, `options.html`, which gives the users various options for resetting the color of the text on this Web page (the `"Color this text."` text). Although you can't see it in glorious black and white, the text is green here.

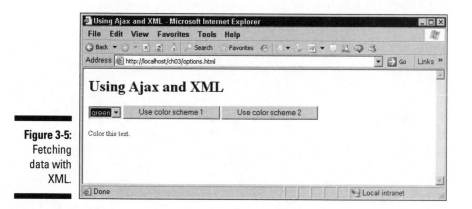

Figure 3-5:
Fetching data with XML.

The various colors in the drop-down list in this application are fetched by using Ajax methods and data formatted as XML. This application has two different color schemes.

Color scheme 1:

✔ red

✔ green

✔ blue

And color scheme 2:

✔ black

✔ white

✔ orange

The user can select between these two (admittedly rather arbitrary) schemes just by clicking the buttons you see in Figure 3-5; when he clicks a button, the colors for that color scheme are loaded into the drop-down list at left. The user can select a color, and when he does, the `"Color this text."` text is colored to match.

Getting XML from a PHP script

Now, how does the application in Figure 3-5 work again? Two PHP scripts supply the colors in each color scheme, `options1.php` and `options2.php`. These scripts send back their data by using XML from `options1.php`, like this (this is the XML that `options1.php` ends up sending back to the browser):

```
<?xml version="1.0"?>
<options>
  <option>
    red
  </option>
  <option>
    green
  </option>
  <option>
    blue
  </option>
</options>
```

This is valid XML; it starts with an XML declaration, `<?xml version="1.0"?>`, which all XML documents must have to be legal. All XML documents must also have a *document element,* which encloses all other elements. You make up the names of your elements in XML, and here the document element is the `<options>` element.

Don't worry if you aren't an XML pro. This is as much as you're going to have to know about XML for most of this book — XML documents start with an XML declaration, have one document element that contains all other elements, you make up the names of the elements, and each element can contain text or other elements. There's more to XML, of course, especially when it comes to handling it with JavaScript. For the full details on XML and how to work with it in JavaScript, take a look at Chapter 8.

The `<options>` element encloses three `<option>` elements, each of which contain text corresponding to a color: red, green, and blue here. This first XML document is a simple one, but it gets the job done — the idea is to list three different colors, and it does that.

How do you send this XML back from the server by using a PHP script? The first thing you have to do is to set the content-type header in the document you're creating to `"text/xml"`. This informs the browser that this data is XML data, and should be treated as such. (This is a necessary step — otherwise the browser will not consider your data as XML.) Here's how you do it:

```
<?
header("Content-type: text/xml");



        .
        .
        .
?>
```

Then you have to construct the rest of the XML document. Here's how you store the names of the colors in an array, and then loop over that array, sending each color in an `<option>` element back to the browser:

```
<?
header("Content-type: text/xml");
$options = array('red', 'green', 'blue');
echo '<?xml version="1.0"?>';
echo '<options>';
foreach ($options as $value)
{
    echo '<option>';
    echo $value;
    echo '</option>';
}
echo '</options>';
?>
```

Perfect. And here's what `options2.php` looks like, for the second color scheme:

```
<?
header("Content-type: text/xml");
$options = array('black', 'white', 'orange');
echo '<?xml version="1.0"?>';
echo '<options>';
foreach ($options as $value)
{
    echo '<option>';
    echo $value;
    echo '</option>';
}
echo '</options>';
?>
```

Setting up a Web page to read XML

Now what about the important part of this application, the Ajax part? That takes place in `options.html`. Two buttons let the user select between color schemes, and those buttons call two functions, `getOptions1` for color scheme 1 and `getOptions2` for color scheme 2, like this:

```
<body>

   <h1>Using Ajax and XML</h1>

   <form>
       <select size="1" id="optionList"
         onchange="setOption()">
         <option>Select a scheme</option>
       </select>
     <input type = "button" value = "Use color scheme 1"
       onclick = "getOptions1()">
     <input type = "button" value = "Use color scheme 2"
       onclick = "getOptions2()">
   </form>

   <div id="targetDiv" width =100 height=100>Color this text.</div>

</body>
```

The `getOptions1` function connects to the `options1.php` script like this:

```
    var options;

    function getOptions1()
    {
      if(XMLHttpRequestObject) {
```

```
XMLHttpRequestObject.open("GET",
"options1.php", true);
        .
        .
        .
    }
}
```

Handling the XML you read from the server

When the response from the server comes back as XML, not just text, you read that response by using the `responseXML` property of the `XML HttpRequest` object, like so:

```
var options;

function getOptions1()
{
  if(XMLHttpRequestObject) {
    XMLHttpRequestObject.open("GET",
    "options1.php", true);

    XMLHttpRequestObject.onreadystatechange = function()
    {
      if (XMLHttpRequestObject.readyState == 4 &&
        XMLHttpRequestObject.status == 200) {
        var xmlDocument = XMLHttpRequestObject.responseXML;
        .

        .

        .
      }
    }

    XMLHttpRequestObject.send(null);
  }
}
```

The bold line of JavaScript in the preceding code stores the XML that `options1.php` sent back in a variable named `xmlDocument`. How can you handle that XML in JavaScript?

That turns out not to be hard. Just as you can use the built-in `getElement ById` function to get an element by its ID value, so you can use the built-in `getElementsByTagName` function to get all the elements with a certain name. In this case, the elements with the data you want are the `<option>` elements, so you can get them and store them all in a variable named `options` like this:

```
var options;

function getOptions1()
{
  if(XMLHttpRequestObject) {
    XMLHttpRequestObject.open("GET",
    "options1.php", true);

    XMLHttpRequestObject.onreadystatechange = function()
    {
      if (XMLHttpRequestObject.readyState == 4 &&
        XMLHttpRequestObject.status == 200) {
      var xmlDocument = XMLHttpRequestObject.responseXML;
      options = xmlDocument.getElementsByTagName("option");
        .
        .
        .
      }
    }

    XMLHttpRequestObject.send(null);
  }
}
```

So far so good — you've stored the colors that were returned from the server in the variable named options. Now how do you unpack the actual names of those colors? Well, take a look at the following section.

Extracting data from XML

To extract information from XML, this example calls another function called `listOptions`, which will unpack the colors and store them in the drop-down list:

```
var options;

function getOptions1()
{
  if(XMLHttpRequestObject) {
    XMLHttpRequestObject.open("GET",
    "options1.php", true);

    XMLHttpRequestObject.onreadystatechange = function()
    {
      if (XMLHttpRequestObject.readyState == 4 &&
```

```
            XMLHttpRequestObject.status == 200) {
         var xmlDocument = XMLHttpRequestObject.responseXML;
         options = xmlDocument.getElementsByTagName("option");
         listOptions();
         }
      }

   XMLHttpRequestObject.send(null);
   }
}
```

How does the `listOptions` function unpack the colors from the options variable and store them in the drop-down HTML `<select>` control where the
user can select them? (The `<select>` controls display a drop-down list, such
as the one in this example.) Right now, the options variable contains this data:

```
<option>
  red
</option>
<option>
  green
</option>
<option>
  blue
</option>
```

This data is actually stored as an array of `<option>` elements, which makes
things easier because you can loop over that array. (I introduce looping in
arrays in Chapter 2.) You can find the number of items in an array by using
the array's length property, so here's how to loop over all the `<option>` elements in the `listOptions` function:

```
function listOptions ()
{
    var loopIndex;

    for (loopIndex = 0; loopIndex < options.length; loopIndex++ )
    {
        .
        .
        .
    }
}
```

Good so far. As you loop, you can refer to each `<option>` element in the
options variable this way: `options[loopIndex]` — that picks out the current `<option>` element each time through the loop. The first such element
looks like this:

```
<option>
  red
</option>
```

How do you pick out the color from this XML element? JavaScript is set up to handle elements like this by treating the text in this element as a *child node* of the element — that is, as a node contained inside the element. To get that child node, you can use the element's `firstChild` property (Chapter 8 has all the details on handling XML with JavaScript in depth), so here's how you recover the current `<option>` element's text as an XML node: `options[loopIndex].firstChild`. This gives you a *text node* — a node that contains only text, believe it or not — that holds the text for the color red. How do you actually extract the text corresponding to the color? You use the text node's data property, so (finally!) you can use this expression to extract the color from the current `<option>` element: `options[loopIndex].firstChild.data`.

Whew. So now you can get the colors from each `<option>` element in the `options` variable.

Listing the colors in the drop-down control

How do you store those colors in the drop-down `<select>` control the one named `optionList` — so the user can select the color she wants? In JavaScript, you can get an object that corresponds to the drop-down control like this:

```
function listOptions ()
{
    var loopIndex;
    var selectControl = document.getElementById('optionList');

    for (loopIndex = 0; loopIndex < options.length; loopIndex++ )
    {
        .
        .
        .
    }
}
```

To add the colors to the `<select>` control, you use the control's `options` property, which holds the items listed in the control. Each item you want to add to the list is an `option` object that corresponds to an HTML `<option>` element, so you can add all the colors to the `<select>` control like this:

```
function listOptions ()
{
    var loopIndex;
    var selectControl = document.getElementById('optionList');

    for (loopIndex = 0; loopIndex < options.length; loopIndex++ )
```

```
        {
            selectControl.options[loopIndex] = new
                Option(options[loopIndex].firstChild.data);
        }
    }
```

And that's it. Now the drop-down list displays the available colors for the color scheme that the user chose.

You have to take one last step. When the user selects a color in the drop-down list, the code has to color the displayed text to match. When the user makes a selection in the drop-down list of colors, the list's onchange event occurs, which calls a function named setOption, as you see here:

```
<form>
    <select size="1" id="optionList"
      onchange="setOption()">
      <option>Select a scheme</option>
    </select>
  <input type = "button" value = "Use color scheme 1"
    onclick = "getOptions1()">
  <input type = "button" value = "Use color scheme 2"
    onclick = "getOptions2()">
</form>
```

The setOption function's job is to color the "Color this text." text, stored in a <div> element named "targetDiv", to match the color the user selected. Which color did the user select? You can determine the number of the item the user selected using the <select> control's selectedIndex property. If the user selected the first item, this property will hold 0; if he selected the second item, this property will hold 1; and so on. You can use this property together with the options variable (which holds all the <option> elements you got from the server) to determine what the appropriate color is to use. So here's how to get the color the user selected (whoever said JavaScript is a lightweight language never had to deal with expressions like this one):

```
options[document.getElementById('optionList').selectedIndex].firstChild.data
```

How do you color the text in the targetDiv <div> element to match this color? You can use the <div> element's style property to recover its style setting. And to access to the <div> element's text color, you can refer to it with the style attribute color. So here's how you refer to the color of the text in the targetDiv <div> element from JavaScript:

```
document.getElementById('targetDiv').style.color
```

That means that to set the color of the text in the `targetDiv` `<div>` element to match the color the user selected in the `setOption` function, you can do this:

```
function setOption()
{
    document.getElementById('targetDiv').style.color =
        options[document.getElementById
            ('optionList').selectedIndex].firstChild.data;
}
```

Yep, it looks complex, but as you get to know JavaScript, or if you're a JavaScript guru already, this kind of stuff will become second nature. It just takes some time. And that's it — this example is a success.

But if you take a step back and assess the situation as an Ajax programmer, you might want to know why you need two PHP scripts to handle the two different color schemes. Why can't you just pass some data to a *single* PHP script to indicate which color scheme we want? That's a very good question. You can indeed pass data to server-side scripts from JavaScript, and that's an important skill because Ajax applications often need to send data to the server to get the response they need.

Passing Data to the Server with GET

No good reason exists for having two server-side PHP scripts, `options1.php` and `options2.php`, to pass back the colors in the two color schemes. All you really need is one server-side script — `options.php` — but you have to tell it which color scheme you're interested in. And doing that means passing data to the server.

Although these examples use PHP, the way Ajax passes data back to the server is the same for just about any server-side programming language, from PHP to Perl, from JSP to Python. So how do you pass data to a server-side program in Ajax? One way of doing this is to use the GET method and *URL encoding*. But one issue here is worth noting — if you use URL encoding and the GET method, your data is pretty public. As it zings around the Internet, it could conceivably be read by others. You can protect against that by using the POST method instead of GET.

However, to use POST, you still need to understand GET. The following sections have all the details.

When you use the GET method of fetching data from the server, as all the Ajax examples in this book have so far, data is sent from Web pages back to the server by using URL encoding, which means that data is appended to the actual URL that is read from the server.

For example, if you're using the GET method and you have a text field named
a that contains the number 5, a text field named b that contains the number
6, and a text field named c that contains the text "Now is the time", all
that data would be encoded and added to the URL you're accessing. When
data is URL encoded, a question mark (?) is added to the end of the URL, and
the data, in *name=data* format, is added after that question mark. Spaces in
text are converted to a plus sign (+), and you separate pairs of *name=data*
items with ampersands (&). So to encode the data from the a, b, and c text
fields and send it to http://www.*servername*.com/*user*/*scriptname*,
you'd use this URL:

```
http://www.servername.com/user/scriptname?a=5&b=6&c=Now+is+the+time
```

Note that the data you send this way is always text — even if you're sending
numbers, they're treated as text.

The JavaScript escape function will encode data for appending to the end
of an URL, and it'll handle things like converting spaces into + signs automatically. For example, if you want to prepare the text from a text field for
appending to a URL, you would use code like this: var urlReadyText =
escape(textField.value);.

In this particular example, the goal is to tell a single online script, options.
php, which color scheme you want to use, scheme 1 or scheme 2. The idea
is to send the value "1" or "2" to options.php. How you recover those
values in your server-side script depends on what language you're using. In
PHP, for example, you can recover those values by using an array named
$_GET (because you're using the GET method — if you were using the POST
method, you'd use $_POST). So if you name the data you're sending to the
script scheme in a URL something like this

```
http://localhost/ch03/options.php?scheme=1
```

you can then recover the setting of the scheme argument in your PHP as
$_GET["scheme"]. For scheme = "1", you want to send back the colors
'red', 'green', and 'blue'; for scheme = "2", you send back the values
'black', 'white', and 'orange'. Here's what options.php looks like —
note the part that checks what scheme is being requested:

```php
<?
header("Content-type: text/xml");
if ($_GET["scheme"] == "1")
  $options = array('red', 'green', 'blue');
if ($_GET["scheme"] == "2")
  $options = array('black', 'white', 'orange');
echo '<?xml version="1.0"?>';
echo '<options>';
foreach ($options as $value)
{
```

```
  echo '<option>';
  echo $value;
  echo '</option>';
}
echo '</options>';
?>
```

Okay, this PHP script sends back two different XML documents, depending on which color scheme you choose — 1 or 2. The next step is to design a new HTML document, options2.html, that will call options2.php correctly. In options2.html, the buttons the user can click to select the color scheme will pass the number of the selected scheme, 1 or 2, to the getOptions function, like this:

```
<body>

    <h1>Passing data using Ajax and XML</h1>

    <form>
        <select size="1" id="optionList"
          onchange="setOption()">
          <option>Select a scheme</option>
        </select>
      <input type = "button" value = "Use color scheme 1"
        onclick = "getOptions('1')">
      <input type = "button" value = "Use color scheme 2"
        onclick = "getOptions('2')">
    </form>

    <div id="targetDiv" width =100 height=100>Color this text.</div>

</body>
```

The getOptions function accepts that one argument, the scheme number:

```
function getOptions(scheme)
{
    .
    .
    .
}
```

The first step is to URL encode the scheme number, setting the scheme argument to "1" or "2", as the options.php script will expect:

```
function getOptions(scheme)
{
  var url = "options2.php?scheme=" + scheme;
    .
    .
    .
}
```

Excellent. Now all you've got to do is to open the URL by using the GET method and then use the data from the server to fill the drop-down list:

```
function getOptions(scheme)
{
  var url = "options2.php?scheme=" + scheme;

  if(XMLHttpRequestObject) {
    XMLHttpRequestObject.open("GET", url, true);

    XMLHttpRequestObject.onreadystatechange = function()
    {
      if (XMLHttpRequestObject.readyState == 4 &&
        XMLHttpRequestObject.status == 200) {
      var xmlDocument = XMLHttpRequestObject.responseXML;
      options = xmlDocument.getElementsByTagName("option");
      listOptions();
      }
    }

    XMLHttpRequestObject.send(null);
  }
}
```

And that's it — options2.html will call options.php on the server, passing the number of the color scheme the user selected. And options.php will send back the data for the colors in that scheme. Very nice. This works as it should. Now you're sending data to the server.

Passing Data to the Server with POST

When you pass data to a URL by using the POST method, it's encoded internally (in the HTTP request sent to the server), which makes sending data more secure than with GET (although not as secure as using a secure HTTPS connection to the server).

In the following sections, you see how using the POST method works.

Passing data by using the POST method in Ajax is a little different than using GET. As far as the PHP goes, you can recover data sent to a PHP script by using POST with the $_POST array, not $_GET. Here's what that looks like in a new PHP script, options3.php:

```
<?
header("Content-type: text/xml");
if ($_POST["scheme"] == "1")
  $options = array('red', 'green', 'blue');
if ($_POST["scheme"] == "2")
  $options = array('black', 'white', 'orange');
```

```
echo '<?xml version="1.0"?>';
echo '<options>';
foreach ($options as $value)
{
  echo '<option>';
  echo $value;
  echo '</option>';
}
echo '</options>';
?>
```

I've heard of rare PHP installations where $_POST wouldn't work with Ajax applications when you use the POST method, in which case you have to use $HTTP_RAW_POST_DATA instead. This technique gives you the raw data string sent to the PHP script (such as "a=5&b=6&c=Now+is+the+time"), and it's up to you to extract your data from it.

How do you use the POST method in your JavaScript? It isn't as easy as just changing "GET" to "POST" when you open the connection to the server:

```
XMLHttpRequestObject.open("POST", url);    //Won't work by itself!
```

It isn't as easy as that, because you don't URL-encode your data when you use POST. Instead, you have to explicitly send that data by using the XMLHttpRequest object's send method.

Here's what you do. You set up the URL to open without any URL encoding this way in the getOptions function, which is the function that communicates with the server:

```
function getOptions(scheme)
{
  var url = "options3.php";
      .
      .
      .
}
```

Then you configure the XMLHttpRequest object to use this URL. You do this by using the open method and by specifying that you want to use the POST method:

```
function getOptions(scheme)
{
  var url = "options3.php";

  if(XMLHttpRequestObject) {
    XMLHttpRequestObject.open("POST", url);
```

```
    .
    .
    .
  }
```

To use the POST method, you should also set an HTTP header for the request that indicates the data in the request will be set up in the standard POST way. Here's what that looks like:

```
function getOptions(scheme)
{
  var url = "options3.php";

  if(XMLHttpRequestObject) {
    XMLHttpRequestObject.open("POST", url);
    XMLHttpRequestObject.setRequestHeader('Content-Type',
      'application/x-www-form-urlencoded');
    .
    .
    .
  }
}
```

Then you can connect an anonymous function to the XMLHttpRequest object's onreadystatechange property as before to handle asynchronous requests, as shown here:

```
function getOptions(scheme)
{
  var url = "options3.php";

  if(XMLHttpRequestObject) {
    XMLHttpRequestObject.open("POST", url);
    XMLHttpRequestObject.setRequestHeader('Content-Type',
      'application/x-www-form-urlencoded');

    XMLHttpRequestObject.onreadystatechange = function()
    {
      if (XMLHttpRequestObject.readyState == 4 &&
        XMLHttpRequestObject.status == 200) {
        var xmlDocument = XMLHttpRequestObject.responseXML;
        options = xmlDocument.getElementsByTagName("option");
        listoptions();
      }
    }
    .
    .
    .
  }
}
```

And now comes the crux. Instead of sending a `null` value as you would if you were using the GET method, you now send the data you want the script to get. In this case, that's `scheme = 1`, like this:

```
function getOptions(scheme)
{
  var url = "options3.php";

  if(XMLHttpRequestObject) {
    XMLHttpRequestObject.open("POST", url);
    XMLHttpRequestObject.setRequestHeader('Content-Type',
      'application/x-www-form-urlencoded');

    XMLHttpRequestObject.onreadystatechange = function()
    {
      if (XMLHttpRequestObject.readyState == 4 &&
        XMLHttpRequestObject.status == 200) {
      var xmlDocument = XMLHttpRequestObject.responseXML;
      options = xmlDocument.getElementsByTagName("option");
      listOptions();
      }
    }

    XMLHttpRequestObject.send("scheme=" + scheme);

  }
}
```

There you go. Now this new version of the Ajax application, `options3. html`, will use the POST method to send its data to `options3.php`, which will return its data in XML format. Very neat.

If you want to use XML to send your data to the server-side program, the POST method works, too. That's because you don't have to explicitly encode the data you send to the server yourself, appending it to the end of an URL. (Some servers have limits on how long URLs can be.)

To send your data as XML, you set a Request header so that the content type of your request will be `"text/xml"` instead of `"application/x-www-form-urlencoded"`:

```
XMLHttpRequestObject.setRequestHeader("Content-Type", "text/xml")
```

Then you can send your XML directly to the server by using the `send` method, which goes something like this:

```
XMLHttpRequestObject.send("<doc><name>limit</name><data>5</data></doc>");
```

Chapter 4

Ajax in Depth

. . . .

In This Chapter

▶ Returning JavaScript from the server

▶ Returning JavaScript objects

▶ Connecting to Google Suggest yourself

▶ Creating a live search

▶ Performing server-side validation

▶ Handling head requests

▶ Handling multiple XMLHttp requests at the same time

. . . .

"**H**ey!" says the highly-paid master Ajax programmer, "what's all this about? I'm just doing my normal Ajax programming here, and some darn security message keeps popping up."

"The browser's giving you a security warning," the CEO says. "It says your application is trying to access another Web site."

"Well, that's very helpful news," the highly-paid master Ajax programmer says, "I know that."

"You shouldn't try to connect to another Web domain like Google from your JavaScript — didn't you read Chapter 4 in *Ajax For Dummies*?" you say calmly, emerging from the shadows.

"Huh?" asks the master Ajax programmer.

"It's okay," you say, sitting down and taking over, "I'll show you how this should work — for a substantial fee."

You know Ajax adds power to your Web applications, but as this example shows, unless you know the tricks, problems such as this one can drive your users away. This chapter explains how you can best implement powerful Ajax techniques, such as connecting to Google for instant searches, returning JavaScript from the server, sending Http head requests to the server, debugging Ajax, and handling multithreading issues. It's all coming up in this chapter.

Returning JavaScript from the Server

In Chapter 3, I explain how to deal with text sent back to an Ajax application from the server and how to work with simple XML sent back from the server as well. But there's another technique you sometimes see — the server can send back JavaScript for you to execute. This isn't as wacky as it sounds, because you can use the built-in JavaScript function named `eval` to evaluate text sent back to you from the server, and if that text is JavaScript, you're in business.

When do you send back JavaScript from the server?

You can sometimes see this technique used when an Ajax application sends multiple requests to a server, and you don't know which one will return first. In such a case, programmers sometimes have the server return the actual JavaScript to be executed that will call the correct function — one function for one asynchronous request, another function for another.

I don't recommend this technique except in one case — where you don't have any control over the server-side code, and you have to deal with the JavaScript it sends you (as when connecting to Google Suggest, which I explain later in this chapter). Otherwise, it's not the best programming form to have the server return code to execute — the server-side program shouldn't have to know the details of your JavaScript code, and getting code from outside sources makes your application that much harder to debug and maintain. Instead, I recommend that your call to the server return a value that can be tested, and the JavaScript code in the browser can then call the correct function.

On the other hand, this is a common Ajax technique that's sometimes unavoidable when you have to deal with a server over which you have no control that returns JavaScript code, so you should get to know how this works.

How does returning JavaScript work?

To show you how this technique works, here's an example — `javascript. html` in the code for this book. This example displays a button with the caption `Fetch JavaScript`, as you can see in Figure 4-1.

Figure 4-1:
Fetching
JavaScript
by using
Ajax.

Here's how to create the button in HTML in `javascript.html`:

```
<body>

  <H1>Returning JavaScript</H1>

  <form>
    <input type = "button" value = "Fetch JavaScript"
      onclick = "getData('javascript.php')">
  </form>

  <div id="targetDiv">
    <p>The fetched data will go here.</p>
  </div>

</body>
```

Note that when the user clicks the button, a function named `getData` is called with the relative URL to get the JavaScript from, `javascript.php`. Here's how the `getData` function calls that URL:

```
<html>
  <head>
    <title>Returning JavaScript</title>

    <script language = "javascript">
      var XMLHttpRequestObject = false;

      if (window.XMLHttpRequest) {
        XMLHttpRequestObject = new XMLHttpRequest();
      } else if (window.ActiveXObject) {
        XMLHttpRequestObject = new ActiveXObject("Microsoft.XMLHttp");
```

```
  }

  function getData(dataSource)
  {
    if(XMLHttpRequestObject) {
      XMLHttpRequestObject.open("GET", dataSource);

      XMLHttpRequestObject.onreadystatechange = function()
      {
        if (XMLHttpRequestObject.readyState == 4 &&
          XMLHttpRequestObject.status == 200) {
          .
          .
          .
        }
      }

      XMLHttpRequestObject.send(null);
    }
  }
  .
  .
  .
```

The server-side script, `javascript.php`, is very simple. It sends back a line of JavaScript that will call a function named `alerter`:

```php
<?php
    echo 'alerter()';
?>
```

So when `javascript.html` calls `javascript.php` behind the scenes, the `XMLHttpRequest` object will end up with the text `"alerter()"` in its `responseText` property. You can execute that JavaScript easily — just pass it to the JavaScript `eval` function in the `getData` function this way:

```
  function getData(dataSource)
  {
    if(XMLHttpRequestObject) {
      XMLHttpRequestObject.open("GET", dataSource);

      XMLHttpRequestObject.onreadystatechange = function()
      {
        if (XMLHttpRequestObject.readyState == 4 &&
          XMLHttpRequestObject.status == 200) {

          eval(XMLHttpRequestObject.responseText);
        }
      }

      XMLHttpRequestObject.send(null);
    }
  }
```

Excellent, all that's left now is to add the `alerter` function to `javascript.html`. That function just displays a friendly message, `"Got the JavaScript OK."`, on the page by writing that text to a `<div>` element:

```
function alerter()
{
  var targetDiv = document.getElementById("targetDiv");

  targetDiv.innerHTML = "Got the JavaScript OK.";
}
```

This is the function that will be called when the server-side script sends back the line of JavaScript to be executed, `"alerter()"`. The `<div>` element where the message is displayed looks like this in the `<body>` section of the page:

```
<body>

  <H1>Returning JavaScript</H1>

  <form>
    <input type = "button" value = "Fetch JavaScript"
      onclick = "getData('javascript.php')">
  </form>

  <div id="targetDiv">
    <p>The fetched data will go here.</p>
  </div>

</body>
```

And that's all there is to it. Now when the user clicks the button, this Ajax application fetches JavaScript to execute from the server, and it executes that JavaScript, calling a function that displays a success message, as you see in Figure 4-2.

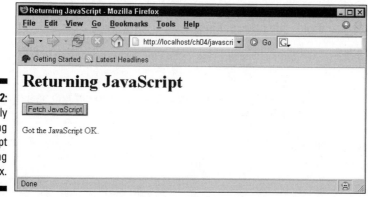

Figure 4-2: Successfully fetching JavaScript by using Ajax.

Returning a JavaScript object

You can do more than simply returning lines of JavaScript code to be executed in an Ajax application — you can return JavaScript objects from the server, as well.

But wait — can't you only return text and text formatted as XML to an Ajax application from the server? Yep, but you can format a JavaScript object as text to be converted back into an object after you get your hands on it in your JavaScript code.

Here's an example, object.html in the code for this book, to show how that works. (See this book's Introduction for details about the code on this book's companion Web site.) Say you have function named adder, as in this example, which adds two numbers and displays the sum in an alert box:

```
function adder(op1, op2)
{
  var sum = op1 + op2;
  alert(op1 + " + " + op2 + " = " + sum);
}
```

Then say you wanted to create an object that held the name of the function to call, along with the two operands to pass to that function — this is the kind of object a server-side program might pass back to you. In this case, the object being passed back to your script might have these three properties:

- ✔ function: The function to call, such as "alerter".

- ✔ operand1: The first operand to pass to the alerter function, 2 in this example.

- ✔ operand2: The second operand to pass to the alerter function, 3 in this example.

You can create an object with these three properties from text in JavaScript. The variable named text holds the text to use, and the variable named jSObject holds the object that will be created:

```
var text = "{function: 'adder', operand1: 2, operand2: 3};";
var jSObject;
```

You can use the eval function to create the new object and assign it to the jSObject variable this way:

```
eval('jSObject = '+ text);
```

Then you can call the `adder` function by using the properties of the newly created object:

```html
<html>
  <head>
    <title>
      Converting text to a JavaScript object
    </title>

    <script>
      var text = "{method: 'adder', operand1: 2, operand2: 3};";
      var jSObject;

      eval('jSObject = '+ text);

      eval(jSObject.method + '(' + jSObject.operand1 + ',' +
        jSObject.operand2 + ');');

      function adder(op1, op2)
      {
        var sum = op1 + op2;
        alert(op1 + " + " + op2 + " = " + sum);
      }
    </script>
  </head>

  <body>
    <h1>
      Converting text to a JavaScript object
    </h1>
  </body>
</html>
```

You can see the results in Figure 4-3. Apparently, 2 + 3 = 5.

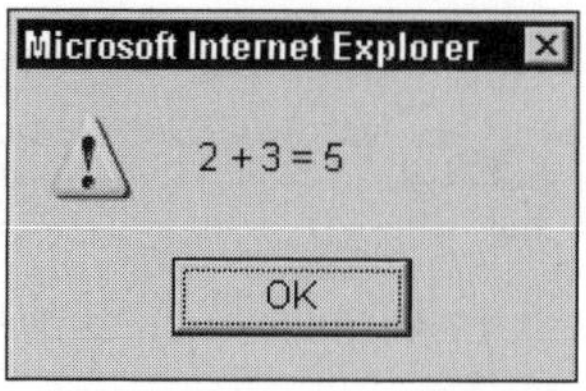

Figure 4-3:
Creating a
JavaScript
object from
text.

That's how you can pass back a JavaScript object from the server to an Ajax application — pass back the text that you can convert into an object by using the JavaScript `eval` function.

Connecting to Google for a Live Search

I'm not really an advocate of using JavaScript sent to you from the server in Ajax applications, except in one case — if the server you're dealing with gives you no choice. And that's the case with the example I show you in this section: connecting directly to Google to implement a live search.

One of the famous Ajax applications is Google Suggest, which you can see at work in Figure 4-4. To use Google Suggest, just navigate to it (as of this writing, its URL is `www.google.com/webhp?complete=1&hl=en`), and start entering a search term. As you see in the figure, Google gives you suggestions as you type — if you click a suggestion, Google searches for that term.

This application is one of the flagships of Ajax because the drop-down menu you see in the figure just appears — no page refreshes needed. This kind of live search application is what wowed people about Ajax in the first place.

As it turns out, you can implement the same kind of live search yourself, tying directly into Google Suggest, as you see in the next example, `google.html` in the code for this book, which appears in Figure 4-5. Just as when you enter a search term in the Google page, you see a menu of clickable items in this local version, which updates as you type.

How can you connect to Google Suggest yourself? Say that you placed the search term you wanted to search for in a variable named `term`. You could then open this URL:

```
http://www.google.com/complete/search?hl=en&js=true&qu=" + term;
```

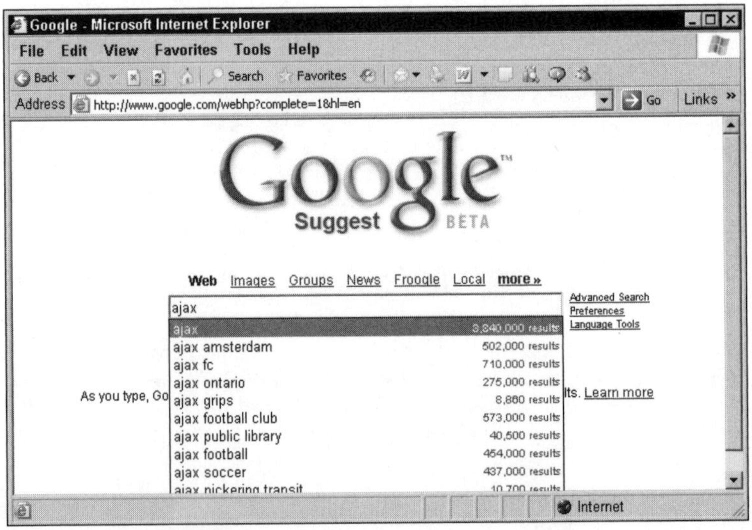

Figure 4-4:
Google
Suggest.

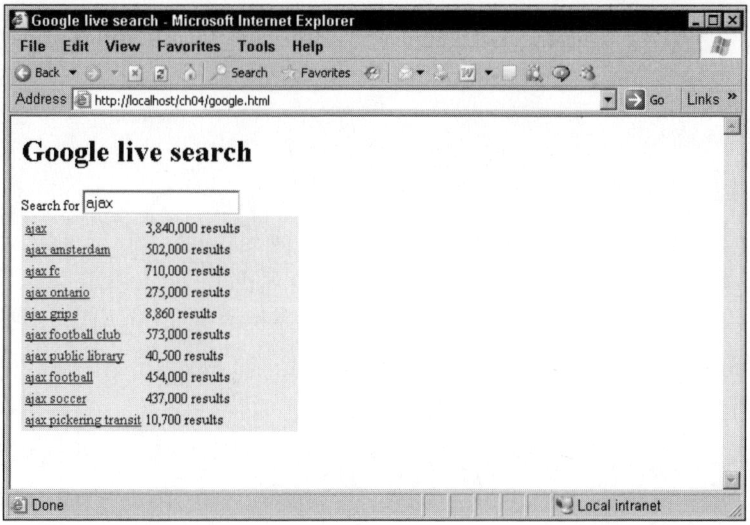

Figure 4-5:
A local
version of
Google
Suggest.

You get back a line of JavaScript from Google Suggest that calls a function named `sendRPCDone`. Here are the parameters passed to that function:

```
sendRPCDone(unusedVariable, searchTerm, arrayTerm, arrayResults, unusedArray)
```

What does the actual JavaScript you get back from Google Suggest look like? If you're searching for `"ajax"`, this is the JavaScript you'll get back from Google as of this writing:

```
sendRPCDone(frameElement, "ajax", new Array("ajax", "ajax amsterdam",
"ajax fc", "ajax ontario", "ajax grips", "ajax football club", "ajax public
library", "ajax football", "ajax soccer", "ajax pickering transit"), new
Array("3,840,000 results", "502,000 results", "710,000 results", "275,000
results", "8,860 results", "573,000 results", "40,500 results", "454,000
results", "437,000 results", "10,700 results"), new Array(""));
```

You can handle this by putting together a function named `sendRPCDone` that will display this data as you see in Figure 4-5 (shown earlier). Cool.

Handling the data Google sends you

What does the code look like in `google.html`? The text field where the user enters text is tied to a function named `getSuggest` by using the `onkeyup` event. As a result, `getSuggest` will be called every time the user types and releases a key. (Note that the event object is passed to `getSuggest` by this code, because that object holds information about which key was pressed, and also note the `<div>` element where the suggestions will appear, `targetDiv`.) Here's what the code looks like:

```
<body>

  <H1>Google live search</H1>

  Search for <input id = "textField" type = "text"
    name = "textField" onkeyup = "getSuggest(event)">

    <div id = "targetDiv"><div></div></div>

</body>
```

Detecting keystrokes

The `getSuggest` function is supposed to be passed an event object that it will refer to as `keyEvent`, which holds data about the key event that just took place:

```
function getSuggest(keyEvent)
{
    .
    .
    .
}
```

However, this method of passing the event object doesn't work in the Internet Explorer, which means `getSuggest` won't be passed anything in that browser. You have to use the `window.event` object instead in the Internet Explorer. So the first line of `getSuggest` is a typical line of JavaScript that uses the JavaScript conditional operator (flip to Chapter 2 and check out Table 2-1) to make sure you have an event object to work with. Here's an example that shows how to use this operator:

```
var temperature = condition ? 72 : 55;
```

If condition is true, the temperature variable will be assigned the value 72; if condition is false, temperature will be assigned 55. In the `getSuggest` function, you can use the conditional operator to test whether `keyEvent` has a non-zero value. If it doesn't, you should use `window.event` instead:

```
function getSuggest(keyEvent)
{
    keyEvent = (keyEvent) ? keyEvent: window.event;
    .
    .
    .
}
```

You can also determine which control the user was typing into, but that depends on which browser the user has. In the Internet Explorer, you use the `srcElement` property of the `keyEvent` object, but otherwise, you use the target property to get the control the user was typing into:

```
function getSuggest(keyEvent)
{
function getSuggest(keyEvent)
{
  keyEvent = (keyEvent) ? keyEvent: window.event;
  input = (keyEvent.target) ? keyEvent.target :
    keyEvent.srcElement;               .
    .
    .
}
```

Excellent. You have all the data you need about the key event. Now you can use the following code to check whether the event was a key up event:

```
function getSuggest(keyEvent)
{
  keyEvent = (keyEvent) ? keyEvent: window.event;
  input = (keyEvent.target) ? keyEvent.target :
    keyEvent.srcElement;

  if (keyEvent.type == "keyup") {
    .
    .
    .
  }
}
```

If the event was a key up event, it's time to read the struck key. If there is some text in the text field, it's time to connect to Google Suggest.

Connecting to Google Suggest

To connect to Google Suggest, you call a function named `getData` which does exactly that — gets the live search data, like this:

```
function getSuggest(keyEvent)
{
  keyEvent = (keyEvent) ? keyEvent: window.event;
  input = (keyEvent.target) ? keyEvent.target :
    keyEvent.srcElement;

  if (keyEvent.type == "keyup") {
    if (input.value) {
      getData("google.php?qu=" +
```

```
        input.value);
    }
    .
    .
    .
  }
}
```

If no text exists in the text field, the user deleted that text, so you can clear the suggestions (which appear in a `<div>` element named `targetDiv`) as follows:

```
function getSuggest(keyEvent)
{
  keyEvent = (keyEvent) ? keyEvent: window.event;
  input = (keyEvent.target) ? keyEvent.target :
    keyEvent.srcElement;

  if (keyEvent.type == "keyup") {
    if (input.value) {
      getData("google.php?qu=" +
        input.value);
    }
    else {
      var targetDiv = document.getElementById("targetDiv");

      targetDiv.innerHTML = "<div></div>";
    }
  }
}
```

How does the `getData` function work? This function calls the PHP script that actually interacts with Google Select, and passes on the current search term on to that script. This function is called with the relative URL to call, which is this (where term holds the search term):

```
google.php?qu=" + term;
```

That URL is opened in the `getData` function this way:

```
<script language = "javascript">
  var XMLHttpRequestObject = false;

  if (window.XMLHttpRequest) {
    XMLHttpRequestObject = new XMLHttpRequest();
  } else if (window.ActiveXObject) {
    XMLHttpRequestObject = new ActiveXObject("Microsoft.XMLHttp");
  }
```

```
function getData(dataSource)
{
  if(XMLHttpRequestObject) {
    XMLHttpRequestObject.open("GET", dataSource);
      .
      .
      .
  }
}
```

Showing Google's response

When you have the search data, you need to show the response from Google, which will be JavaScript. The response is executed with the JavaScript `eval` function:

```
function getData(dataSource)
{
  if(XMLHttpRequestObject) {
    XMLHttpRequestObject.open("GET", dataSource);

    XMLHttpRequestObject.onreadystatechange = function()
    {
      if (XMLHttpRequestObject.readyState == 4 &&
        XMLHttpRequestObject.status == 200) {
          eval(XMLHttpRequestObject.responseText);
      }
    }

    XMLHttpRequestObject.send(null);
  }
}
```

This calls the `sendRPCDone` function. All that's left in `google.html` is to set up that function in this way:

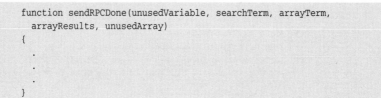

```
function sendRPCDone(unusedVariable, searchTerm, arrayTerm,
  arrayResults, unusedArray)
{
  .
  .
  .
}
```

You fill the `<div>` element, `targetDiv`, with data you get from Google in the `sendRPCDone` function, using an HTML table to align the columns. Here's how to create the table and start looping over the suggestions Google returned:

```
function sendRPCDone(unusedVariable, searchTerm, arrayTerm,
  arrayResults, unusedArray)
{
  var data = "<table>";
  var loopIndex;

  if (arrayResults.length != 0) {
    for (var loopIndex = 0; loopIndex < arrayResults.length;
      loopIndex++) {
      .
      .
      .

    }
  }

  data += "</table>";

  var targetDiv = document.getElementById("targetDiv");

  targetDiv.innerHTML = data;
}
```

Next, you give each suggestion its own hyperlink which — when clicked — searches Google, redirecting the browser to the Google Web site like this:

```
function sendRPCDone(unusedVariable, searchTerm, arrayTerm,
  arrayResults, unusedArray)
{
  var data = "<table>";
  var loopIndex;

  if (arrayResults.length != 0) {
    for (var loopIndex = 0; loopIndex < arrayResults.length;
      loopIndex++) {
      data += "<tr><td>" +
      "<a href='http://www.google.com/search?q=" +
      arrayTerm[loopIndex] + "'>" + arrayTerm[loopIndex] +
      '</a></td><td>' + arrayResults[loopIndex] + "</td></tr>";
    }
  }

  data += "</table>";

  var targetDiv = document.getElementById("targetDiv");

  targetDiv.innerHTML = data;
}
```

The last touch: the `targetDiv` `<div>` element is given a light yellow background in the `<style>` element in the `<head>` section (you can find out more on how to use styles with Ajax in Chapter 9):

```html
<html>
  <head>

    <title>Google live search</title>

    <style>
    #targetDiv {
      background-color: #FFEEAA;
      width: 30%;
    }
    </style>
        .
        .
        .
```

And that's all it takes.

Because this Google example is a complicated one, Listing 4-1 shows the whole code to help you put things in place:

Listing 4-1:   Connecting to Google Suggest

```html
<html>
  <head>

    <title>Google live search</title>
        .
    <style>
    #targetDiv {
      background-color: #FFEEAA;
      width: 30%;
    }
    </style>

    <script language = "javascript">
      var XMLHttpRequestObject = false;

      if (window.XMLHttpRequest) {
        XMLHttpRequestObject = new XMLHttpRequest();
      } else if (window.ActiveXObject) {
        XMLHttpRequestObject = new ActiveXObject("Microsoft.XMLHttp");
      }

      function getData(dataSource)
      {
```

(continued)

Listing 4-1 *(continued)*

```
  if(XMLHttpRequestObject) {
    XMLHttpRequestObject.open("GET", dataSource);

    XMLHttpRequestObject.onreadystatechange = function()
    {
      if (XMLHttpRequestObject.readyState == 4 &&
        XMLHttpRequestObject.status == 200) {
          eval(XMLHttpRequestObject.responseText);
      }
    }

    XMLHttpRequestObject.send(null);
  }
}

function getSuggest(keyEvent)
{
  keyEvent = (keyEvent) ? keyEvent: window.event;
  input = (keyEvent.target) ? keyEvent.target :
    keyEvent.srcElement;

  if (keyEvent.type == "keyup") {
    if (input.value) {
      getData("google.php?qu=" +
        input.value);
    }
    else {
      var targetDiv = document.getElementById("targetDiv");

      targetDiv.innerHTML = "<div></div>";
    }
  }
}

function sendRPCDone(unusedVariable, searchTerm, arrayTerm,
  arrayResults, unusedArray)
{
  var data = "<table>";
  var loopIndex;

  if (arrayResults.length != 0) {
    for (var loopIndex = 0; loopIndex < arrayResults.length;
      loopIndex++) {
      data += "<tr><td>" +
      "<a href='http://www.google.com/search?q=" +
      arrayTerm[loopIndex] + "'>" + arrayTerm[loopIndex] +
      '</a></td><td>' + arrayResults[loopIndex] + "</td></tr>";
    }
```

```
        }

        data += "</table>";

        var targetDiv = document.getElementById("targetDiv");

        targetDiv.innerHTML = data;
    }
  </script>

</head>

<body>

  <H1>Google live search</H1>

  Search for <input id = "textField" type = "text"
    name = "textField" onkeyup = "getSuggest(event)">

    <div id = "targetDiv"><div></div></div>

</body>

</html>
```

Check out the PHP script, `google.php`, which is the script that actually does the communicating with Google. This one takes a little PHP of the kind that appears in detail in Chapter 10. This script is passed the term the user has entered into the text field, and it should get some suggestions from Google, which it does like this with the PHP `fopen` (file open) statement:

```php
<?php
    $handle = fopen("http://www.google.com/complete/search?hl=en&js=true&qu=" .
      $_GET["qu"], "r");
        .

        .

        .
```

This gives you a PHP *file handle,* which you can use in PHP to read from the Google URL. Here's how that looks in PHP, where a `while` loop keeps reading data from Google as long as the end of the data marker isn't seen. You can check if you've reached the end of the data with the `feof` function, which returns `true` if the end of the data has been reached:

```php
<?php
    $handle = fopen("http://www.google.com/complete/search?hl=en&js=true&qu=" .
      $_GET["qu"], "r");
    while (!feof($handle)){
```

```
        .
        .
        .
    }
?>
```

To get the data from Google, you can use the `fgets` (file get string) function, and echo the fetched text, which sends that text back to the browser. Here's how you can make that happen:

```
<?php
    $handle = fopen("http://www.google.com/complete/search?hl=en&js=true&qu=" .
      $_GET["qu"], "r");
    while (!feof($handle)){
        $text = fgets($handle);
        echo $text;
    }
    fclose($handle);
?>
```

And that's all you need. Now this script, `google.php`, will read the suggestion data from Google and send it back to your script.

Everything works as expected. (Note, however, that this example can execute slowly; Google Suggest is still in beta version as I write this book.) But why was it necessary to use a PHP script at all? Why couldn't the Ajax part have called Google directly to get the suggestions from Google? The answer is coming up in the next section.

Calling a Different Domain

When an Ajax script tries to access a Web domain that it isn't part of (such as http://www.google.com), browsers these days get suspicious. They've surely been burned enough by malicious scripts. So if your Ajax application is hosted on your own Web site and you try to access an entirely different site in your code, you'll probably see a security warning like the one that appears in Figure 4-6.

If that kind of warning appears each time your Ajax application is going to access data, you have a disaster. What user wants to keep clicking the Yes button over and over?

So what's the solution? You'll see various solutions thrown around in the Ajax community, such as changing the security settings of the user's browser. Clearly, that's a poor suggestion — how are you going to convince the general public to do that so they can use your script? Another suggestion you might see is to mirror the site you're trying to access locally. That's another poor suggestion when it comes to working with a site like Google. (Can you imagine your ISP's response when you say you need an additional 10,000GB of hard drive space — and that's just for starters?)

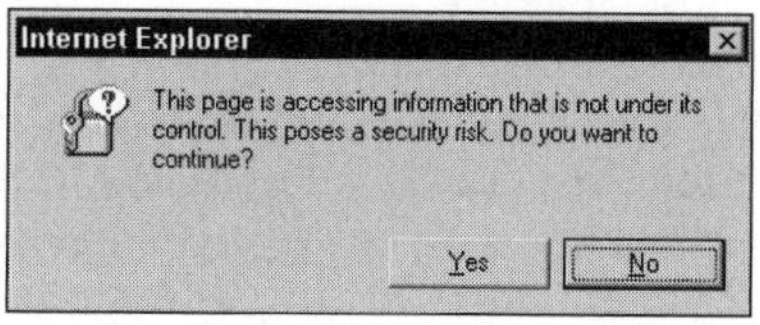

Figure 4-6:
You get a
security
warning
when you
try to
access a
different
domain by
using Ajax.

As far as Ajax goes, the fix to this problem isn't really all that difficult, even though browsers have become somewhat sticky in regards to security. The fix is to let a server-side script, not your code executing in the browser, access the different domain for you. That's why it was necessary to have `google.html` use `google.php` to access the Google URL. Here's how it does that:

```php
<?php
    $handle = fopen("http://www.google.com/complete/search?hl=en&js=true&qu=" .
    $_GET["qu"], "r");
        .
        .
        .
```

Accessing a Web domain different from the one the browser got your Ajax application from will cause the browser to display a security warning. To avoid that, use sever-side code to access that different domain and send any data back to you.

Reversing the Roles: Performing Validation on the Server

As I explain in "Connecting to Google for a Live Search" earlier in this chapter, you can literally check the user's input character by character as they type.

This capability is important to Ajax. To save bandwidth, you might not want to do that all the time, but it can come in handy. For example, you might want to validate the user's input as she's typing.

Data validation is often done by JavaScript in the browser these days, but a script in the browser can't check certain things without contacting the server, such as a database on the server or a list of usernames and passwords that you don't want to download to the browser for obvious security reasons. Instead, you can use Ajax for a little server-side validation.

The code for this book has an example for that — login.html and login.php, which let a new user select a username. When you open login.html and enter a tentative username, the code checks with login.php on the server and makes sure the name the user entered isn't already taken, as you see in Figure 4-7.

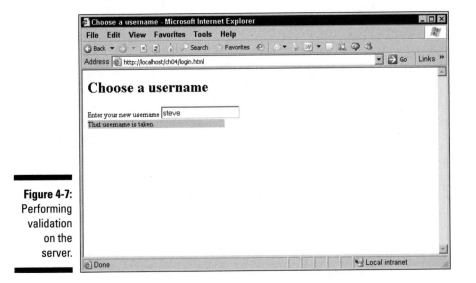

Figure 4-7: Performing validation on the server.

The following code shows what login.php looks like. As you can see, only one taboo name exists: "steve". If you try to take that username, this PHP script will return a value of "taken".

```php
<?php
    if ($_GET["qu"] == "steve"){
      echo "taken";
    }
    else {
      echo "ok";
    }
?>
```

The `login.html` file asks the user to enter the possible new username in a text field, and every time there's a new keystroke, the `checkUsername` function is called, as you see here:

```
<body>

  <H1>Choose a username</H1>

  Enter your new username <input id = "textField" type = "text"
    name = "textField" onkeyup = "checkUsername(event)">

    <div id = "targetDiv"><div></div></div>

</body>
```

The `checkUsername` function passes control onto the `getData` function to check the username the user has entered so far, like so:

```
function checkUsername(keyEvent)
{
  keyEvent = (keyEvent) ? keyEvent: window.event;
  input = (keyEvent.target) ? keyEvent.target :
    keyEvent.srcElement;

  if (keyEvent.type == "keyup") {
    var targetDiv = document.getElementById("targetDiv");
    targetDiv.innerHTML = "<div></div>";

    if (input.value) {
      getData("login.php?qu=" +
        input.value);
    }
  }
}
```

And the `getData` function asks `login.php` if the user's current suggested username is taken. If it is, the code displays the message `"That username is taken."`. this way:

```
function getData(dataSource)
{
  if(XMLHttpRequestObject) {
    XMLHttpRequestObject.open("GET", dataSource);

    XMLHttpRequestObject.onreadystatechange = function()
    {
      if (XMLHttpRequestObject.readyState == 4 &&
        XMLHttpRequestObject.status == 200) {
        if(XMLHttpRequestObject.responseText == "taken"){
```

```
                    var targetDiv = document.getElementById("targetDiv");

                    targetDiv.innerHTML = "<div>That username is taken.</div>";
                }
            }
        }

        XMLHttpRequestObject.send(null);
    }
}
```

You can see this server-side validation at work in Figure 4-7, which appears earlier in the chapter. Now you're using Ajax to check user input character by character. Very cool.

Checking every character the user types is okay only for limited, specific uses like the one in this example. You don't want to overwhelm the server with endless requests for data.

Getting Some Amazing Data with HEAD Requests

In Chapter 3, I explain how to use the GET method when you primarily need to fetch some data from the server, and the POST method when the idea was primarily to send data to the server. Another option is to use HEAD requests, which gets data about a document, and about the server.

How do you make a HEAD request? You just use HEAD as the method to get data with. You can see an example, head.html, at work in Figure 4-8.

As you see in the figure, this example displays data on the server, last-modified date of the document, the current date, the type of the document being accessed, and so on. Here's what that data looks like:

```
Server: Microsoft-IIS/5.1 Date: Tue, 09 Aug 2005 16:17:03 GMT
Content-Type: text/plain Accept-Ranges: bytes Last-Modified: Thu, 28 Jul
2005 16:29:44 GMT Etag: "94125909193c51:911" Content-Length: 38
```

This data represents the values of the Http headers that an Ajax script gets when it tries to read a text file on the server, data.txt. If you sent a GET request, you'd get the text inside data.txt. But if you send a HEAD request, you get data *about* data.txt and the server. For example, the "Last-Modified" Http header holds the text "Thu, 28 Jul 2005", which is the date on which data.txt was last modified.

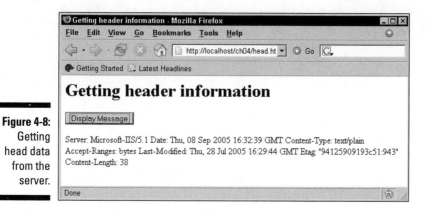

Figure 4-8:
Getting
head data
from the
server.

You can grab all this data or just the tidbits that you need. The following sections have the details.

Returning all the header data you can get

How do you get access to this kind of data? When the user clicks the button you see in Figure 4-8 (shown earlier), the code calls the `getData` function (responsible for interacting with the server) with the relative URL `data.txt`:

```
<form>
  <input type = "button" value = "Display Message"
    onclick = "getData('data.txt', 'targetDiv')">
</form>
```

The code in the `getData` function sends a `HEAD` request for that URL to the server like this:

```
<html>
  <head>
    <title>Getting header information</title>

    <script language = "javascript">
      var XMLHttpRequestObject = false;

      if (window.XMLHttpRequest) {
        XMLHttpRequestObject = new XMLHttpRequest();
      } else if (window.ActiveXObject) {
        XMLHttpRequestObject = new ActiveXObject("Microsoft.XMLHttp");
      }

      function getData(dataSource, divID)
```

```
    {
      if(XMLHttpRequestObject) {
        var obj = document.getElementById(divID);
        XMLHttpRequestObject.open("HEAD", dataSource);
            .
            .
            .

    }
  </script>
</head>
    .
    .
    .
```

When the data comes back from the server, the data will be in the `XMLHttp RequestObject` object, and you can use that object's `getAllResponse Headers` method to get the list of all headers and header data that appears in Figure 4-7. Here's how:

```
function getData(dataSource, divID)
{
  if(XMLHttpRequestObject) {
    var obj = document.getElementById(divID);
    XMLHttpRequestObject.open("HEAD", dataSource);

    XMLHttpRequestObject.onreadystatechange = function()
    {
      if (XMLHttpRequestObject.readyState == 4 &&
        XMLHttpRequestObject.status == 200) {
          obj.innerHTML = XMLHttpRequestObject.getAllResponseHeaders();
      }
    }

    XMLHttpRequestObject.send(null);
  }
}
```

This example gets all the header data that's available from the server, but what if you wanted to extract only data from a specific header, such as the `"Last-Modified"` header to determine when a file on the server was last modified? It turns out there's a method for that too.

Finding the last-modified date

How do you find the data for a specific header, such as the `"Last-Modified"` header for a file on the server? Here's how that works in a new example, `date.html`, which you can see at work in Figure 4-9. This example checks the date on which the target file on the server, `date.txt`, was last modified, and displays that date, as you see in the figure.

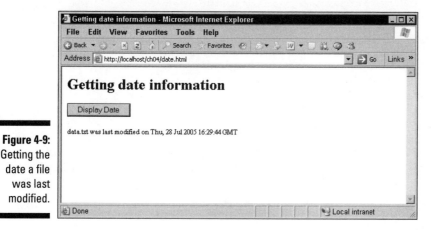

Figure 4-9:
Getting the
date a file
was last
modified.

As in the previous example, this example gets all Http headers for the `data.txt` file:

```
<script language = "javascript">
var XMLHttpRequestObject = false;

if (window.XMLHttpRequest) {
  XMLHttpRequestObject = new XMLHttpRequest();
} else if (window.ActiveXObject) {
  XMLHttpRequestObject = new ActiveXObject("Microsoft.XMLHttp");
}

function getData(dataSource, divID)
{
  if(XMLHttpRequestObject) {
    var obj = document.getElementById(divID);
    XMLHttpRequestObject.open("HEAD", dataSource);
      .

      .

      .
  }
}
</script>
```

But then, instead of using the `getAllResponseHeaders` method to get all headers, you can use the `getResponseHeader` method to get only data for a specific header, the `"Last-Modified"` header, like this:

```
XMLHttpRequestObject.getResponseHeader("Last-Modified")
```

The code displays the text returned in that header on the Web page:

```
function getData(dataSource, divID)
{
  if(XMLHttpRequestObject) {
    var obj = document.getElementById(divID);
    XMLHttpRequestObject.open("HEAD", dataSource);

    XMLHttpRequestObject.onreadystatechange = function()
    {
      if (XMLHttpRequestObject.readyState == 4 &&
        XMLHttpRequestObject.status == 200) {
          obj.innerHTML = "data.txt was last modified on " +
            XMLHttpRequestObject.getResponseHeader(
              "Last-Modified");
      }
    }

    XMLHttpRequestObject.send(null);
  }
}
```

As you see in the figure, that gives you a result like `"data.txt was last modified on Thu, 28 Jul 2005 16:29:44 GMT"`. What if you wanted to convert that text to numbers that you can check to make sure a file is after a specific date? You can use the JavaScript Date object for that. Just use the text you get from the Last-Modified header this way to create a new `Date` object named `date`:

```
var date = new Date(XMLHttpRequestObject.getResponseHeader("Last-Modified"));
```

Now you can compare `date` to other `Date` objects by using JavaScript operators such as `>` to determine which date is later than the other. You can also use the built-in Date object methods like `getMonth` to get the month of the `date` object. Here's a sampling of `Date` object methods:

```
alert ("Day (1-31): " + date.getDate());
alert ("Weekday (0-6, 0 = Sunday): " + date.getDay());
alert ("Month (0-11): " + date.getMonth());
alert ("Year (0-99-31): " + date.getYear());
alert ("Full year (four digits): " + date.getFullYear());
alert ("Day (1-31): " + date.getDate());
alert ("Day (1-31): " + date.getDate());
alert ("Hour (0-23): " + date.getHours());
alert ("Minutes (0-59): " + date.getMinutes());
alert ("Seconds (0-59): " + date.getSeconds());
```

Does a URL exist?

Sometimes, you might want to check to make sure a Web resource exists before trying to download it. If that Web resource is a long one, you might not want to download the whole thing just to check whether it's there. You can use HEAD requests to check whether a Web resource exists, and use up a lot less bandwidth doing so.

The example in the code for the book, exists.html, shows how this works by checking whether or not the data.txt file exists. The following example works by doing a HEAD request on that file, and checking the return Http status code — 200 means everything's fine and the file is there, ready for use, but 404 means nope, file isn't there:

```javascript
<script language = "javascript">
  var XMLHttpRequestObject = false;

  if (window.XMLHttpRequest) {
    XMLHttpRequestObject = new XMLHttpRequest();
  } else if (window.ActiveXObject) {
    XMLHttpRequestObject = new ActiveXObject("Microsoft.XMLHttp");
  }

  function getData(dataSource, divID)
  {
    if(XMLHttpRequestObject) {
      var obj = document.getElementById(divID);
      XMLHttpRequestObject.open("HEAD", dataSource);

      XMLHttpRequestObject.onreadystatechange = function()
      {
        if (XMLHttpRequestObject.readyState == 4) {
          if (XMLHttpRequestObject.status == 200) {
            obj.innerHTML = "URL exists";
          }
          else if (XMLHttpRequestObject.status == 404) {
            obj.innerHTML = "URL does not exist";
          }
        }
      }

      XMLHttpRequestObject.send(null);
    }
  }
</script>
```

You might want to use a technique like the one in this example to check if your server-side program is there and ready to use — and if it isn't available (which might mean your server is down), use a JavaScript alternative instead, this way:

```
if (XMLHttpRequestObject.readyState == 4) {
  if (XMLHttpRequestObject.status == 200) {
    keepGoing();
  }
  else if {(XMLHttpRequestObject.status == 404) {
    callAJavascriptFunctionInstead();
  }
}
```

Finding the Problem: Debugging Ajax

When it comes to debugging JavaScript, Firefox is far superior to Internet Explorer. Firefox has its entire JavaScript console (which you open by choosing Tools⇨JavaScript Console), and which actually tells you what the problems are (as opposed to the unenlightening "Object expected" error you see for almost any problem in the Internet Explorer).

But what about debugging Ajax issues specifically? Is there any tool that lets you watch what's going on with requests to the server and responses from the server? Such tools are starting to appear.

One example is Julien Couvreur's XMLHttpRequest debugger, which is a *Greasemonkey* script. Greasemonkey is an extension to Firefox that lets you add dynamic HTML to change what a particular page does. In the sections that follow, I explain how you set up and use this debugger to polish your Ajax code.

This is not to say that Greasemonkey is worry-free — some security issues have appeared. For example, such issues were discovered in Greasemonkey version 0.3.4, which is no longer available. So be careful when using this product.

Setting up your browser for debugging

You can get Greasemonkey from the Mozilla people and set up the debugging script by following these steps:

1. **Open up Firefox and go to http://greasemonkey.mozdev.org.**

2. **Click the Install Greasemonkey link.**

After Greasemonkey is installed, you see a monkey icon in the lower-right corner in Firefox (skip ahead to Figure 4.12 if you want to see that icon). Clicking that icon toggles Greasemonkey on and off. You can get more information on using Greasemonkey at `http://greasemonkey. mozdev.org/using.html`.

3. **Go to `http://blog.monstuff.com/archives/000252.html` to get Julien Couvreur's `XMLHttpRequest` debugger script.**

4. **To install a script like this in Greasemonkey, right-click the link to the script and select the Install User Script menu item.**

   This opens the dialog box you see in Figure 4-10, which installs the script.

5. **You can select which URLs the script should be valid for by entering them in the Included Pages box.**

   When you access such pages, your `XMLHttpRequest` information will appear in the debugger script.

6. **Click OK when you're done.**

After the initial setup, you can also manage the `XMLHttpRequest Debugging` script in Firefox by choosing Tools➪Manage User Scripts to open the dialog box you see in Figure 4-11. In that dialog box, you can add or remove pages you want to track, just as when you first installed the script.

Manage User Scripts   ☒

XmlHttpRequestDebugging   **XmlHttpRequestDebugging**

Allows you to debug XmlHttpRequest calls with an
in-browser UI

┌─ Included pages ──────────────────────────┐
│ http://pick.some.domains/*   [Add...] │
│ http://www.google.com/webhp...   [Edit]   │
│ http://localhost/*   │
│ http://localhost/ch03/*   [Remove] │
│ http://localhost/ch03/options3....   │
└──┘

┌─ Excluded pages ──────────────────────────┐
│   [Add...] │
│   [Edit]   │
│   [Remove] │
│   │
│   │
└──┘

☑ Enabled   [Edit]   [Uninstall]

                   [OK]   [Cancel]

Figure 4-11:
Managing a
Greasemon
key script.

Debugging with Greasemonkey

The debugging part comes in when you navigate to one of the pages you included in Step 5 of the preceding section. For example, if you've included the Google Suggest page (`http://www.google.com/webhp?complete=1&hl=en`), navigate to that page in Firefox and start entering a search term, the `XMLHttpRequestDebugging` script displays what's going on in Ajax terms, as shown in Figure 4-12.

In this case, the user has typed *s*, then *t*, then e in the text field. Each time the user types a character, an Ajax request is sent to the server, and you can track those in the window that the script displays at right, as shown in Figure 4-12.

The script lets you watch every GET request and where it was sent (for example, `"GET /complete/search?hl=en&js=true&qu=s"`), as well as the response that came back from the server (for example, `"Status: completed (200 OK)"`). That kind of window into what's happening in Ajax terms can be very useful when debugging — you can watch, interactively, what your code is sending to the server, and what the server is sending back.

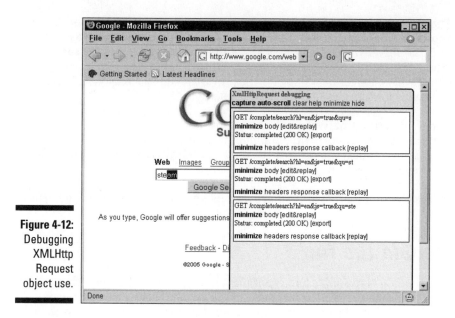

Figure 4-12:
Debugging
XMLHttp
Request
object use.

Overload: Handling Multiple Concurrent Requests

Looking over the user's shoulder, you notice they're clicking different buttons awfully fast in your Ajax application. "Hey," you say, "don't do that."

"Why not?" the user asks.

"Because if you do, you might confuse the application. You might make it start a new request before the previous one has had time to come back from the server."

"I understand," says the user, who doesn't understand at all. As you watch, the user goes back to clicking buttons just as fast as before.

So far, the Ajax applications you've seen here have all used a single XMLHttp Request object, and that hasn't been a big problem. But in the real world, your Ajax applications might have many buttons to click, many images to roll the mouse over, many text fields to check — and that means that your Ajax application might have several requests in to the server at nearly the same time.

That can be an issue if you're using the same XMLHttpRequest object for all your Ajax work. What if the XMLHttpRequest object is waiting for a response from the server when the user clicks another button and forces the same XMLHttpRequest object to start a new request? The XMLHttpRequest object will no longer be waiting for the previous request's response; now it'll be waiting for the current request's response.

And that's a problem. When your Ajax application has only one XMLHttp Request object to work with, but multiple requests can occur at the same time, a new request will destroy the object's ability to handle responses to the previous ones. Yipes.

What's the solution? Well, you have a couple options, and they're coming up.

Double the fun

One solution is to simply have multiple XMLHttpRequest objects that you work with, one per request you send to the server. There's an example of that in the code for this book, double.html, which you can see at work in Figure 4-13.

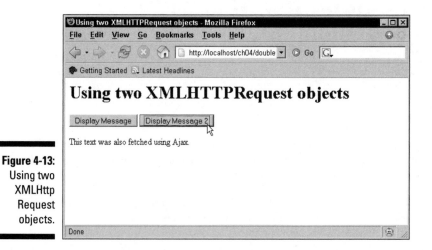

Figure 4-13:
Using two
XMLHttp
Request
objects.

This example fetches text from data.txt ("This text was fetched using Ajax.") and data2.txt ("This text was also fetched using Ajax."), and uses two buttons and two separate XMLHttpRequest objects to do it. Here's what that looks like in the code:

```html
<html>
  <head>
    <title>Ajax at work</title>

    <script language = "javascript">
      var XMLHttpRequestObject = false;
      var XMLHttpRequestObject2 = false;

      if (window.XMLHttpRequest) {
        XMLHttpRequestObject = new XMLHttpRequest();
        XMLHttpRequestObject2 = new XMLHttpRequest();
      } else if (window.ActiveXObject) {
        XMLHttpRequestObject = new ActiveXObject("Microsoft.XMLHttp");
        XMLHttpRequestObject2 = new ActiveXObject("Microsoft.XMLHttp");
      }

      function getData(dataSource)
      {
        if(XMLHttpRequestObject) {
          var obj = document.getElementById("targetDiv");
          XMLHttpRequestObject.open("GET", dataSource);

          XMLHttpRequestObject.onreadystatechange = function()
          {
            if (XMLHttpRequestObject.readyState == 4 &&
              XMLHttpRequestObject.status == 200) {
                obj.innerHTML = XMLHttpRequestObject.responseText;
            }
          }

          XMLHttpRequestObject.send(null);
        }
      }

      function getData2(dataSource, divID)
      {
        if(XMLHttpRequestObject2) {
          var obj = document.getElementById("targetDiv");
          XMLHttpRequestObject2.open("GET", dataSource);

          XMLHttpRequestObject2.onreadystatechange = function()
          {
            if (XMLHttpRequestObject2.readyState == 4 &&
              XMLHttpRequestObject2.status == 200) {
                obj.innerHTML = XMLHttpRequestObject2.responseText;
            }
          }

          XMLHttpRequestObject2.send(null);
        }
      }

    </script>
```

```
</head>

<body>

  <H1>Fetching data with Ajax</H1>

  <form>
    <input type = "button" value = "Display Message"
      onclick = "getData('data.txt')">
    <input type = "button" value = "Display Message 2"
      onclick = "getData2('data2.txt')">
  </form>

  <div id="targetDiv">
    <p>The fetched data will go here.</p>
  </div>

</body>
</html>
```

This is a simple solution that handles multiple requests in many instances. But even this isn't really good enough on some occasions. What if the user clicks the same button more than once? You might be stuck trying to send a new request before the old one has returned from the server. And this only handles two XMLHttpRequest objects. What if you needed dozens?

Packing it all into an array

The best way of handling multiple concurrent requests is with multiple XMLHttpRequest objects, one per request. You can, for example, create an array of such objects and add new objects to the array by using the built-in JavaScript push function each time there's a new request. You can see a way of doing this in the example named objectarray.html in the code for this book. This example declares an array of XMLHttpRequest objects:

```
var XMLHttpRequestObjects = new Array();
```

And then when the application needs a new XMLHttpRequest object, it just uses the push function to add one to the array:

```
if (window.XMLHttpRequest) {
  XMLHttpRequestObjects.push(new XMLHttpRequest());
} else if (window.ActiveXObject) {
  XMLHttpRequestObjects.push(new
    ActiveXObject("Microsoft.XMLHttp"));
}
```

That's how it works. There's a lot more to it than this, of course; you can see the full code in `objectarray.html`. Creating an array of `XMLHttpRequest` objects like this works and lets you handle multiple `XMLHttp` requests without getting them mixed up. But it turns out to be a pretty lengthy way of doing things and, in fact, there's an easier way — using JavaScript *inner functions*.

Getting the inside scoop on inner functions

In JavaScript, an inner function is just a function defined inside another function. Here's an example, where the function named `inner` is an inner function:

```
function outer(data)
{
  var operand1 = data;

  function inner(operand2)
  {
    alert(operand1 + operand2)
  }
}
```

Here's what happens: Say you call the outer function with a value of 3 like this: `outer(3)`. That sets the variable `operand1` in this function to 3. The inner function has access to the outer function's data — even after the call to the outer function has finished. So if you were now to call the inner function, passing a value of 6, that would set `operand2` in the inner function to 6 — and `operand1` is still set to 3. So the result of calling the inner function would be 3 + 6 = 9, which is the value that would be displayed by the JavaScript `alert` function here.

Now here's the fun part. Every time you call the outer function, a *new* copy of the function is created, which means a new value will be stored as `operand1`. And the inner function will have access to that value. So if you make the shift from thinking in terms of `operand1` and start thinking in terms of the variable `XMLHttpRequestObject`, you can see that each time a function like this is called, JavaScript will create a new copy of the function with a new `XMLHttpRequest` object, and that object will be available to any inner functions.

That's perfect here because the code you've been developing in this and the previous chapter already uses an (anonymous) inner function to handle `onreadystatechange` events in the `getData` function. Currently, the way it works is that first, the `XMLHttpRequest` object is created, and then it's used inside the anonymous inner function this way:

```
      var XMLHttpRequestObject = false;

  if (window.XMLHttpRequest) {
    XMLHttpRequestObject = new XMLHttpRequest();
  } else if (window.ActiveXObject) {
    XMLHttpRequestObject = new ActiveXObject("Microsoft.XMLHttp");
  }

  function getData(dataSource, divID)
  {
    if(XMLHttpRequestObject) {
      var obj = document.getElementById(divID);
      XMLHttpRequestObject.open("GET", dataSource);

      XMLHttpRequestObject.onreadystatechange = function()
      {
        if (XMLHttpRequestObject.readyState == 4 &&
          XMLHttpRequestObject.status == 200) {
            obj.innerHTML = XMLHttpRequestObject.responseText;
        }
      }

      XMLHttpRequestObject.send(null);
    }
  }
```

So to use a new XMLHttpRequest object for each request, all you have to do is to use your mastery of inner functions to move the part of the code where the XMLHttpRequest object is created *inside* the getData function, because the getData function is the outer function that encloses the anonymous inner function. That'll create a new XMLHttpRequest object to be used by the anonymous inner function each time getData is called — and each time getData is called, a new copy of getData will be created. That's what you want — a new XMLHttpRequest object for each new request.

Here's what that looks like in an example in the book's code, multiobject. html, where the XMLHttpRequest object creation part has been moved inside the outer function, getData. (Note that this example also deletes each XMLHttpRequest object as it finishes with it. That isn't necessary, but it's a good idea to avoid cluttering up memory with extra XMLHttpRequest objects.)

```
<html>
  <head>
    <title>Using multiple XMLHttpRequest objects</title>

    <script language = "javascript">

    function getData(dataSource)
    {
```

```
      var XMLHttpRequestObject = false;

      if (window.XMLHttpRequest) {
        XMLHttpRequestObject = new XMLHttpRequest();
      } else if (window.ActiveXObject) {
        XMLHttpRequestObject = new
          ActiveXObject("Microsoft.XMLHttp");
      }

      if(XMLHttpRequestObject) {
        XMLHttpRequestObject.open("GET", dataSource);

        XMLHttpRequestObject.onreadystatechange = function()
        {
          if (XMLHttpRequestObject.readyState == 4 &&
            XMLHttpRequestObject.status == 200) {
              document.getElementById("targetDiv").innerHTML =
                XMLHttpRequestObject.responseText;
              delete XMLHttpRequestObject;
              XMLHttpRequestObject = null;
          }
        }

        XMLHttpRequestObject.send(null);
      }
    }
  </script>
</head>

<body>

  <H1>Using multiple XMLHttpRequest objects</H1>

  <form>
    <input type = "button" value = "Display Message"
      onclick = "getData('data.txt')">
    <input type = "button" value = "Display Message 2"
      onclick = "getData('data2.txt')">
  </form>

  <div id="targetDiv">
    <p>The fetched data will go here.</p>
  </div>

</body>
</html>
```

And there you go. This application can handle multiple concurrent XML Http requests, such as when the user is clicking multiple Ajax-enabled buttons in rapid succession. Each time the getData function is called, a new copy of that function is created — and a new XMLHttpRequest object is created, which the anonymous inner function has access to, even after the call to getData (the outer function) has finished. And because each request gets its own XMLHttpRequest object, there won't be any conflicts.

Very cool. You can see multiobject.html at work in Figure 4-14.

Figure 4-14:
Using two
XMLHttp
Request
objects.

Part III
Ajax Frameworks

The 5th Wave   By Rich Tennant

"... and then one day it hit Tarzan, Lord of Jungle - where future in that?"

In this part . . .

The preceding part, Part II, makes it pretty clear that considerable programming can be involved in writing everything from the ground up. But instead of reinventing the wheel every time, you can put some of the many Ajax frameworks to work. An Ajax framework can do most of the programming for you, from the JavaScript to the server-side programming in languages such as PHP or JavaServer pages. Part III puts many of the available Ajax frameworks to work for you, giving you a shortcut when it comes to writing your own code. I share all kinds of handy tricks in this part, such as using Ajax for drag-and-drop operations, pop-up menus, downloading images behind the scenes, and more.

Chapter 5

Introducing Ajax Frameworks

. . . .

. . . .

*T*he Ajax programming team under your supervision isn't getting much done, and you decide to drop in to see what's going on.

"Do we always have to develop all our Ajax code from scratch?" the programmers ask. "We keep forgetting how to spell onreadystatechange and other stuff, and it's slowing us down."

"Hm," you say. "No, you can use one of the many Ajax frameworks available to make developing Ajax code a lot easier, because those frameworks have done all the programming for you. You typically need to call only a few functions."

"Wow," the programmers chorus. "How can we get a framework?"

"Just read this chapter," you say. "Ajax frameworks are usually JavaScript files that you simply include in your own scripts. That's all you need." And you show the programming crew a list of available Ajax frameworks.

"Gee," they say, "there sure are a lot of frameworks out there! It's going to take us a long time to figure out which one to use."

You sigh.

This chapter starts the book's look at the available Ajax frameworks, including one I developed especially for this book (Ajax Gold). These frameworks are mostly free, and they're typically JavaScript libraries of functions you can call to use Ajax techniques without having to remember how all the coding goes.

Some of the examples in this chapter use Ajax frameworks that are available for free online. Before you try to run a particular example, make sure that the files you need for the associated framework are in the same folder on your server as the example you're trying to run. For copyright reasons, the code for the Ajax frameworks that I discuss in this and the next chapter can't be included in the downloadable code for this book, so pick up that code at the supplied URL for a framework before you try to run an example that uses that framework. (The Ajax Gold framework, developed especially for this book, does come in the book's downloadable code.)

A Little More Ajax Power

Now that you're about to start developing your own ready-to-distribute Ajax applications, it's important to bear in mind that Ajax is all about response time. You can get pretty fancy with some of the Ajax frameworks, so be sure you test your applications to make sure they have that Ajax feel as they do everything from writing JavaScript on the fly on the server to downloading dozens of images by using Ajax.

How's that? Downloading *images?* Isn't Ajax just about text and XML? Yes, Ajax itself is all about downloading only text or XML, but the *browser* can download images and display them without a page refresh by using Dynamic HTML. And if you start downloading images or other binary objects, being careful about response time is worthwhile.

How does downloading images by using Ajax with Dynamic HTML work? Your Ajax script might, for example, download the name or URL of the image you should display, and you can construct an HTML <img> tag on the fly to make the browser download the image.

The image.html example in the code for the book demonstrates how this works. This example has two buttons, as you see in Figure 5-1. When the user clicks the first button, the application displays Image1.jpg, as you see in the figure, and when the user clicks the second button, the application displays Image2.jpg. (Both image files are in the ch05 folder of the code available for download from the Web site associated with this book.)

This application works by using Ajax to fetch the name of the image to load from one of two image files — imageName.txt or imageName2.txt — and which one is fetched from the server depends on which button the user clicked. Here's imageName.txt:

```
Image1.jpg
```

and here's imageName2.txt:

```
Image2.jpg
```

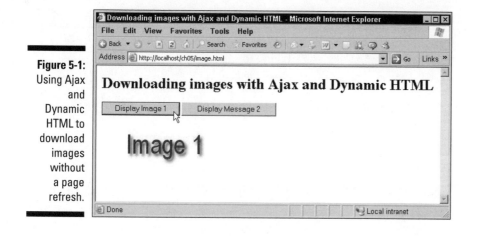

Figure 5-1:
Using Ajax
and
Dynamic
HTML to
download
images
without
a page
refresh.

When the user clicks a button, the text of the corresponding .txt file is fetched from the server, and that text is used to create an <img> element, which is then inserted into the targetDiv <div> element, where the browser will evaluate it and download the image without a page refresh. Listing 5-1 shows what that looks like in image.html.

Listing 5-1:   Using Ajax to Grab Images from Web Servers

```
<html>
  <head>
    <title>Downloading images with Ajax and Dynamic HTML</title>

    <script language = "javascript">

      function getDataReturnText(dataSource, callback)
      {
        var XMLHttpRequestObject = false;

        if (window.XMLHttpRequest) {
          XMLHttpRequestObject = new XMLHttpRequest();
        } else if (window.ActiveXObject) {
          XMLHttpRequestObject = new
            ActiveXObject("Microsoft.XMLHTTP");
        }

        if(XMLHttpRequestObject) {
          XMLHttpRequestObject.open("GET", dataSource);

          XMLHttpRequestObject.onreadystatechange = function()
          {
            if (XMLHttpRequestObject.readyState == 4 &&
              XMLHttpRequestObject.status == 200) {
                callback(XMLHttpRequestObject.responseText);
```

(continued)

Listing 5-1 *(continued)*

```
            delete XMLHttpRequestObject;
            XMLHttpRequestObject = null;
        }
      }

      XMLHttpRequestObject.send(null);
    }
  }

  function callback(text)
  {
    document.getElementById("targetDiv").innerHTML =
      "<img src= " + text + ">";
  }

  </script>
</head>

<body>

  <H1>Downloading images with Ajax and Dynamic HTML</H1>

  <form>
    <input type = "button" value = "Display Image 1"
      onclick =
        "getDataReturnText('imageName.txt', callback)">
    <input type = "button" value = "Display Message 2"
      onclick =
        "getDataReturnText('imageName2.txt', callback)">
  </form>

  <div id="targetDiv">
    <p>The fetched image will go here.</p>
  </div>

</body>
</html>
```

The results appear in Figure 5-1, where, through a combination of Ajax and Dynamic HTML, you're downloading images without a page refresh. The design issue here is to make sure that when you're downloading data like this by writing HTML tags dynamically, you don't slow response time significantly. You can use the technique not only for images but also other binary data objects (such as PDF files, Microsoft Word documents, or Excel spreadsheets) when you use the Internet Explorer <object> element. If you use this technique, be careful about degrading performance.

Introducing the Ajax Gold Framework

Ajax frameworks let you use other people's code to use Ajax. These frameworks range from the very simple to the very complex.

But you've already been creating your own Ajax code in this book, so before taking a look at other people's efforts, how about putting that code to work in an Ajax library written specifically for this book? That library is the Ajax Gold library, and like other Ajax frameworks, it's a JavaScript file — in this case, ajaxgold.js (available in the ch05 folder in the code available for download from the Web site associated with this book). You can use the prewritten functions in this library to make Ajax calls simple as pie. All you have to do is include ajaxgold.js in your Web page's <head> section like this:

```
<script type = "text/javascript" src = "ajaxgold.js"></script>
```

Now you've got the full power of this library at your command — and it'll implement the Ajax techniques you want to use. For example, say that when the user clicks a button, you want to fetch text by using the GET method from the server. You can use the Ajax Gold function getDataReturnText to do that — all you have to do is pass it the URL that will return the text you want like this: http://localhost/ch05/data.txt or http://localhost/ch05/data.php.

How do you handle the text when it comes back from the server? You pass the getDataReturnText the name of a function that you've written that you want to have called with that text — such a function is named a *callback function.*

Here's an example. Say that when the user clicks a button, you want the script to fetch the text in the file data.txt, and when that text has been fetched, you want that text to be sent to a function you've named callback1. Here's how you could set up the button to make all that happen:

```
<form>
  <input type = "button" value = "Display Message"
    onclick =
      "getDataReturnText('data.txt', callback1)">
</form>
```

You don't include quotation marks around the name of the function, because you aren't passing the name of the function here, but actually the function itself.

Then all you have to do is add the function you've named `callback1` to your `<script>` element. That function will be passed the text that was fetched from the URL you indicated. In this example, you might just display that text in a `<div>` element this way in the `callback1` function:

```
function callback1(text)
{
  document.getElementById("targetDiv").innerHTML =
    "Function 1 says " + text;
}
```

So as you can see, easy as pie. If you want to use Ajax to get text from a URL, just call the Ajax Gold function `getDataReturnText`, passing it the URL and the function that should be called to handle the received text like this:

```
getDataReturnText(url, callbackFunction);
```

No problem. Now you're using Ajax and you don't even have to write any Ajax code. That's what Ajax frameworks are all about.

Four functions are built into `ajaxgold.js`, and they're designed to let you get either text or XML from a URL by using either the GET or POST method:

- ✔ `getDataReturnText(url, callback)`: Uses the GET method to get text from the server.
- ✔ `getDataReturnXml(url, callback)`: Uses the GET method to get XML from the server.
- ✔ `postDataReturnText(url, data, callback)`: Uses the POST method to send data to server, gets text back from the server.
- ✔ `postDataReturnXml(url, data, callback)`: Uses the POST method to send data to server, gets XML back from the server.

You can find more details on these functions and how to use them in the following sections.

Using GET to get text

The first function in the Ajax Gold library is `getDataReturnText`, which uses the GET method to get text from the server. The `getDataReturnText` function and the `getDataReturnXml` function, which gets XML from the server, are the two most commonly used. You can find a description of each function in `ajaxgold.js`, and here's the description for `getDataReturnText`:

```
Ajax Gold JavaScript Library supports these functions for using Ajax
  (most commonly used: getDataReturnText and getDataReturnXml):
```

```
getDataReturnText(url, callback)
  ** Uses the GET method to get text from the server. **
  Gets text from url, calls function named callback with that text.
  Use when you just want to get data from an URL, or can easily
  encode the data you want to pass to the server in an URL, such as
  "http://localhost/script.php?a=1&b=2&c=hello+there".
  Example: getDataReturnText("http://localhost/data.txt", doWork);
  Here, the URL is a string, and doWork is a function in your own
  script.
```

How does this function work? You pass a URL to this function so that the script can fetch text from the URL as well as a callback function which then receives the text the browser fetched from the server. Here's how it looks:

```
function getDataReturnText(url, callback)
{
        .
        .
        .
}
```

This function starts by creating an XMLHttpRequest object:

```
function getDataReturnText(url, callback)
{
  var XMLHttpRequestObject = false;

  if (window.XMLHttpRequest) {
    XMLHttpRequestObject = new XMLHttpRequest();
  } else if (window.ActiveXObject) {
    XMLHttpRequestObject = new
      ActiveXObject("Microsoft.XMLHTTP");
  }
        .
        .
        .
}
```

And if the browser created the XMLHttpRequest object successfully, the code primes that object by passing the URL that the user wants to get data from to the open method. Here's what happens:

```
function getDataReturnText(url, callback)
{
  var XMLHttpRequestObject = false;

  if (window.XMLHttpRequest) {
    XMLHttpRequestObject = new XMLHttpRequest();
  } else if (window.ActiveXObject) {
    XMLHttpRequestObject = new
      ActiveXObject("Microsoft.XMLHTTP");
  }
```

```
if(XMLHttpRequestObject) {
  XMLHttpRequestObject.open("GET", url);
        .
        .
        .

  }
}
```

Then the code sets up the anonymous inner function (discussed in Chapter 4) to handle events from the XMLHttpRequest object, like this:

```
function getDataReturnText(url, callback)
{
  var XMLHttpRequestObject = false;

  if (window.XMLHttpRequest) {
    XMLHttpRequestObject = new XMLHttpRequest();
  } else if (window.ActiveXObject) {
    XMLHttpRequestObject = new
      ActiveXObject("Microsoft.XMLHTTP");
  }

  if(XMLHttpRequestObject) {
    XMLHttpRequestObject.open("GET", url);

    XMLHttpRequestObject.onreadystatechange = function()
    {
      if (XMLHttpRequestObject.readyState == 4 &&
        XMLHttpRequestObject.status == 200) {
          callback(XMLHttpRequestObject.responseText);
          delete XMLHttpRequestObject;
          XMLHttpRequestObject = null;
      }
    }
        .
        .
        .

  }
}
```

Finally, the browser fetches the URL, and the code passes null as the data, which is what usually happens with the GET method. Here's how:

```
function getDataReturnText(url, callback)
{
  var XMLHttpRequestObject = false;

  if (window.XMLHttpRequest) {
    XMLHttpRequestObject = new XMLHttpRequest();
  } else if (window.ActiveXObject) {
    XMLHttpRequestObject = new
      ActiveXObject("Microsoft.XMLHTTP");
```

```
    }

  if(XMLHttpRequestObject) {
    XMLHttpRequestObject.open("GET", url);

    XMLHttpRequestObject.onreadystatechange = function()
    {
      if (XMLHttpRequestObject.readyState == 4 &&
        XMLHttpRequestObject.status == 200) {
          callback(XMLHttpRequestObject.responseText);
          delete XMLHttpRequestObject;
          XMLHttpRequestObject = null;
      }
    }

    XMLHttpRequestObject.send(null);
  }
}
```

Okay, it's time to put this new function, `getDataReturnText`, to work. If you want to give it a try, open the HTML document `testGetDataReturnText.html` in the code for this book ms as always, available for download from the Web site associated with this book. You can see this example at work in Figure 5-2. There are two buttons here, and they read text from two different files on the server. After the browser has fetched that text, it's displayed as you see in the figure.

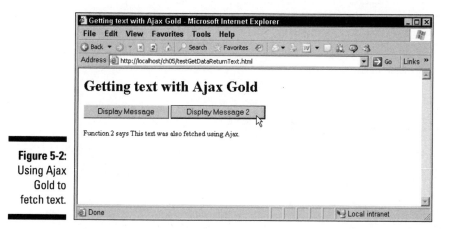

Figure 5-2:
Using Ajax
Gold to
fetch text.

Everything starts by making sure the Ajax Gold library is loaded and available to your JavaScript, using this line in the <head> section of your Web page:

```
<script type = "text/javascript" src = "ajaxgold.js"></script>
```

Each of the two buttons calls its own URL, and has its own callback function to handle the text fetched from its URL. Here's how you can implement that when creating the buttons, simply by using the `getDataReturnText` function:

```
<form>
  <input type = "button" value = "Display Message"
    onclick =
      "getDataReturnText('data.txt', callback1)">
  <input type = "button" value = "Display Message 2"
    onclick =
      "getDataReturnText('data2.txt', callback2)">
</form>
```

The two callback functions just handle the fetched text and display it in the `<div>` element (named `targetDiv`), like so:

```
<script type = "text/javascript" src = "ajaxgold.js"></script>

<script language = "javascript">
  function callback1(text)
  {
    document.getElementById("targetDiv").innerHTML =
      "Function 1 says " + text;
  }

  function callback2(text)
  {
    document.getElementById("targetDiv").innerHTML =
      "Function 2 says " + text;
  }
</script>
```

And that's all there is to it.

Using GET to get XML

What if you didn't want to fetch text, but wanted to get XML instead? In that case, you can use the Ajax Gold `getDataReturnXml` function, which you can find described this way in `ajaxgold.js`:

```
getDataReturnXml(url, callback)
    ** Uses the GET method to get XML from the server. **
    Gets XML from URL, calls function named callback with that XML.
    Use when you just want to get data from an URL, or can easily
```

```
encode the data you want to pass to the server in an URL, such as
"http://localhost/script.php?a=1&b=2&c=hello+there".
Example: getDataReturnXml("http://localhost/data.txt", doWork);
Here, the URL is a string, and doWork is a function in your
own script.
```

This function is the same as the `getDataReturnText` function you just saw,
but fetches XML instead of text. In other words, this function uses the
`XMLHttpRequestObject` object's `responseXML` property, not
`responseText`, as you see in Listing 5-2.

Listing 5-2: The getDataReturnXml Function

```
function getDataReturnXml(url, callback)
{
  var XMLHttpRequestObject = false;

  if (window.XMLHttpRequest) {
    XMLHttpRequestObject = new XMLHttpRequest();
  } else if (window.ActiveXObject) {
    XMLHttpRequestObject = new
      ActiveXObject("Microsoft.XMLHTTP");
  }

  if(XMLHttpRequestObject) {
    XMLHttpRequestObject.open("GET", url);

    XMLHttpRequestObject.onreadystatechange = function()
    {
      if (XMLHttpRequestObject.readyState == 4 &&
        XMLHttpRequestObject.status == 200) {
          callback(XMLHttpRequestObject.responseXML);
          delete XMLHttpRequestObject;
          XMLHttpRequestObject = null;
      }
    }

    XMLHttpRequestObject.send(null);
  }
}
```

What about putting the `getDataReturnXml` function to work reading some
XML? For example, what about rewriting the Chapter 3 example that grabbed
XML for the two different color schemes from the scripts `options1.php` and
`options2.php`? No problem at all — you can see the Ajax Gold version,
`testGetDataReturnXml.html`, in Figure 5-3.

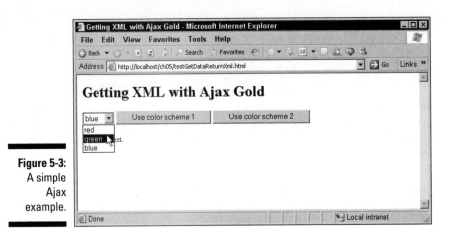

The PHP scripts in this example return XML like this:

```
<? xml version = "1.0" ?>
<options>
  <option>
    red
  </option>
  <option>
    green
  </option>
  <option>
    blue
  </option>
</options>
```

Writing this example by using the Ajax Gold function `getDataReturnXml` is simplicity itself. You want to fetch XML from `options1.php` or `options2.php` when the user clicks a button, and call a function, say `getOptions1` or `getOptions2`, that will handle that XML when it's fetched. Easy. Here's how that looks:

```
<input type = "button" value = "Use color scheme 1"
  onclick =
    "getDataReturnXml('options1.php', getOptions1)">
<input type = "button" value = "Use color scheme 2"
  onclick =
    "getDataReturnXml('options2.php', getOptions2)">
```

The getOptions1 and getOptions2 functions are passed the XML that the PHP scripts send back, and all they have to do is store the <option> elements in an array and pass that array on to the listOptions function developed in Chapter 3, which will list the available options in the application's drop-down list control. Check this out:

```
function getOptions1(xml)
{
  options = xml.getElementsByTagName("option");
  listOptions(options);
}

function getOptions2(xml)
{
  options = xml.getElementsByTagName("option");
  listOptions(options);
}
```

As in the original version of this example, the listOptions function lists the color options in the drop-down list control:

```
function listOptions ()
{
  var loopIndex;
  var selectControl = document.getElementById('optionList');

  for (loopIndex = 0; loopIndex < options.length; loopIndex++ )
  {
      selectControl.options[loopIndex] = new
         Option(options[loopIndex].firstChild.data);
  }
}
```

And there you have it — after the users make a selection from the color scheme they've chosen, the text in the page is colored to match.

```
function setOption()
{
  document.getElementById('targetDiv').style.color =
    options[document.getElementById
      ('optionList').selectedIndex].firstChild.data;
}
```

So as you can see, using getDataReturnXml is very easy — just pass the URL and the callback function that should be called with the XML you get. No trouble at all. If you want to send data to the server while using the GET method, just encode that data as part of the URL you're accessing.

Using POST to post data and get text

In the Ajax Gold library, you can post data to the server and get text back using the `postDataReturnText` function. Here's how:

```
postDataReturnText(url, data, callback)
```

All you have to do is to pass the URL you want to reach on the server, the data you want to post, and the `callback` function that will be passed the text recovered from the server. Here's the description for `postDataReturnText` that appears in `ajaxgold.js`:

```
postDataReturnText(url, data, callback)
   ** Uses the POST method to send data to server, gets text back. **
   Posts data to url, calls function callback with the returned text.
   Uses the POST method, use this when you have more text data to send
   to the server than can be easily encoded into an URL.
   Example: postDataReturnText("http://localhost/data.php",
      "parameter=5", doWork);
   Here, the URL is a string; the data sent to the server
   ("parameter=5") is a string;and doWork is a function in
   your own script.
```

How does this function work? You pass it three arguments: the URL to fetch, the data to post, and the `callback` function that you want called with the returned text. Here's what `postDataReturnText` looks like in action:

```
function postDataReturnText(url, data, callback)
{



        .
        .
        .


}
```

You start by getting a local `XMLHttpRequest` object to handle the POST operations:

```
function postDataReturnText(url, data, callback)
{
  var XMLHttpRequestObject = false;

  if (window.XMLHttpRequest) {
    XMLHttpRequestObject = new XMLHttpRequest();
  } else if (window.ActiveXObject) {
    XMLHttpRequestObject = new
      ActiveXObject("Microsoft.XMLHTTP");
  }
```

```
      .
      .
      .
}
```

Then you open the `XMLHttpRequest` object for use with the `POST` method and use the `setRequestHeader` method so the server will know that the data you're sending is encoded in the request in the standard way for the `POST` method:

```
function postDataReturnText(url, data, callback)
{
      .
      .
      .

  if(XMLHttpRequestObject) {
    XMLHttpRequestObject.open("POST", url);
    XMLHttpRequestObject.setRequestHeader('Content-Type',
      'application/x-www-form-urlencoded');
      .
      .
      .

}
```

To complete the preparations, you set up the anonymous inner function that will handle the text that comes from the server. The inner function will also call the `callback` function with that text:

```
function postDataReturnText(url, data, callback)
{
      .
      .
      .

  if(XMLHttpRequestObject) {
    XMLHttpRequestObject.open("POST", url);
    XMLHttpRequestObject.setRequestHeader('Content-Type',
      'application/x-www-form-urlencoded');

    XMLHttpRequestObject.onreadystatechange = function()
    {
      if (XMLHttpRequestObject.readyState == 4 &&
        XMLHttpRequestObject.status == 200) {
          callback(XMLHttpRequestObject.responseText);
          delete XMLHttpRequestObject;
          XMLHttpRequestObject = null;
      }
    }
      .
      .
      .

}
```

And you're set — all you have to do now is to send the request and wait confidently for the returned text to show up. Here's how you start off your request:

```
function postDataReturnText(url, data, callback)
{
        .
        .
        .

    XMLHttpRequestObject.onreadystatechange = function()
    {
      if (XMLHttpRequestObject.readyState == 4 &&
        XMLHttpRequestObject.status == 200) {
          callback(XMLHttpRequestObject.responseText);
          delete XMLHttpRequestObject;
          XMLHttpRequestObject = null;
      }
    }

    XMLHttpRequestObject.send(data);
  }
}
```

How might you use `postDataReturnText`? Here's an example, `testPostDataReturnText.html` in the code available for download from the Web site associated with this book. This example posts data to a small PHP script named `echo.php`, which simply echoes back the data sent in a parameter named `message`:

```
<?
echo ($_POST["message"]);
?>
```

The `testPostDataReturnText.html` example posts the data `message=Good afternoon.` to `echo.php` by using the Ajax Gold `postDataReturnText` function when the user clicks a button. Here's how it does that:

```
<input type = "button" value = "Get the message"
  onclick = "postDataReturnText('echo.php', 'message=Good afternoon.',
    display)">
```

When the browser posts the data `message=Good afternoon.` to `echo.php`, that script will send back the text `Good afternoon.`, and the callback function display will show that text in a `<div>` element. Listing 5-3 shows how to post data using Ajax Gold.

Listing 5-3:   Posting Data to a Web Server with Ajax Gold

```html
<html>
  <head>

    <title>Posting data and returning text with Ajax Gold</title>

    <script type = "text/javascript" src = "ajaxgold.js"></script>

    <script language = "javascript">

      function display(text)
      {
        document.getElementById('targetDiv').innerHTML = text;
      }

    </script>
  </head>

  <body>

    <h1>Posting data and returning text with Ajax Gold</h1>

    <form>
      <input type = "button" value = "Get the message"
        onclick = "postDataReturnText('echo.php', 'message=Good afternoon.',
              display)">
    </form>

    <div id="targetDiv">The fetched text will go here.</div>

  </body>

</html>
```

You can see the results in Figure 5-4. When the user clicks the button, the post
DataReturnText function posts the data "message=Good afternoon."
to echo.php and calls the display function with the text returned from the
server ("Good afternoon."), and that text appears in the <div> element
on the Web page, as you see in Figure 5-4.

Cool. Now you're posting data to Web servers and handling the returned
text — all without any Ajax programming on your part when you put the
Ajax Gold library to work.

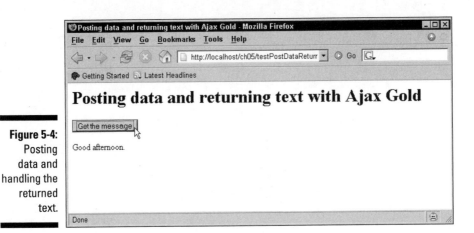

Figure 5-4:
Posting
data and
handling the
returned
text.

Using POST to post data and get XML

What if you want to post data and get XML back? The `postDataReturnXml` function in the Ajax Gold library lets you post data to a server using Ajax techniques. In return, you get XML. Here's how you use it:

```
postDataReturnXml(url, data, callback)
```

To use this function, you pass it the URL you want to access, the data you want to post, and the `callback` function that you want passed the XML returned from the server. Here's the description of `postDataReturnXml` from `ajaxgold.js`:

```
postDataReturnXml(url, data, callback)
  ** Uses the POST method to send data to server, gets XML back. **
  Posts data to url, calls function callback with the returned XML.
  Uses the POST method, use this when you have more text data to send
  to the server than can be easily encoded into an URL.
  Example: postDataReturnXml("http://localhost/data.php",
    "parameter=5", doWork);
  Here, the URL is a string; the data sent to the server
  ("parameter=5") is a string; and doWork is a function in
  your own script.
```

As you'd expect, this function works very much like its counterpart, `postDataReturnText`, except that it returns XML, not text. In other words, where `postDataReturnText` uses the `responseText` property of the `XMLHttpRequest` object, `postDataReturnXml` uses the `responseXML` property:

```
function postDataReturnXml(url, data, callback)
{
  var XMLHttpRequestObject = false;
```

```
if (window.XMLHttpRequest) {
  XMLHttpRequestObject = new XMLHttpRequest();
} else if (window.ActiveXObject) {
  XMLHttpRequestObject = new
    ActiveXObject("Microsoft.XMLHTTP");
}


if(XMLHttpRequestObject) {
  XMLHttpRequestObject.open("POST", url);
  XMLHttpRequestObject.setRequestHeader('Content-Type',
    'application/x-www-form-urlencoded');

  XMLHttpRequestObject.onreadystatechange = function()
  {
    if (XMLHttpRequestObject.readyState == 4 &&
      XMLHttpRequestObject.status == 200) {
        callback(XMLHttpRequestObject.responseXML);
        delete XMLHttpRequestObject;
        XMLHttpRequestObject = null;
    }
  }

  XMLHttpRequestObject.send(data);
}
}
```

How about putting `postDataReturnXml` to work? Take a look at `textpost DataReturnXml.html` for an example that does that. This example modifies the color scheme application to handle posted data, using `options3.php`. Posting `"scheme=1"` will return color scheme one, and posting `"scheme=2"` will return color scheme two:

```php
<?
header("Content-type: text/xml");
if ($_POST["scheme"] == "1")
  $options = array('red', 'green', 'blue');
if ($_POST["scheme"] == "2")
  $options = array('black', 'white', 'orange');
echo '<?xml version="1.0"?>';
echo '<options>';
foreach ($options as $value)
{
  echo '<option>';
  echo $value;
  echo '</option>';
}
echo '</options>';
?>
```

The `textpostDataReturnXml.html` example posts the data `"scheme=1"` or `"scheme=2"` to `options3.php` (depending on which color scheme the user selects), using the Ajax Gold `postDataReturnXml` function:

```
<input type = "button" value = "Use color scheme 1"
  onclick = "postDataReturnXml('options3.php', 'scheme=1', getOptions)">
<input type = "button" value = "Use color scheme 2"
  onclick = "postDataReturnXml('options3.php', 'scheme=2', getOptions)">
```

And when `options3.php` returns its XML for the appropriate color scheme, the `postDataReturnXml` calls the `getOptions` function to handle that XML:

```
<html>
  <head>

    <title>Posting data and returning XML with Ajax Gold</title>

    <script type = "text/javascript" src = "ajaxgold.js"></script>

    <script language = "javascript">

      var options;

      function getOptions(xml)
      {
        options = xml.getElementsByTagName("option");
        listOptions();
      }

      function listOptions ()
      {
        var loopIndex;
        var selectControl = document.getElementById('optionList');

        for (loopIndex = 0; loopIndex < options.length; loopIndex++ )
        {
            selectControl.options[loopIndex] = new
              Option(options[loopIndex].firstChild.data);
        }
      }

      function setOption()
      {
        document.getElementById('targetDiv').style.color =
          options[document.getElementById
            ('optionList').selectedIndex].firstChild.data;
      }

    </script>
  </head>

  <body>
```

```
<h1>Posting data and returning XML with Ajax Gold</h1>

<form>
    <select size="1" id="optionList"
      onchange="setOption()">
      <option>Select a scheme</option>
    </select>
   <input type = "button" value = "Use color scheme 1"
     onclick = "postDataReturnXml('options3.php', 'scheme=1', getOptions)">
   <input type = "button" value = "Use color scheme 2"
     onclick = "postDataReturnXml('options3.php', 'scheme=2', getOptions)">
</form>

   <div id="targetDiv" width =100 height=100>Color this text.</div>

</body>

</html>
```

You can see this example at work in Figure 5-5. When the user clicks a button, this application uses `postDataReturnXml` to post data to the server, which returns a color scheme by using XML. And that color scheme appears in the drop-down list box, as you can see in Figure 5-5.

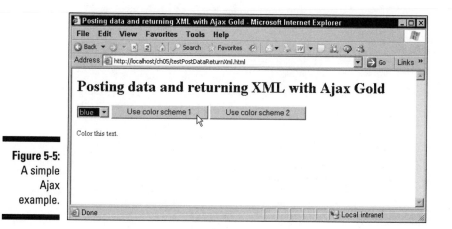

Figure 5-5:
A simple
Ajax
example.

Finding Ajax Frameworks in the Wild

The Ajax Gold JavaScript library written for this book (and covered in the previous sections) is one example of an Ajax framework that lets you put Ajax to work in Web pages without actually having to write any Ajax code yourself. Many other Ajax frameworks are available as well, and I cover two of them in the following sections.

Easy Ajax with AJAXLib

AJAXLib is a very simple Ajax framework that you can pick up for free at `http://karaszewski.com/tools/ajaxlib`. The actual framework is named `ajaxlib.js`.

How do you use it? It's easy — you just call its `loadXMLDoc` function, passing that function the URL it should fetch XML from, as well as the `callback` function you want called with that XML, and a `true/false` argument that you set to `true` if you want extra white space removed from the fetched XML automatically.

PHP scripts can return XML (such as `options1.php` from Chapter 3, which returns three colors) in an XML document. Here's an example:

```
<?
header("Content-type: text/xml");
$options = array('red', 'green', 'blue');
echo '<?xml version="1.0"?>';
echo '<options>';
foreach ($options as $value)
{
    echo '<option>';
    echo $value;
    echo '</option>';
}
echo '</options>';
?>
```

How about trying to read the XML from `options1.php` by using AJAXLib? To include `ajaxlib.js` in a new page — `textAjaxlib.html`, to be precise — you use this line:

```
<html>
  <head>
    <title>Testing ajaxlib</title>

    <script type = "text/javascript" src = "ajaxlib.js"></script>
        .
        .
        .
```

Now you can use AJAXLib's `loadXMLDoc` function to load the XML received from `options1.php` and to call a function named `decodeXML` in your code with the XML like this:

```
<html>
  <head>
    <title>Testing ajaxlib</title>

    <script type = "text/javascript" src = "ajaxlib.js"></script>
```

```
          .
          .
          .
   </head>

   <body>

     <H1>Testing ajaxlib</H1>

     <form>
       <input type = "button" value = "Display Message"
         onclick = "loadXMLDoc('options1.php', decodeXml, false)">
     </form>

     <div id="targetDiv">
       <p>The fetched data will go here.</p>
     </div>

   </body>
</html>
```

All that's left is to decode the XML. For example, in this case, you might display the first color received from `options1.php`, which is `"red"`. I show you how in Listing 5-4.

Listing 5-4:   Putting AJAXLib to Work

```
<html>
  <head>
    <title>Testing AJAXLib</title>

    <script type = "text/javascript" src = "ajaxlib.js"></script>

    <script language = "javascript">

      function decodeXml()
      {
        var options = resultXML.getElementsByTagName("option");

        var loopIndex;
        var div = document.getElementById('targetDiv');

        div.innerHTML = "The first color is " +
          options[0].firstChild.data;

      }
    </script>
  </head>

  <body>
```

(continued)

Listing 5-4 *(continued)*

```
<H1>Testing AJAXLib</H1>

<form>
  <input type = "button" value = "Display Message"
    onclick = "loadXMLDoc('options1.php', decodeXml, false)">
</form>

<div id="targetDiv">
  <p>The fetched data will go here.</p>
</div>

</body>
</html>
```

You can see the results in Figure 5-6, where you see that the first color retrieved in the XML from `options1.php` is indeed red.

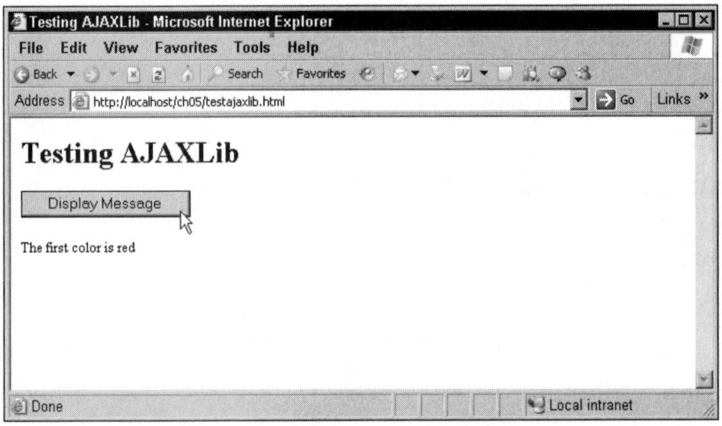

Figure 5-6:
Using
AJAXLib to
get XML
from the
server.

Not bad, now you've put the AJAXLib framework to work. This framework is a very simple one, offering only the `loadXMLDoc` function, but it gets things started with Ajax frameworks.

Grabbing XML with libXmlRequest

You can get the Ajax `libXmlRequest` framework for free at www.white frost.com/reference/2003/06/17/libXmlRequest.html. This framework has two main methods, the `getXML` and `postXML` methods, which use the `GET` and `POST` methods to retrieve XML from the server. This library features pooling of `XMLHttpRequest` objects, so the browser doesn't create too many such objects — which can be a drain on memory — and also lets you cache the response XML you get from the server.

Here are the main functions in this library, from the `libXmlRequest` documentation:

- ✔ `getXml(sPath)`: A synchronous `GET` request; returns `null` or an XML document object.

- ✔ `getXml(sPath, fHandler,1)`: An asynchronous `GET` request; returns 1 if the request was made and invokes handler `fHandler` when the XML document is loaded.

- ✔ `postXml(sPath, vData)`: A synchronous `POST` request; returns `null` or an XML document object. Note that this function expects the server will respond with well-formed XML. If the server doesn't respond with well-formed XML, the response XML object will be `null`.

- ✔ `postXml(sPath, vData, fHandler, 1)`: An asynchronous `POST` request. This returns 1 if the request was made, and invokes handler `'fHandler'` when the XML document is loaded. Note that this function expects the server to respond with well-formed XML. If the server doesn't respond with well-formed XML, the response XML object will be null. The `responseText` isn't queried.

You call the `callback` function, named `fHandler` here, with two parameters, and the second parameter is a JavaScript object that holds the XML data that you want. This object supports two properties:

- ✔ `id`: The request ID if you've supplied one.
- ✔ `xdom`: The XML object that holds your data.

You can also control caching (see Chapter 6 for more on avoiding browser caching of data) and pooling with these functions, which the `libXmlRequest` documentation explains in this way:

- ✔ `setCacheEnabled([true | false])`: Enables caching.
- ✔ `getCacheEnabled()`: Returns `true` if caching is enabled.
- ✔ `setPoolEnabled([true | false])`: Enables pooling.
- ✔ `getPoolEnabled()`: Returns `true` if pooling is enabled.
- ✔ `getXmlHttpArray()`: Returns an array of pool objects.
- ✔ `clearCache()`: Clears cached XML DOM references.
- ✔ `testXmlHttpObject()`: Tests whether an `XmlHttpObject` can be created; returns `true` if so.

The `libXmlRequest` library also gives you some utility functions that help you work with the XML you get from the server:

- ✔ `newXmlDocument(sNodeName)`: Returns a new XML document object with the specified root node name.

- ✔ `serialize(oNode)`: Returns the string representation of a node.

- ✔ `selectNodes(xmlDocument, sXpath, oNode)`: Returns an array of results based on the specified XPath for a given XML document.

- ✔ `selectSingleNode(xmlDocument, sXpath, oNode)`: Returns a single XML node based on the specified *XPath* — the special XML language that lets you specify the location of an exact node or set of nodes in an XML document — for a given XML document. ***Note:*** The node reference is required for this implementation to work with Mozilla.

- ✔ `removeChildren(node)`: Removes all children from an HTML or XML DOM node.

- ✔ `setInnerXHTML(target_node, source_node, preserve)`: Copies the `source_node` (XML or HTML) structure into `target_node` (HTML).

- ✔ `transformNode([xml_dom | xml_path], [xsl_dom | xsl_path] {, node_reference, xml_request_id, xsl_request_id, bool_cache_xsl})`: Transforms nodes using XSL. (See Chapter 8 for more on transforming XML.)

Note that in this library, you must preface the name of all these functions with the text `org.cote.js.xml.` to call them; for example, if you want to call the `getXml` function, you call `org.cote.js.xml.getXml`.

How about an example putting this library to work? Take a look at `libXmlRequest.html` — available for download from the Web site associated with this book — which connects to the `libXmlRequest` library like this:

```html
<html>
  <head>
    <title>Testing libXmlRequest</title>

    <script type = "text/javascript" src = "libXmlRequest.js"></script>
        .
        .
        .
```

As in the previous example, you can retrieve XML from `options1.php` here too. You can do that with the `libXmlRequest org.cote.js.xml.getXml` function this way, passing the location from which to get the XML (that's the relative URL `options1.php` here), the callback function (`decodeXML`, as in the previous example), and a 1 to indicate you want this to be an asynchronous data fetch:

```
<html>
  <head>
    <title>Testing libXmlRequest</title>

    <script type = "text/javascript" src = "libXmlRequest.js"></script>
        .
        .
        .
  </head>

  <body>

    <H1>Testing libXmlRequest</H1>

    <form>
      <input type = "button" value = "Display Message"
        onclick = "org.cote.js.xml.getXml('options1.php', decodeXml, 1)">
    </form>

    <div id="targetDiv">
      <p>The fetched data will go here.</p>
    </div>

  </body>
</html>
```

The decodeXML function handles the XML, much as in the previous example — but in this case, this callback function is passed two arguments. The second of these arguments is a JavaScript object with a property named xmldom that holds the XML data you want. Listing 5-5 shows how you can recover the <option> elements from the XML data by using that property.

Listing 5-5:   Putting libXmlRequest to Work

```
<html>
  <head>
    <title>Testing libXmlRequest</title>

    <script type = "text/javascript" src = "libXmlRequest.js"></script>

    <script language = "javascript">

      function decodeXml(a, b)
      {
        var options = b.xdom.getElementsByTagName("option");

        var loopIndex;
```

(continued)

Listing 5-5 *(continued)*

```
            var div = document.getElementById('targetDiv');

            div.innerHTML = "The first color is " +
              options[0].firstChild.data;


        }
    </script>
</head>

<body>

    <H1>Testing libXmlRequest</H1>

    <form>
      <input type = "button" value = "Display Message"
        onclick = "org.cote.js.xml.getXml('options1.php', decodeXml, 1)">
    </form>

    <div id="targetDiv">
      <p>The fetched data will go here.</p>
    </div>

  </body>
</html>
```

What does this look like in action? You can see the answer in Figure 5-7, where the `getXml` function did its thing and grabbed the XML. The `libXmlRequest` framework gives you a way of getting XML from the server by using the GET and POST methods, and also provides you with some added functions to handle that XML when you get it.

Figure 5-7:
Using libXml
Request to
get XML
from the
server.

Chapter 6

More Powerful Ajax Frameworks

....

In This Chapter

▶ Dragging and dropping with online shopping carts

▶ Using the XHConn framework

▶ Using the Sack framework

▶ Handling older browsers with `HTMLHttpRequest`

▶ Handling XML with Sarissa

▶ Working with Rico

....

*T*he CEO comes to you and says, "We need an easier way for customers to purchase televisions from our Web site. Too many customers don't like the multistage process of moving from page to page with a shopping cart to buy things. We're losing money."

"Okay," you say, "how about using Ajax?"

"Great idea!" says the CEO. "How?"

"Well, you could let the users just drag and drop the articles they want to purchase into a shopping cart visually. That way they could buy as many televisions as they want without leaving the same page."

"Great!" says the CEO. "Now we can finally get our $19,995 televisions moving."

"$19,995 for a television?" you ask. "Hmm. I think I know the reason you're not moving televisions, and it has nothing to do with shopping carts."

 Some of the examples in this chapter use Ajax frameworks that are available for free online. Before you try to run a particular example, make sure that the files needed for the associated framework is in the same folder on your server as the example you're trying to run. For copyright reasons, the code for the Ajax frameworks that I discuss in this and the previous chapter can't be included in the downloadable code for this book, so pick up that code at the supplied URL for a framework before you try to run an example that uses that framework.

Dragging and Dropping with Shopping Carts

One of the popular uses for Ajax is to let users drag and drop items, such as when they want to put the items into a shopping cart, and to update the server with those new items in the shopping cart.

You can build drag-and-drop applications with a number of the Ajax frameworks in this chapter, and they're good for that kind of purpose. However, for the most part, you still have to write the drag-and-drop part of the code yourself. For that reason, I start this chapter with a homegrown drag-and-drop application to make life a little easier if you want to implement this for yourself.

You can see the Ajax application, `drag.html`, in Figure 6-1. The code for the application is included in the code for this book. (See the Introduction for details about downloading the code from this book's companion Web site.)

In this case, the user sees a television (represented by a `<div>` element in this case, but it could as easily be an image using an `<img>` element), and a shopping cart (also represented by a `<div>` element in this example). The user can drag the television with the mouse, as you see in Figure 6-2.

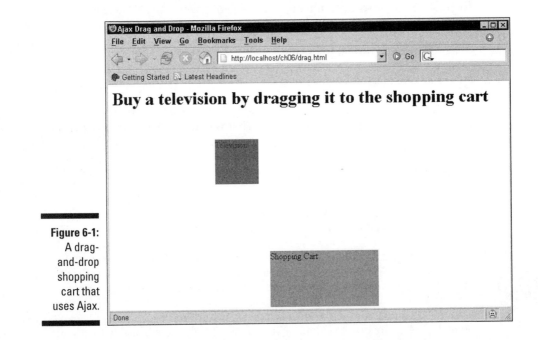

Figure 6-1:
A drag-and-drop shopping cart that uses Ajax.

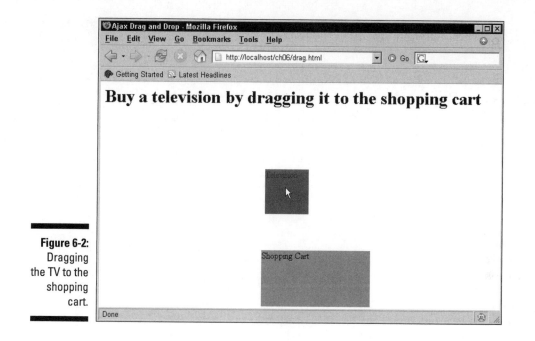

Figure 6-2:
Dragging
the TV to the
shopping
cart.

When the user drops the television in the shopping cart, the application uses Ajax to communicate with the server, and it displays the text you see in Figure 6-3 — You just bought a nice television.

That's how this example works — the user can drop items into the shopping cart, and the server will be notified immediately of the new shopping cart contents, no need for the user to click buttons and go from page to page. (If you're going to use this kind of code for the front end of a real shopping cart application, you've obviously got to spiff up the images and the appearance of this application, but it shows how to get drag and drop working and how to connect dragging and dropping to Ajax.) Handling mouse events like dragging and dropping differs significantly from browser to browser, and knowing how to handle the major browsers when creating Ajax applications like this one is very useful.

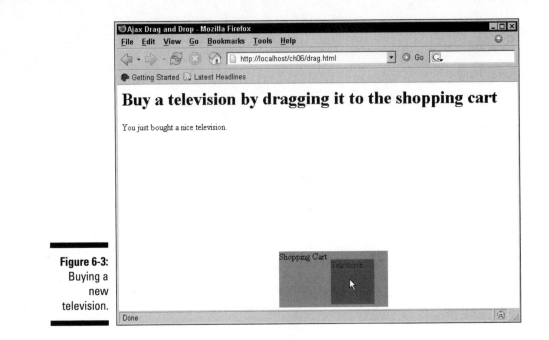

Figure 6-3:
Buying a
new
television.

This example starts by displaying the television and shopping cart, using `<div>` elements. Note that the television `<div>` element also connects its `onmousedown` event handler to a function named `handleDown`, which means that when the mouse is over the television and the user is pressing down the mouse button, the `handleDown` function is called, like this:

```
<body>
  <h1>Buy a television by dragging it to the shopping cart</h1>
    <div id="targetDiv"></div>

    <div id="television"
      style="left:200px; top:100px; width:80px; height:80px;"
      onmousedown="handleDown(event);">Television</div>

    <div id="target"
      style="left:300px; top:300px; width:200px; height:100px;">
      Shopping Cart</div>

</body>
```

To color the television and the shopping cart, you can apply CSS styles (see Chapter 9 for the details on how to use CSS styles with Ajax elements). You can connect a style to an HTML element by using a `<style>` element, and prefacing the element's ID with a # sign. The next bit of code shows how to set up the television and shopping cart by using styles.

```
<head>
  <title>Ajax Drag and Drop</title>

  <style type="text/css">
    #television {
      position:absolute;
      z-index:200;
      background: #FF0000;
      color:#0000FF;
    }

    #target {
      position:absolute;
      background: #00FF00;
      color:#000000;
    }
  </style>
      .
      .
      .
```

Note the television `<div>` is given a z-index value of `200` in this `<style>` element, which will makes sure it stays on top of other elements like the shopping cart when the user drags it. That seem wacky to you? You can find the details on how this kind of styling works in Chapter 9.

Handling mouse events

Now it's time to start working with the mouse when the user drags the television — and this is where the difference between browsers comes in. Handling events like mouse presses and movements always takes a little work when you want to target more than one browser.

In browsers like Firefox, this line in the television `<div>` element will cause the `handleDown` function to be called with an object named `event` that will contain the details of the mouse's present position:

```
<div id="television"
  style="left:200px; top:100px; width:80px; height:80px;"
  onmousedown="handleDown(event);">
  Television</div>
```

In Internet Explorer, on the other hand, the `handleDown` function will be called without being passed an `event` object. You use the window object's `event` object instead. To find the X and Y location of the mouse in the `television` `<div>`, you use the `pageX` and `pageY` properties of the `event` object in Firefox, but `clientX` and `clientY` in Internet Explorer. And to find which element the mouse clicked, you use the `target` property in Firefox, but `srcElement` in Internet Explorer.

That's all pretty crazy, so this example starts by supporting its own type of event, named MouseEvent. That way, the rest of the code can work with this type of event and not always have to keep checking which browser is being used.

You pass the event object you got when the mouse event occurred (the event object will be null in Internet Explorer, because event handler functions aren't passed an event object) to the MouseEvent function, and it'll create a new JavaScript object with these main properties:

- ✔ x: The x location of the mouse.
- ✔ y: The y location of the mouse.
- ✔ target: The HTML element that the mouse is in.

Here's the code that creates the MouseEvent object that the rest of the application can use without having to worry about what browser is involved. Note the use of the keyword this here, which is how you refer to the current object in JavaScript:

```
<script type="text/javascript">
    .
    .
    .
    function MouseEvent(e)
    {
      if(e) {
        this.e = e;
      } else {
        this.e = window.event;
      }

      if(e.pageX) {
        this.x = e.pageX;
      } else {
        this.x = e.clientX;
      }

      if(e.pageY) {
        this.y = e.pageY;
      } else {
        this.y = e.clientY;
      }

      if(e.target) {
        this.target = e.target;
      } else {
        this.target = e.srcElement;
      }
    }
```

Handling mouse down events

When the user presses the mouse to start the drag operation, the
handleDown function will be called:

```
<div id="television"
   style="left:200px; top:100px; width:80px; height:80px;"
   onmousedown="handleDown(event);">
   Television</div>
```

The handleDown function is passed an event object in Firefox, but not in
Internet Explorer, and the first thing to do is to create a new MouseEvent
object this way:

```
function handleDown(e)
{
  var e = new MouseEvent(e);
  .
  .
  .
}
```

Now you can use the MouseEvent object's properties, such as the target
property, which is the HTML element where the mouse was in. (That's the
television <div> in this case, but in a general shopping cart application, it
could be any of the items you're offering for sale.)

Now that the mouse is down, the user might be starting to drag an item, so
the next step is to make the browser "listen" for moveMove events, which
happen when the user drags an item, and mouseUp events, which occur
when the user drops a dragged item. To make the browser listen for those
events, you have to use *listener* functions. How you connect such functions to
the current document depends on which browser you're using, so this example adds a new function, addListener, to connect the mouseMove event to
a function named handleMove, and the mouseUp event to a function named
handleUp:

```
function handleDown(e)
{
  var e = new MouseEvent(e);
  addListener("mousemove", handleMove);
  addListener("mouseup", handleUp);
  .
  .
  .
}
```

The `addListener` function connects events to functions you want called when those events occur, and how you do that depends on which browser the user has. Here's what this function looks like:

```
function addListener(type, callback)
{
  if (document.addEventListener) {
    document.addEventListener(type, callback, false);
  } else if (document.attachEvent) {
    document.attachEvent("on" + type, callback, false);
  }
}
```

After calling the `addListener` function for the `mouseMove` and `mouseUp` events, your code will be called when those events occur. So far, so good.

When the user moves the mouse, you have to move the HTML element they're dragging. To do that, you should record the location at which the mouse was pressed inside that element. The reason for doing so is that when the user moves an element, you want to make the element's new location match the new mouse location. To move an element by using styles, you can position its top-left corner to match the new mouse location, but if the user pressed the mouse somewhere inside the element, you have to keep in mind that the upper-left corner doesn't necessarily correspond to the mouse location in the element. To account for that, you can store the X and Y offset of the mouse with respect to the upper-left corner of the dragged element, like this:

```
<script type="text/javascript">

  var offsetX, offsetY;
      .
      .
      .
  function handleDown(e)
  {
    var e = new MouseEvent(e);
    addListener("mousemove", handleMove);
    addListener("mouseup", handleUp);
    offsetX = e.x - parseInt(television.style.left);
    offsetY = e.y - parseInt(television.style.top);
    document.getElementById("targetDiv").innerHTML = "";
  }
```

Note also that the last line here clears the text in the `<div>` element that displays the message `You just bought a nice television`.

Congratulations, you've set up everything to handle the rest of the dragging operations, starting with mouse-move events, which I cover in the following section.

Handling mouse-move events

When the user drags the mouse, your `handleMove` function will be called. In that function, you should move the `television` `<div>` to match the new location of the mouse (after taking into account the offset of the mouse inside the `<div>`). The `handleMove` function starts by creating a new `MouseEvent` object so it can decode where the mouse is:

```
function handleMove(e)
{
  var e = new MouseEvent(e);
      .
      .
      .
}
```

Now you can move the dragged HTML element to its new location by using dynamic styles this way:

```
function handleMove(e)
{
  var e = new MouseEvent(e);
  var x = e.x - offsetX;
  e.target.style.left = x + "px";
  var y = e.y - offsetY;
  e.target.style.top = y + "px";
}
```

That's fine. Now you're dragging the item the user has selected. But what about when he drops that item? Check out the next section for more information.

Handling mouse up events

When the user drops the item he's dragging, the `handleUp` function will be called, and the first order of business is to create a `MouseEvent` object to get the location at which the user dropped the dragged HTML element. Here's how:

```
function handleUp(e)
{
  var e = new MouseEvent(e);
      .
      .
      .
}
```

Now that the user has released the mouse button, any dragging operation that was going on is over, so you can stop responding to mouse events until the next mouse down event. To stop responding to `mouseMove` and `mouseUp` events, you can remove the listener functions you connected to those events earlier by using a new function, `removeListener`, like so:

```
function handleUp(e)
{
   var e = new MouseEvent(e);
   removeListener("mousemove", handleMove);
   removeListener("mouseup", handleUp);
      .
      .
      .
}
```

Here's what the `removeListener` function looks like in this example:

```
function removeListener (type, callback)
{
   if (document.removeEventListener) {
      document.removeEventListener(type, callback, false);
   } else if (document.detachEvent) {
      document.detachEvent("on" + type, callback, false);
   }
}
```

But did the user drop the television in the shopping cart? You need the location and dimensions of the shopping cart to check. The ID of the shopping cart `<div>` element is `"target"`, so you can get an object that corresponds to the shopping cart on the screen this way:

```
function handleUp(e)
{
   var e = new MouseEvent(e);
   removeListener("mousemove", handleMove);
   removeListener("mouseup", handleUp);

   var target = document.getElementById("target");
      .
      .
      .
```

You can get the X and Y location of the upper-left corner of the shopping cart with the left and top styles of the shopping cart `<div>` element, and its width and height with the `width` and `height` styles. Those styles are stored as text, however, and you need them to be numbers to see whether the user dropped the television in the shopping cart. The way to make JavaScript turn a text string like `"220"` into the corresponding number, 220, is to use the JavaScript `parseInt` (parse integer) function, so here's how to get the location and dimensions of the shopping cart:

```
function handleUp(e)
{
  var e = new MouseEvent(e);
  removeListener("mousemove", handleMove);
  removeListener("mouseup", handleUp);

  var target = document.getElementById("target");
  var x = parseInt(target.style.left);
  var y = parseInt(target.style.top);
  var width = parseInt(target.style.width);
  var height = parseInt(target.style.height);
    .
    .
    .
```

Great . . . so did the user drop the television in the shopping cart? You can check whether the final location of the mouse was inside the shopping cart in this way:

```
function handleUp(e)
{
  var e = new MouseEvent(e);
  removeListener("mousemove", handleMove);
  removeListener("mouseup", handleUp);

  var target = document.getElementById("target");
  var x = parseInt(target.style.left);
  var y = parseInt(target.style.top);
  var width = parseInt(target.style.width);
  var height = parseInt(target.style.height);

  if(e.x > x && e.x < x + width &&
    e.y > y && e.y < y + height){
      .
      .
      .
  }
}
```

If this `if` statement is executed, the user dropped the TV in the shopping cart, and it's time to let the server know about it (see the next section).

Updating the shopping cart

Okay, a new item is in the shopping cart, and you should update the server-side program with that information. You can do that in the normal Ajax way, getting an `XMLHttpRequest` object this:

```
function handleUp(e)
{
  var e = new MouseEvent(e);
  removeListener("mousemove", handleMove);
  removeListener("mouseup", handleUp);

  var target = document.getElementById("target");
  var x = parseInt(target.style.left);
  var y = parseInt(target.style.top);
  var width = parseInt(target.style.width);
  var height = parseInt(target.style.height);

  if(e.x > x && e.x < x + width &&
    e.y > y && e.y < y + height){

    var XMLHttpRequestObject = false;

    if (window.XMLHttpRequest) {
      XMLHttpRequestObject = new XMLHttpRequest();
    } else if (window.ActiveXObject) {
      XMLHttpRequestObject = new
      ActiveXObject("Microsoft.XMLHTTP");
    }

    if(XMLHttpRequestObject) {
      XMLHttpRequestObject.open("GET", "text.txt");

      XMLHttpRequestObject.onreadystatechange = function()
      {
        if (XMLHttpRequestObject.readyState == 4 &&
          XMLHttpRequestObject.status == 200) {
          .
          .
          .
            delete XMLHttpRequestObject;
            XMLHttpRequestObject = null;
        }
      }

      XMLHttpRequestObject.send(null);
    }
  }
}
```

The Ajax code just retrieves the text in the file `text.txt`, which is `"You
just bought a nice television."`, and displays that text in a `<div>`
named `targetDiv`:

```
function handleUp(e)
{
  var e = new MouseEvent(e);
  removeListener("mousemove", handleMove);
  removeListener("mouseup", handleUp);
         .
         .
         .

  if(XMLHttpRequestObject) {
    XMLHttpRequestObject.open("GET", "text.txt");

    XMLHttpRequestObject.onreadystatechange = function()
    {
      if (XMLHttpRequestObject.readyState == 4 &&
        XMLHttpRequestObject.status == 200) {
          document.getElementById("targetDiv").innerHTML =
            XMLHttpRequestObject.responseText;
          delete XMLHttpRequestObject;
          XMLHttpRequestObject = null;
      }
    }

    XMLHttpRequestObject.send(null);
  }
 }
}
```

The text that this Ajax code fetches from the server appears on the Web page (refer to Figure 6-3).

There it is — the wave of the future as far as shopping carts go. The users no longer have to push a lot of buttons and move from page to page, and then back to the shopping pages, just to add something to a shopping cart. All they have to do now is to drag the item to the cart, and Ajax does the rest. Very nice. When you've built your user interface by using drag-and-drop techniques like this, the Ajax frameworks in this chapter will handle the Ajax operations for you.

In this case, only one page was involved, which is going to be impractical if you're Amazon.com with millions of books to offer. But the principle still holds: Each book's page can include a shopping cart icon, in the upper-left corner for example, and all you'd have to do is to drag the book's picture there to add it to the shopping cart, which would instantly update itself by displaying the items in the cart.

Looking at Some Heavier-Weight Frameworks

The available Ajax frameworks make developing your own applications a snap, and plenty of them are out there. In Chapter 5, I introduce what Ajax frameworks can do. In the sections that follow, I continue that survey by pointing you to some of the more powerful frameworks, among the many that are available. When it comes time to write your own Ajax applications, these frameworks can save you a lot of time. The following sections are intended to help you understand how they work so that you can decide which frameworks you want to use.

Getting XMLHttpRequest objects with XHConn

XHConn is an Ajax framework with a twist: It passes you the entire `XMLHttpRequest` object instead of just the data from that object. You can get the data yourself by using the `XMLHttpRequest` object's `responseText` and `responseXML` properties. You can pick up XHConn for free at `http://xkr.us/code/javascript/XHConn`. You can use GET or POST with XHConn.

How do you use XHConn? XHConn gives you a JavaScript object that will do all the work for you. You start by creating that object:

```
var xhconn = new XHConn();
```

To use this new object, you call its `connect` method. Here are the arguments you pass to the `connect` method:

URL	The URL of the server-side resource you want to connect to.
method	The HTTP method you want to use to connect; `"GET"` or `"POST"`
variables	The URL-encoded variables you want to send to the server, given as a string. For example, `"color=red&number=3...."`.
function	The function that is called after the data is downloaded. This function is passed the `XMLHttpRequest` object.

So here's how you might use the XHConn object:

```
xhconn.connect("data.php", "POST", "color=red&number=3", handlerFunction);
```

Listing 6-1 shows an example, testXHConn.html, which you can download
with the code for this book. This example puts XHConn to work by fetching
the text from a file named xhconn.txt (also in the code for this book),
which has these contents:

```
This data was fetched using XHConn.
```

This example creates an XHConn object, sets up a function to be called when
the data (xhconn.txt in this example) has been fetched, and displays the
fetched data.

Listing 6-1: Using the XHConn Ajax Framework

```html
<html>
  <head>

    <script type = "text/javascript" src = "XHConn.js"></script>

    <script language = "javascript">

      function testXHConn()
      {
        var myConn = new XHConn();

        if (!myConn) {
          alert("XHConn creation failed.");
        }

        var fnWhenDone = function (XMLHTTPRequestObject)
        {
          document.getElementById("targetDiv").innerHTML
            = XMLHTTPRequestObject.responseText;
        };

        myConn.connect("xhconn.txt", "GET",
          "", fnWhenDone);
      }
    </script>
  </head>

  <body>
    <h1> Testing XHConn</h1>


    <form>
      <input type = "button" value = "Display Message"
        onclick = "testXHConn()">
    </form>


    <div id="targetDiv">
```

(continued)

Listing 6-1 *(continued)*

```
    <p>The fetched data will go here.</p>
  </div>

 </body>
</html>
```

TIP

When you want to run this example, make sure that `xhconn.js` is located in the same directory on your server as this example's code. The results appear in Figure 6-4, where XHConn was successful in grabbing some text for you.

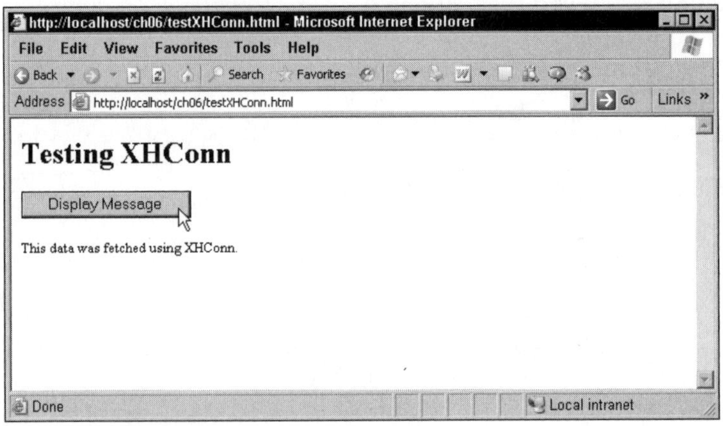

Figure 6-4:
Using XHConn to fetch data.

> **http://localhost/ch06/testXHConn.html - Microsoft Internet Explorer**
> File   Edit   View   Favorites   Tools   Help
> Back ▾   ▾   Search   Favorites
> Address http://localhost/ch06/testXHConn.html   Go   Links »
>
> ## Testing XHConn
>
> [Display Message]
>
> This data was fetched using XHConn.
>
> Done   Local intranet

The Simple AJAX Code Kit: Sack

Here's another useful, and simple-to-use Ajax framework — Sack, which stands for Simple AJAX Code Kit. You can get Sack for free at `http://twilightuniverse.com/projects/sack`.

When you create a Sack object, you can configure it (setting the method to `"GET"`, for example) by using the `setVar` method. Then you can fetch your data with the `runAJAX` method.

The idea here is that you create a Sack object, set the parameters you want, and call `runAjax` to perform the Ajax operation. Say, for example, that you wanted to use Sack to fetch the following text, stored in a file named `sack.txt` on the server:

```
This data was fetched using Sack.
```

Here's how that would work in an example in the code for the book, named testSack.html, which shows one way of working with Sack. After you create a new Sack object, you configure various properties of that object to indicate that the text file you want to read is sack.txt, the HTTP method you want to use is the GET method, and the HTML element in your Web page you want to display the fetched text in is the element with the ID "targetDiv":

```
sackObject = new sack();
var vars = "";
sackObject.requestFile = "sack.txt";
sackObject.method = "GET";
sackObject.element = "targetDiv";
sackObject.runAJAX(vars);
```

You can see the entire code for this example in Listing 6-2.

Listing 6-2: Using the Sack Ajax Framework

```
<html>
  <head>
    <title>Testing Sack</title>

    <script type = "text/javascript" src = "tw-sack.js"></script>

    <script language = "javascript">

      function getData(dataSource, divID)
      {
        sackObject = new sack();
        var vars = "";
        sackObject.requestFile = "sack.txt";
        sackObject.method = "GET";
        sackObject.element = "targetDiv";
        sackObject.runAJAX(vars);
      }
    </script>
  </head>

<body>

  <H1>Testing Sack</H1>

  <form>
    <input type = "button" value = "Display Message"
      onclick = "getData('sack.txt', 'targetDiv')">
  </form>

  <div id="targetDiv">
    <p>The fetched data will go here.</p>
  </div>

  </body>
</html>
```

And the results appear in Figure 6-5, where Sack is fetching data for you by using Ajax. Sack is a nice framework that's easy to use.

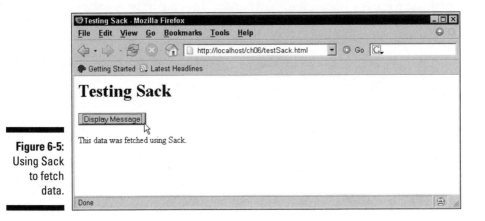

Testing Sack - Mozilla Firefox

File   Edit   View   Go   Bookmarks   Tools   Help

http://localhost/ch06/testSack.html   Go

Getting Started   Latest Headlines

Testing Sack

Display Message

This data was fetched using Sack.

Done

Figure 6-5:
Using Sack
to fetch
data.

Parsing XML with Interactive Website Framework

The Interactive Website Framework (IWF) is a multipurpose Ajax framework that includes a custom XML parser and other features. You can get IWF for free at `http://sourceforge.net/projects/iwf`.

This framework allows multiple `XMLHttp` requests at the same time, and prevents caching by sending unique URLs to the server. Its custom XML parser can make it easier to handle XML, so that you can extract data from an XML document using syntax like this in JavaScript:

```
var dressing = doc.food.sandwich[0].dressing;
```

instead of something like this (see Chapter 8 for the details on extracting XML data from XML documents by using JavaScript like this):

```
var dressing = doc.documentElement.firstChild.getAttribute("dressing");
```

IWF gives you many built-in tools, such as functions that let you move elements around a Web page to support drag-and-drop operations or functions that let you grab XML data and insert it into an HTML element on a Web page.

You can also use IWF to perform other actions, such as moving elements around a Web page with a function named `iwfMoveTo`. An example of that, `iwfajax.html`, comes with IWF, and you can see it at work in Figure 6-6. When you click the various hyperlinks, a small orange box moves around in the page, as you see in Figure 6-6.

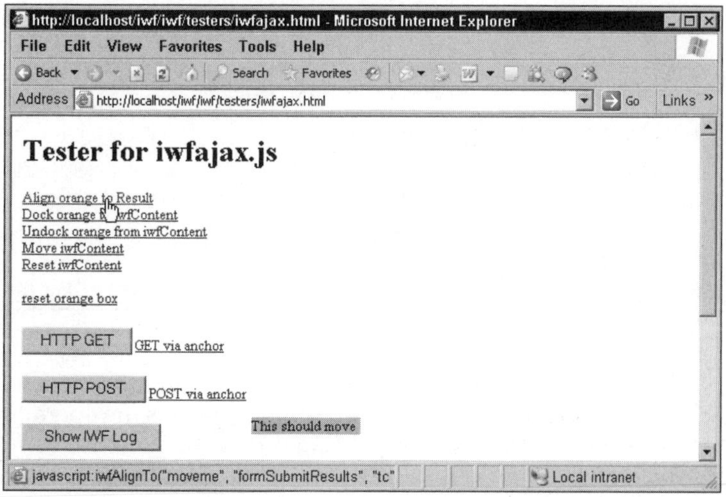

Figure 6-6: Using IWF to move page elements.

Handling older browsers with HTMLHttpRequest

The `HTMLHttpRequest` Ajax framework, which you can pick up for free at `www.twinhelix.com/javascript/htmlhttprequest`, supports not only Ajax, but also uses hidden `IFrame` elements to mimic Ajax in older browsers that don't support `XMLHttpRequest` objects.

You can see a demo of `HTMLHttpRequest` at `www.twinhelix.com/javascript/htmlhttprequest/demo`, as shown in Figure 6-7. There's some standard Ajax stuff here. When you click the tabs in this demo, text is loaded into the area under the tabs, as you can see in Figure 6-7.

Figure 6-7:
Using
HTMLHttp
Request to
load text.

Another demo on the same page passes a math operation, such as multiplication, and two operands to the server, which performs the operation. You can see that at the bottom of the page in Figure 6-8, where `HTMLHttpRequest` tells you that 2 x 6 = 12.

If you're working with older browsers that don't support `XMLHttpRequest` objects, take a look at this framework.

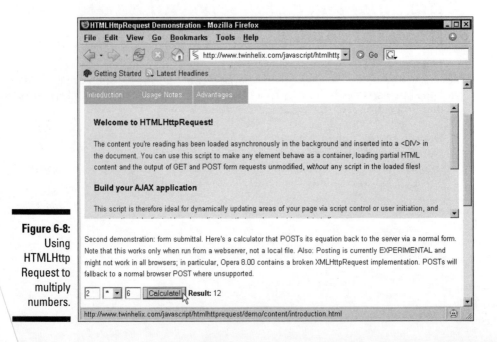

Figure 6-8:
Using
HTMLHttp
Request to
multiply
numbers.

Decoding XML with Sarissa

Sarissa is a JavaScript library (although it calls JavaScript by its formal name, ECMAScript) that specializes in working with XML — and recently, that's included some Ajax power.

Sarissa lets you

✔ Create or load XML documents and manipulate them.

✔ Use XML's XPath (see Chapter 8) to extract data from XML documents.

✔ Use XSLT to transform XML (also see Chapter 8) into other forms, such as HTML.

✔ Use `XMLHttpRequest` objects to download XML using Ajax.

You can get Sarissa at `http://sourceforge.net/projects/sarissa`.

Sarissa is useful because it can help you easily deal with the XML you download. Here's an example, `testSarissa.html` in the code for this book. This example reads in this XML file, `sarissa.xml`, and extracts the text from the element named `<span>`:

```
<?xml version="1.0" ?>
<ajax>
  <response>
    <span>Hello from Sarissa.</span>
  </response>
</ajax>
```

You can see this example at work in Figure 6-9. When the user clicks the button, `sarissa.xml` is downloaded, and Sarissa extracts the text in the `<span>` element, which is displayed. That's great, because using JavaScript to handle the XML you download can be an involved process (as I explain in Chapter 8).

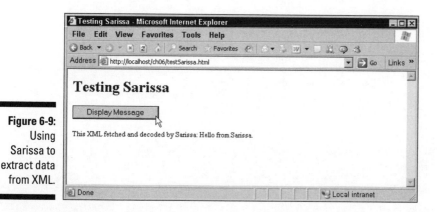

Figure 6-9:
Using
Sarissa to
extract data
from XML.

This example works by creating a Sarissa DomDocument object that will hold the XML:

```
var domDocument = Sarissa.getDomDocument();
    .
    .
    .
```

To indicate that you want to download data asynchronously, you set the DomDocument object's async property to true:

```
var domDocument = Sarissa.getDomDocument();
domDocument.async = true;
    .
    .
    .
```

Next, you set up the callback function using the DomDocument object's onreadystatechange property:

```
var domDocument = Sarissa.getDomDocument();
domDocument.async = true;

domDocument.onreadystatechange = function myHandler()
{
    .
    .
    .
}
    .
    .
    .
```

When the XML has been fetched, you can use the Sarissa method select SingleNode to extract the <span> element. You do that by passing an XML XPath expression (see Chapter 8) to selectSingleNode; in this case, that's "//span", which will match the <span> element anywhere in the document:

```
var domDocument = Sarissa.getDomDocument();
domDocument.async = true;

domDocument.onreadystatechange = function myHandler()
{
    if (domDocument.readyState == 4) {
        var element = domDocument.selectSingleNode("//span");
        .
        .
        .
    }
}
    .
    .
    .
```

This variable, `element`, now contains an object holding the XML `<span>` element. To extract the text in that element, you can use Sarissa's `serialize` method, which converts XML objects into text. The text then gets displayed in a `<div>` element named `targetDiv`:

```
var domDocument = Sarissa.getDomDocument();
domDocument.async = true;

domDocument.onreadystatechange = function myHandler()
{
  if (domDocument.readyState == 4) {
    var element = domDocument.selectSingleNode("//span");
    document.getElementById("targetDiv").innerHTML =
      "This XML fetched and decoded by Sarissa: " +
      Sarissa.serialize(element);
  }
}
    .
    .
    .
```

All that's left is to load the XML file asynchronously, which you do with the Sarissa `load` method, include the Sarissa JavaScript files, and set up the rest of the Web page. Check out Listing 6-3.

Listing 6-3: Using the Sarissa Ajax Framework

```
<html>
  <head>
    <title>Testing Sarissa</title>

    <script type = "text/javascript" src = "sarissa.js"></script>
    <script type = "text/javascript" src = "sarissa_ieemu_xpath.js">

    </script>

    <script language = "javascript">

      function getData(dataSource, divID)
      {
        var domDocument = Sarissa.getDomDocument();
        domDocument.async = true;

        domDocument.onreadystatechange = function myHandler()
        {
          if (domDocument.readyState == 4) {
            var element = domDocument.selectSingleNode("//span");
            document.getElementById("targetDiv").innerHTML =
              "This XML fetched and decoded by Sarissa: " +
              Sarissa.serialize(element.firstChild);
          }
```

(continued)

Listing 6-3 *(continued)*

```
        }

        domDocument.load("sarissa.xml");
    }
    </script>
</head>

<body>

    <H1>Testing Sarissa</H1>

    <form>
      <input type = "button" value = "Display Message"
        onclick = "getData('data.txt', 'targetDiv')">
    </form>

    <div id="targetDiv">
      <p>The fetched data will go here.</p>
    </div>

</body>
</html>
```

And the results appear in Figure 6-9 (shown earlier).

Creating visual effects with Rico

Rico is a popular JavaScript framework that offers a number of cool visual effects, such as dragging and dropping. For example, check out the demo page, shown in Figure 6-10, which you can find at

```
http://openrico.org/rico/demos.page?demo=ricoDragAndDropSimple.html
```

Rico also has a control it calls a *LiveGrid*, which can display and sort data in a table that it fetches behind the scenes. You can see a Rico LiveGrid control at work in Figure 6-11, which shows part of `http://openrico.org/rico/livegrid.page`, displaying a table of movie titles. If you click a column header, the table sort itself automatically, based on that header.

Figure 6-12 shows another LiveGrid example, `http://openrico.org/rico/yahooSearch.page`, which uses Ajax methods to perform a Yahoo! search. When you click the button, the search results appear in the table without a page refresh.

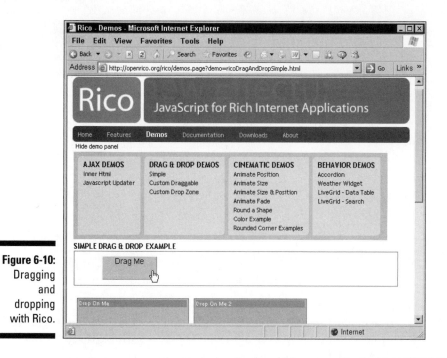

Figure 6-10:
Dragging
and
dropping
with Rico.

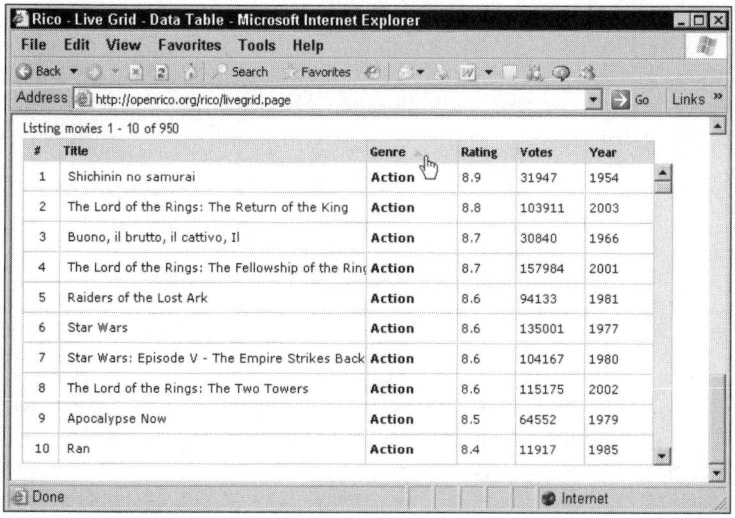

Figure 6-11:
A Rico
LiveGrid.

Besides these techniques, Rico offers other visual effects, such as making elements fade in and out of view, and an "accordion" control that can display several panes of text which you can slide open or closed with a draggable bar.

Displaying data in an HTML element

The Rico library files, `prototype.js`, `rico.js`, `util.js`, include support for directly fetching text and XML data by using Ajax. For example, say that you wanted to recover the text in an XML document named `rico.xml`, which looks like this:

```
<?xml version = "1.0" ?>
<ajax-response>
  <response type="element" id="targetDiv">
    <span>This data fetched using RICO methods.</span>
  </response>
</ajax-response>
```

In this case, the XML `<response>` element indicates that its content should be displayed in an HTML element named `"targetDiv"`. To make that happen, you use the Rico library files. You can connect the name of a request (`"request1"` in this example) to the XML document that's using the Rico `ajaxEngine` object's `registerRequest` method, and indicate in which HTML element to display the fetched data with the `registerAjaxElement` method in an example named `testRico.html`. You can see how all this works in the following code:

```
<script language="javascript">

  function init()
  {
      ajaxEngine.registerRequest("request1", "rico.xml");
      ajaxEngine.registerAjaxElement("targetDiv");
  }


</script>
        .
        .
        .
<body onload="init()">
        .
        .
        .
</body>
```

After you've set up the request, you can execute that request with
ajaxEngine object's sendRequest method when the user clicks a button to
fetch the data this way:

```
<html>
  <head>
    <title>Testing Rico</title>

    <script src="prototype.js"></script>
    <script src="rico.js"></script>
    <script src="util.js"></script>

    <script language="javascript">

      function init()
      {
        ajaxEngine.registerRequest("request1", "rico.xml");
        ajaxEngine.registerAjaxElement("targetDiv");
      }

      function getData()
      {
        ajaxEngine.sendRequest("request1", "");
      }

    </script>
  </head>

  <body onload="init()">
```

```
    <h1>Testing RICO</h1>

    <form>
      <input type="button" value="Display Message" onclick="getData()">
    </form>

    <div id="targetDiv">The fetched data will go here.</div>
  </body>
</html>
```

You can see the results of `testRico.html` in Figure 6-13, where the code used Rico methods to fetch the text, "`This data was fetched using RICO methods.`" from `rico.xml` on the server.

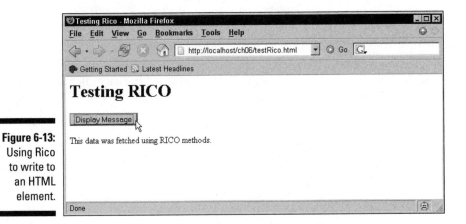

Figure 6-13:
Using Rico
to write to
an HTML
element.

Letting JavaScript objects handle your data

Rico also lets you fetch XML data and handle that data by using JavaScript objects, which is handy if you want to put that data to use rather than simply display it. For example, say that you had an XML document, `rico2.xml`, and you wanted to recover the text assigned to the `day` attribute of the `<response>` element (which is "`Friday`"):

```
<?xml version = "1.0" ?>
<ajax-response>
  <response type="object" id="displayHandler" day="Friday">
    <span>Here is some text.</span>
  </response>
</ajax-response>
```

You can do this task by using a JavaScript object to handle the fetched data by using Rico. The `<response>` element in the preceding code indicates you want to use an object named `displayHandler`, which is what you'll do here.

Rico is set up so that the JavaScript object you use to handle data should have a method named `ajaxUpdate`, which is passed the XML data. This example uses a JavaScript object of a type named `DisplayHandler` that supports an `ajaxUpdate` method. The goal in this method is to recover the text assigned to the `<response>` element's `day` attribute and to display that data, which works like this (see Chapter 8 for more on handling XML by using JavaScript this way):

```
<script language="javascript">

  function DisplayHandler () {}

  DisplayHandler.prototype =
  {
    ajaxUpdate: function(ajaxResponse)
    {
      var attrs = ajaxResponse.attributes;
      document.getElementById("targetDiv").innerHTML =
        "Today is " + attrs.getNamedItem("day").value;
    }
  }
    .
    .
    .
```

Now you can create the `displayHandler` object and set up the request so that it'll fetch the data in `rico2.xml`. Next, you use a Rico method named `registerAjaxObject` to register the JavaScript object whose `ajaxUpdate` method should be called with the XML data:

```
<html>
  <head>
      .
      .
      .
    <script language="javascript">
      .
      .
      .
    function init()
    {
      displayHandler = new DisplayHandler();
      ajaxEngine.registerRequest("request1", "rico2.xml");
      ajaxEngine.registerAjaxObject(
```

```
          "displayHandler", displayHandler);
      }

    </script>
  </head>

  <body onload="init()">
        .
        .
        .
```

Now when the user clicks a button, the `ajaxEngine sendRequest` method is called to fetch the data, as you see here:

```
<html>
  <head>
    <title>Testing RICO with JavaScript objects</title>

        .
        .
        .

      function init()
      {
        displayHandler = new DisplayHandler();
        ajaxEngine.registerRequest("request1", "rico2.xml");
        ajaxEngine.registerAjaxObject(
          "displayHandler", displayHandler);
      }

      function getData()
      {
        ajaxEngine.sendRequest("request1", "");
      }

    </script>
  </head>

  <body onload="init()">
    <h1>Testing RICO with JavaScript objects</h1>

    <form>
      <input type="button" value="Display message" onclick="getData()">
    </form>

    <div id="targetDiv">The fetched data will be displayed here.</div>

  </body>
</html>
```

When the data is fetched, it'll be passed to the `displayHandler` object's `ajaxUpdate` method, which will extract and display the text assigned to the `day` attribute in `rico2.xml`, as shown in Figure 6-14.

Figure 6-14:
Using Rico
to handle
XML data by
using a
JavaScript
object.

This example is a success. Passing data to a JavaScript object like this can be a useful technique when you want to process the data you fetch from the server before displaying it.

Overcoming caching with the Http framework

Got problems with caching? Internet Explorer caches the data it gets from the server, so you'll often see that same data over and over, even if you change the actual data the server sends back. One solution is to use Firefox for development, instead of Internet Explorer. But you're going to have to deal with Internet Explorer at some point, and if you still have caching issues when development is done, you might take a look at the Http framework, which you can get for free at `http://adamv.com/dev/javascript/http_request`.

This framework supports forced caching in Firefox as well as forced non-caching in Internet Explorer.

You can see an example at `http://adamv.com/dev/javascript/files/time`, which displays the current time (in milliseconds), as shown in Figure 6-15. Internet Explorer caches the response from the server by default, so clicking the top Get Time button always gives you the same time. But the Http package can avoid caching (which it does by appending unique data to the end of an URL each time you call the URL). For example, when you click the second button from the top in the figure, the time is updated for each button click, even in Internet Explorer.

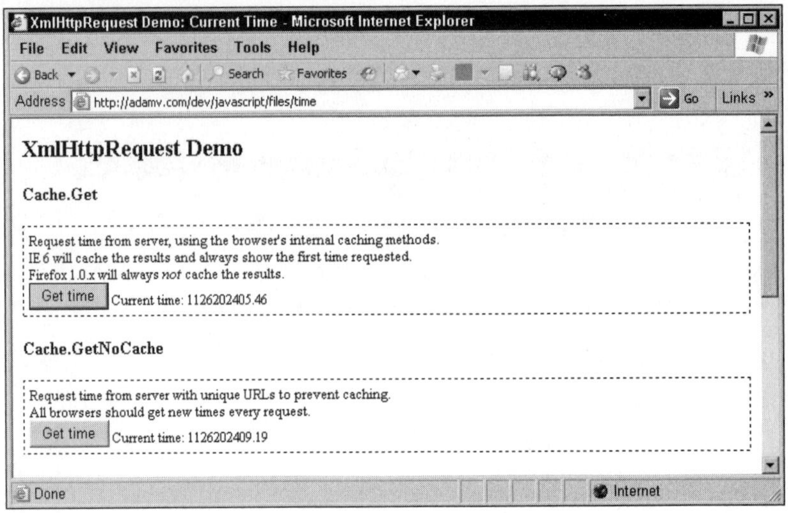

Figure 6-15:
Avoiding
caching
with the
Http
framework.

This is a useful package when data caching becomes an issue, but you can often handle this issue yourself just by appending unique data to the end of an URL, as already discussed.

Chapter 7

Server-Side Ajax Frameworks

"*H*m," says the CEO, "all those JavaScript-oriented Ajax frameworks are very nice — "

"Great," you say. "So we're in business?"

"Well, I have a question," says the CEO. "As I was saying, those JavaScript–oriented Ajax frameworks are very nice, but you still have to develop the server-side code too."

"Sure," you say, "unless you just want to fetch data from a simple data file."

"Aren't there any Ajax packages that let you develop just the server-side code and automatically create the JavaScript for you?"

"Glad you asked," you say. "In fact, that's what this whole chapter is all about."

Writing JavaScript by Using Ajax Frameworks

Working with Ajax often means using JavaScript in the browser and a language like PHP or JavaServer Pages on the server. In earlier chapters, I show you Ajax packages that let you develop the browser-side part of the application. But some Ajax packages are designed to be used on the server — and they can write JavaScript for you. That's what you see in this chapter.

Although some server-side frameworks are based on exotic server-side languages, most of the ones you see use the popular PHP (see Chapter 10 for more on PHP) and Java languages, especially JavaServer Pages. Those are the ones I stick to here, starting with Sajax. Note that many of the following frameworks do much the same thing: let you work with Ajax by using server-side programming. When you see how these packages work in this chapter, you'll know which one is right for you.

Sajax and PHP

Sajax is an Ajax framework (available for download from www.modern method.com/sajax) that lets you create Ajax JavaScript on the server by using various server-side languages.

How does Sajax work? You can use it on the server to create the JavaScript that will support Ajax in your browser. Currently, Sajax lets you connect to ASP, ColdFusion, Io, Lua, Perl, PHP, Python, and Ruby on the server.

For example, you can use it to create a JavaScript function in a Web page, connecting that function to a PHP method on the server, which in turn handles your data and then sends its data to another JavaScript function back in the browser. So when the user opens the PHP page, Sajax generates all the JavaScript to handle Ajax operations in the created Web page.

For example, take a look at the addition example, addem.php — available for download from the Web site associated with this book — which appears in Figure 7-1. When you enter two values and click the Calculate button, the page uses Ajax to add the values on the server and display the result without a page refresh.

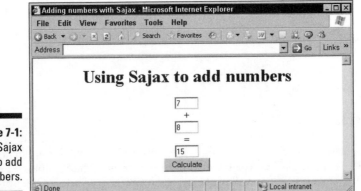

Figure 7-1:
Using Sajax
to add
numbers.

How does it work? In this example, `addem.php`, you start by including `Sajax.php`:

```
<?
  require("Sajax.php");
    .
    .
    .
```

Then you define a PHP function named `addem` to add two numbers (this is the PHP function that will run on the server):

```
<?
  require("Sajax.php");

  function addem($op1, $op2)
  {
    return $op1 + $op2;
  }
    .
    .
?>
```

You'll be able to call this function from the JavaScript in a Web page, except that you refer to it as x_addem. In other words, if you define a PHP function named `addem`, you can call it in JavaScript as x_addem by using Sajax.

Next, set up Sajax by calling `sajax_init`, and *export* the `addem` function:

```
<?
  require("Sajax.php");

  function addem($op1, $op2)
  {
    return $op1 + $op2;
  }

  sajax_init();
  sajax_export("addem");
    .
    .
?>
```

Exporting the `addem` function means that you'll be able to access the `addem` function in JavaScript (as x_addem). Finally, the code calls the `sajax_handle_client_request` method to connect the `addem` function to Sajax and start setting up the JavaScript that will appear in the browser:

```
<?
  require("Sajax.php");

  function addem($op1, $op2)
  {
    return $op1 + $op2;
  }

  sajax_init();
  sajax_export("addem");
  sajax_handle_client_request();

?>
```

Sajax generates much of the JavaScript needed in this example, and it does that with the PHP function `sajax_show_javascript`, which you execute by using PHP inside an HTML `<script>` element so the generated JavaScript will be inside that `<script>` element:

```
<script>
  <?
    sajax_show_javascript();
  ?>
    .
    .
    .
```

This example also includes the HTML for the controls you see in Figure 7-1: three text fields and a button. The text fields for the two operands to add are named `op1` and `op2`, and the text field where the answer will appear is named `result`.

```
<body>
  <center>
    <h1>Using Sajax to add numbers</h1>
    <input type="text" name="op1" id="op1" value="7" size="3">
    <br>
              +
    <br>
    <input type="text" name="op2" id="op2" value="8" size="3">
    <br>
      =
    <br>
    <input type="text" name="result" id="result" value="" size="3">
    <br>
    <input type="button" name="check" value="Calculate"
      onclick="do_addem(); return false;">
  </center>
</body>
```

Note that the button here is tied to a JavaScript function named do_addem, which calls x_addem, the generated JavaScript function that connects back to the PHP function addem on the server. When the user clicks the button to perform the multiplication, the operands are read from the first two text fields, and the x_addem function is called, which passes the operands to the PHP function named addem back on the server.

```
<script>
  <?
    sajax_show_javascript();
  ?>

  function do_addem()
  {
    var op1, op2;

    op1 = document.getElementById("op1").value;
    op2 = document.getElementById("op2").value;
    x_addem(op1, op2, show_results);
  }
</script>
```

Note that the x_addem function not only passes the operands back to the addem function on the server, but also takes the name of a JavaScript function that will be called with the results of the multiplication. In this example, that callback function is named show_results, as you can see in the preceding code.

This callback function, show_results, is passed an argument from the PHP addem function and displays it in the third text field, which is named result. Here's what the code looks like:

```
<script>
  <?
    sajax_show_javascript();
  ?>

  function show_results(result)
  {
    document.getElementById("result").value = result;
  }

  function do_addem()
  {
    var op1, op2;

    op1 = document.getElementById("op1").value;
    op2 = document.getElementById("op2").value;
    x_addem(op1, op2, show_results);
  }
</script>
```

As you can see, Sajax lets you create JavaScript on the server and tie that JavaScript to server-side functions by using Ajax. Very cool. You might also take a look at `http://cyberdummy.co.uk/test/dd.php`, which uses Sajax for drag-and-drop operations.

Xajax and PHP

Xajax, which you can get for free at `http://xajax.sf.net`, is an Ajax framework that lets you use server-side methods to create Ajax JavaScript for use in a browser. Xajax uses PHP on the server, and you can get an idea about how it works by taking a look at my handy `addem.php` example — available for download from the Web site associated with this book — which will add two numbers. You can see this example at work in Figure 7-2.

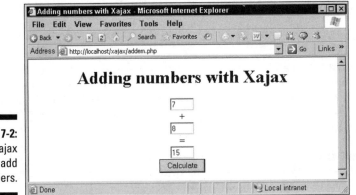

Figure 7-2:
Using Xajax
to add
numbers.

Much like the Sajax example in the preceding section, this Xajax example uses a PHP function named `addem`, which adds the values passed to it and assigns the result a variable named `"result"`. Here's what the PHP code looks like:

```
function addem($op1, $op2)
{
  $objResponse = new xajaxResponse();
  $objResponse->addAssign("result", "value", $op1 + $op2);
  return $objResponse->getXML();
}
```

Then the code creates an new object named `$xajax`.

```
function addem($op1, $op2)
{
  $objResponse = new xajaxResponse();
  $objResponse->addAssign("result", "value", $op1 + $op2);
  return $objResponse->getXML();
}

$xajax = new xajax("addem.server.php");
          .
          .
          .
```

And the code registers the `addem` function with the `$xajax` object.

```
function addem($op1, $op2)
{
  $objResponse = new xajaxResponse();
  $objResponse->addAssign("result", "value", $op1 + $op2);
  return $objResponse->getXML();
}

$xajax = new xajax("addem.server.php");
$xajax->registerFunction("addem");
          .
          .
          .
```

Then the code calls the Xajax method `processRequests`, which is much like the Sajax `sajax_handle_client_request` method, to prepare for the JavaScript generation.

```
function addem($op1, $op2)
{
  $objResponse = new xajaxResponse();
  $objResponse->addAssign("result", "value", $op1 + $op2);
  return $objResponse->getXML();
}

$xajax = new xajax("addem.server.php");
$xajax->registerFunction("addem");
$xajax->processRequests();
          .
          .
          .
```

In the HTML part of this example, the code uses an Xajax method named
printJavascript to create the JavaScript that Xajax will use.

```
<html>
<html>
  <head>
    <title>Adding numbers with Xajax</title>
    <?php $xajax->printJavascript(); ?>
  </head>
      .
      .
      .
```

The HTML part also sets up the HTML controls shown in Figure 7-2 and calls
a generated function named xajax_addem that will call the PHP function
addem on the server:

```
<body>
  <center>
    <h1>Adding numbers with Xajax</h1>
    <input type="text" name="op1" id="op1" value="7" size="3" />
    <br>
    +
    <br>
    <input type="text" name="op2" id="op2" value="8" size="3" />
    <br>
    =
    <br>
    <input type="text" name="result" id="result" value="" size="3" />
    <br>
    <input type="button" value="Calculate"
            onclick="xajax_addem(document.getElementById('op1').value,document
            .getElementById('op2').value);return false;" />
  </center>
</body>
```

How is the result of the addition displayed in the third text field, named
"result"? The PHP addem function uses an Xajax method named
addAssign to assign the answer to the value property of the "result"
text field:

```
function addem($op1, $op2)
{
  $objResponse = new xajaxResponse();
  $objResponse->addAssign("result", "value", $op1 + $op2);
  return $objResponse->getXML();
}
```

And that's it. The data the user enters is sent to the server by using Ajax
techniques, and the result is displayed without a page refresh, as you see in
Figure 7-2. If you're interested in generating JavaScript on the server this way,
take a look at both Sajax and Xajax.

LibAjax and PHP

Here's another PHP-based Ajax server-side framework: LibAjax, which you can get for free from `http://sourceforge.net/projects/libajax`. The documentation appears at `http://libajax.sourceforge.net/documentation.html`. To demonstrate how LibAjax works, I show you an addition example here as well, which you can see in Figure 7-3.

Keep in mind that the files for the script I highlight here extract to a `php` folder by default. The code for this chapter (available for download from the Web site associated with this book) assumes that `addem.php` and `libajax.php` are in the same directory, so be sure that you do in fact place these files in the same directory.

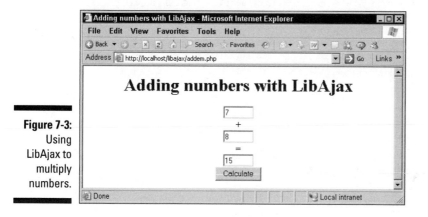

Figure 7-3:
Using
LibAjax to
multiply
numbers.

How does this example — `addem.php`, downloadable from the Web site associated with this book — work? In the PHP, you start by creating a new LibAjax object (named, in this case, `$ajax`) this way:

```php
<?php
require_once("libajax.php");
$ajax = new ajax();
          .
          .
          .
```

This example then uses a PHP function named `addem` that adds the operands passed to it:

```php
function addem($op1, $op2)
{
    print $op1 + $op2;
}
```

Then you configure the $ajax object to select the HTML method, GET or POST, to send data with, and you export the addem function to make that function available in JavaScript.

```
$ajax->mode = "POST";
$ajax->export = array("addem");
    .
    .
    .
```

Now you can access the addem function from JavaScript. If you have other PHP functions to export, you can list them with commas, like this:

```
array("addem", "subtractem");
```

After exporting the addem function, you call the LibAjax client_request method to set up the callback from JavaScript to the PHP code.

```
$ajax->mode = "POST";
$ajax->export = array("addem");
$ajax->client_request();
    .
    .
    .
?>
```

LibAjax automatically writes the JavaScript for you when you call the $ajax->output() method:

```
<html>
  <head>
    <title>Adding numbers with LibAjax</title>
    <script type="text/javascript">
    <?php $ajax->output(); ?>
        .
        .
        .
```

Okay so far. Now what about reading actual data from the user, as shown in Figure 7-3? In this example, I use HTML text fields named op1, op2, and result for that:

```
<body>
  <center>
    <h1>Adding numbers with LibAjax</h1>
    <form>
      <input type="text" name="op1" id="op1" value="7" size="5">
      <br>
      +
      <br>
      <input type="text" name="op2" id="op2" value="8" size="5">
```

```
        <br>
        =
        <br>
        <input type="text" name="result" id="result" value="" size="5">
        <br>
        <input type="button" name="check" value="Calculate" onclick="addem();
            return false;">
    </form>
  </center>
 </body>
</html>
```

When the user clicks the button, a JavaScript function named addem is called. That function is the interface to the server-side PHP function named addem (which you call in JavaScript by calling the generated function ajax_addem). In the JavaScript addem function, the code starts by getting the two operands to multiply, like this:

```
function addem()
{
  var op1 = document.getElementById("op1").value;
  var op2 = document.getElementById("op2").value;
      .
      .
      .
}
```

Then the code calls ajax_addem, which calls the PHP addem function on the server. The two operands, op1 and op2, are passed to ajax_addem, along with a callback function that will handle the answer sent back from the server-side code.

```
function addem()
{
  var op1 = document.getElementById("op1").value;
  var op2 = document.getElementById("op2").value;
  ajax_addem(op1, op2, addem_init);
}
```

The callback function is passed with the result and displays it in the result text field.

That's how LibAjax works — you export a PHP function and can call it by prefacing the name of the function in your JavaScript code with "ajax_". The last argument passed to ajax_addem is the name of a callback function that the PHP code on the server will call in the JavaScript in the browser, and in this case, that's a function named addem_init. The addem_init function simply takes the value passed to it and displays it in the third text field, which is named `"result"`. Here's how the code appears in this example:

```
function addem_init(result)
{
    document.getElementById("result").value = result;
}
```

And that's all it takes. All you have to do is write a server-side PHP function (such as `phpFunction`), export it, and call the `client_request` method; then you can call that function from JavaScript as `ajax_phpFunction`. When you call `ajax_phpFunction`, you pass the arguments you want to pass to `phpFunction`, as well as a JavaScript function to call with the result. In that JavaScript function, you can handle the result as you see fit, such as displaying it in a text field, as in the preceding example.

JPSpan and PHP

Another Ajax framework based in PHP is JPSpan, which you can get from `http://sourceforge.net/projects/jpspan`. The documentation is at `http://jpspan.sourceforge.net/api`.

JPSpan is a relatively complicated framework and uses considerable code to get things running, but it offers a great deal of Ajax support. You can see an autocompletion example (available in the JPSpan download) at work in Figure 7-4, where the application responds to the user's keystrokes by giving possible matches to a country name.

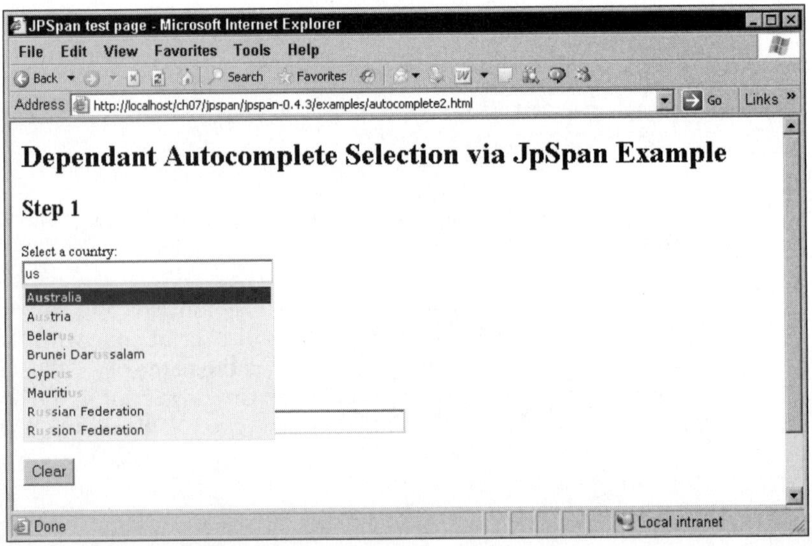

Figure 7-4: Using JPSpan for auto-completion.

Accessing Java with Direct Web Remoting

Direct Web Remoting (DWR) uses Java on the server (as do the following frameworks in this chapter) instead of PHP. You can pick up DWR at `http://getahead.ltd.uk/dwr` for free and read the documentation at `http://getahead.ltd.uk/dwr/documentation`. Also check out the introduction at `http://getahead.ltd.uk/dwr/intro.html`.

Direct Web Remoting is an Ajax framework for calling Java methods directly from JavaScript code. Because DWR uses Ajax, you can access the full power of Java (not otherwise available to you in a browser) behind the scenes on the server and display your results in the server. That's great because Java is a far more powerful language, with a lot more built into it, than JavaScript.

Setting up for Java on the Web

To work with DWR and other Java-based Ajax frameworks, you need a Web server that supports Java. Many such servers exist on the Internet. In fact, your ISP might already support Java, or you can find ISPs by searching for *"Java hosting"* with Google. Java-based Web servers support applications that use JavaServer Pages (JSP) and Java *servlets* (Java server-side programs), and the server-side code you write to connect to your Ajax code will be made up of JSP or servlets.

 One popular Java-based server is Apache Tomcat, which you can get for free at `http://jakarta.apache.org/tomcat`. You can install this server on your own machine and test your applications instantly. Installation is easy; to start the server on a Windows machine, simply open Apache Tomcat and click the Start button.

Connecting to Java by using DWR

DWR is an open-source code library that does much of what the PHP packages do — it lets JavaScript code call Java functions back on the server.

DWR has two parts: code you use in the browser to connect to Java back on the server and code you can use in the browser to make displaying the data you fetched easier. The main part of the DWR code is the part that lets you call Java functions on the server. Like the other frameworks you've seen in this chapter, you can call server-side functions, and DWR will handle the details of connecting your code to those functions. And when your data has been fetched, DWR will call the callback function you've given it with that data.

After you've fetched the data you want, you might also consider using the DWR JavaScript libraries that let you use dynamic HTML to display that data and create interactive Web pages.

You can see an example in Figure 7-5 from the DWR Web site at `http://getahead.ltd.uk/dwr/examples/text`. This simple Ajax example checks the server type and details, and uses Ajax to fetch that data and display it on a Web page, as you see in Figure 7-5.

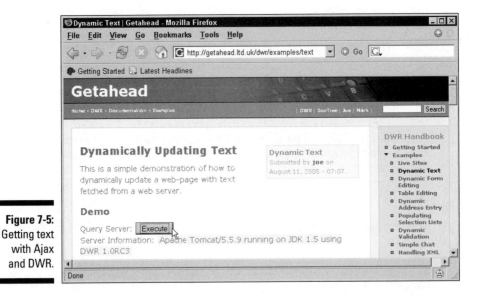

Figure 7-5:
Getting text
with Ajax
and DWR.

You can find other DWR examples on the DWR Web site as well. For example, in Figure 7-6, you can see a DWR chat application, at `http://getahead.ltd.uk/dwr/examples/chat`, that uses Ajax to fetch data and display it in a text-area control. All you have to do is enter your text, which is sent to the server, by clicking the Send button. Your text, along with the text others have entered, appears in the text area.

You can see another DWR example in Figure 7-7, where a list box is filled with values by using Ajax techniques to fetch data from the server. If you click the check box in this example, the application fetches some numbers to fill the list box with, as you can see in Figure 7-7.

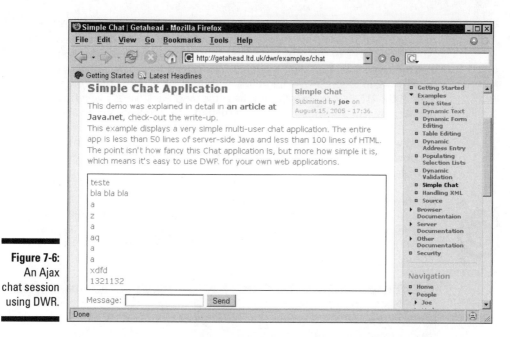

Figure 7-6:
An Ajax
chat session
using DWR.

Figure 7-7:
Populating a
list box with
Ajax and
DWR.

Here's another DWR example, which you can see at `http://getahead.ltd.uk/dwr/examples/table`. This example lets you edit the contents of a table (your edits of the table are stored by using cookies in your browser), and the table is redisplayed by using Ajax techniques. You can see this example at work in Figure 7-8 — just click Edit in a row of the table, edit the row's data in the HTML controls below the table, and click Save. Everything is updated by using Ajax, so no page refreshes are required. Very handy.

If you want to connect Java to your Ajax applications, take a look at DWR. It's powerful and extensive. It does take some work to install it (see the directions at `http://getahead.ltd.uk/dwr/getstarted`).

TIP

Here's a shortcut: Download the `dwr.war` file (see `http://getahead.ltd.uk/dwr/download`) and then put it in the main directory of your Java-based Web server (in Apache Tomcat, that's the `webapps` directory). The Web server will expand `dwr.war` into a working DWR installation for you.

Figure 7-8:
Editing a
table with
Ajax and
DWR.

Building Web Applications with Echo2

Echo2 is a framework you can use to create applications, and it's recently been upgraded to support Ajax. Echo2 is a package for creating Web-based applications that work much like the applications you'd find on a desktop computer. In version 2, the creators of the Echo package have made dramatic improvements in performance and capabilities. When you use Echo2, you don't even need to know anything about HTML, HTTP, or even JavaScript.

Building full applications with Echo2 is beyond the scope of this book, but you can take a look at an online demo at `http://demo.nextapp.com/Email/app`, a Web-based e-mail program that appears in Figure 7-9.

This application uses Ajax to download the text for various e-mail messages. All you have to do is select an e-mail message in the top box at right, and the text of that message appears in the box beneath it, as you see in the figure.

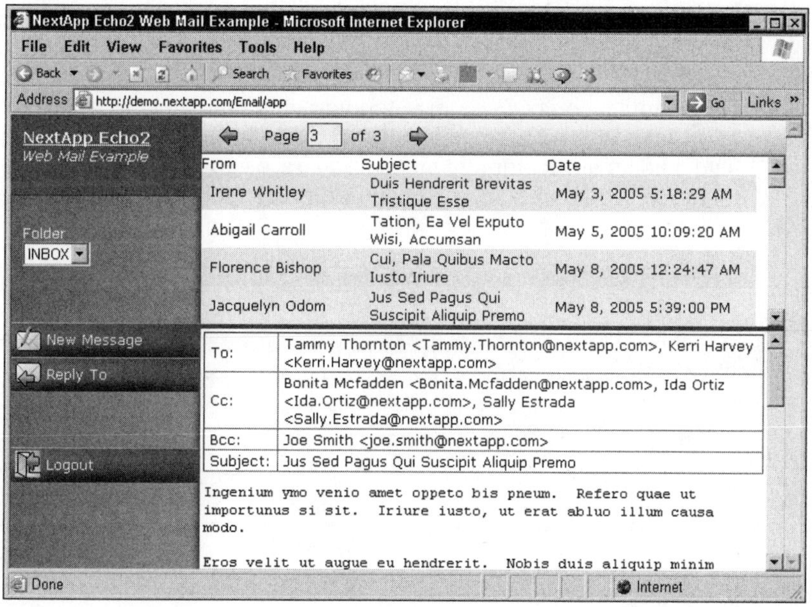

Figure 7-9:
A Web mail
client using
Echo2.

Handling Ajax and JavaServer Pages with Ajax Tags

Here's another interesting framework — the Ajax Tag Library, which you can get at `http://ajaxtags.sourceforge.net`. This Ajax framework relies on JSP tags on the server to create the JavaScript you'll need. In JSP, you can create your own custom tags to tell the server what you want to do, and you tie those tags to Java code that the server runs before it sends the page back to the browser.

This library comes with built-in JSP tags that you can use to implement standard Ajax applications. Here's the list of the tags:

- ✔ **Autocomplete:** Gets a list of possible items that match the text the user has entered in a field for autocompletion.

- ✔ **Callout:** Displays a pop-up balloon connected to a particular element in a Web page.

- ✔ **Select/dropdown:** Sets the contents of a drop-down control based on the user's selection in another drop-down control.

- ✔ **Toggle:** Lets you switch images between two different sources.

- ✔ **Update Field:** Updates the text in a field based on the data the user enters in another field.

For example, you can see an autocomplete demo at work at `http://ajax tags.no-ip.info`. You can enter the first letter of a name of car in the text field, and an autocomplete menu appears, as you see in Figure 7-10. A second text field, which also supports autocomplete, lets you enter the make of a car.

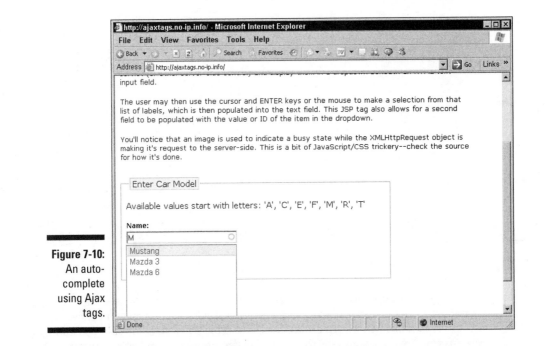

Figure 7-10: An autocomplete using Ajax tags.

Here's how it works: You construct a JSP page that uses the Ajax Tag Library to support various Ajax functionality, such as autocompletion, populating a `<select>` control, or displaying text fetched by using Ajax in an HTML element. Then you write the Java support on the server to supply the XML that holds the data you want to present. For in-depth details on the Ajax Tags Library, take a look at the usage guide at `http://ajaxtags.sourceforge. net/usage.html`.

Handling Java with SWATO

Another Java-based Ajax framework is SWATO, which you can get from `https://swato.dev.java.net`. You can find an introduction to SWATO at `https://swato.dev.java.net/doc/html/quickstart.html`.

SWATO comes with built-in components for common Ajax operations, such as an autocomplete text field, a live form, live lists, and so on. In Figure 7-11, you can see the autocompletion control in an example that comes with SWATO.

SWATO is an interesting framework. It relies on plain old Java objects (called POJOs by Java programmers) on the server, so the server-side programming can be a little less involved.

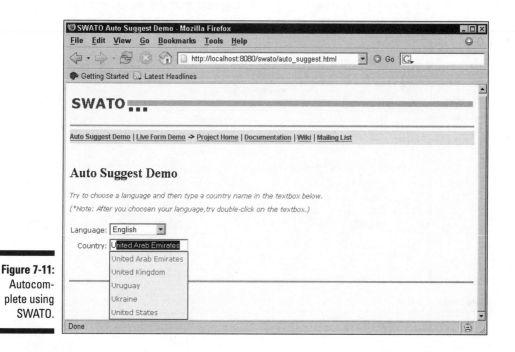

Figure 7-11: Autocomplete using SWATO.

Tracking Down the Many Other Frameworks Available

Plenty of other Ajax frameworks are out there, in a variety of languages. I briefly cover some of them in the following sections. More and more Ajax power is coming online all the time — the future looks bright indeed!

Developing amazing applications with WebORB

You can find WebORB at www.themidnightcoders.com/weborb/aboutweborb.htm. WebORB specializes in creating rich Internet applications that are professional-level quality. Using WebORB, you can integrate Ajax and other technologies such as Flash into your application seamlessly.

WebORB can connect to various languages on the server, from .NET to Java. In Figure 7-12, you can see a shopping-cart example from www.themidnightcoders.com/examples/session-activation.htm.

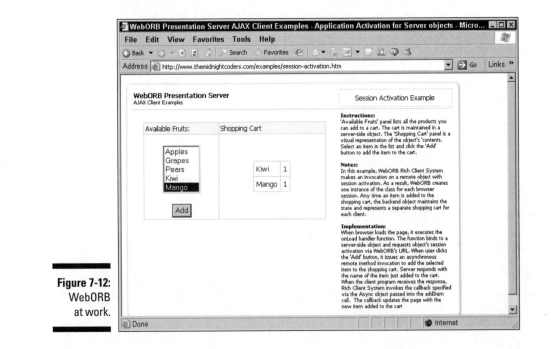

Figure 7-12: WebORB at work.

All you have to do in this example is select an item in the `<select>` control at left and click the Add button. Thanks to Ajax, the selected item appears in the shopping cart at right without the need for a page refresh.

Ruby on Rails

Ruby on Rails (`www.rubyonrails.org`) is an Ajax-enabled framework heavyweight. Instead of PHP or Java, it uses its own proprietary language on the server. It has all kinds of built-in support for Ajax.

When it comes to acting like a server-side Ajax framework, Ruby on Rails functions much like the other frameworks shown in this chapter, except that it uses its own language on the server. As is normal for Ajax applications, you can send data asynchronously to the server by using an `XMLHttpRequest` object. After the data you've requested is sent back to you in the browser, JavaScript generated by Rails will let you handle that data easily — for example, you can display that data by using a `<div>` element.

You can see a Ruby on Rails demo that uses Ajax at `www.papermountain.org/demos/live`, as shown in Figure 7-13. For example, take a look at the autocomplete demo at left in the figure, where the user has typed **he** and the application has suggested various words.

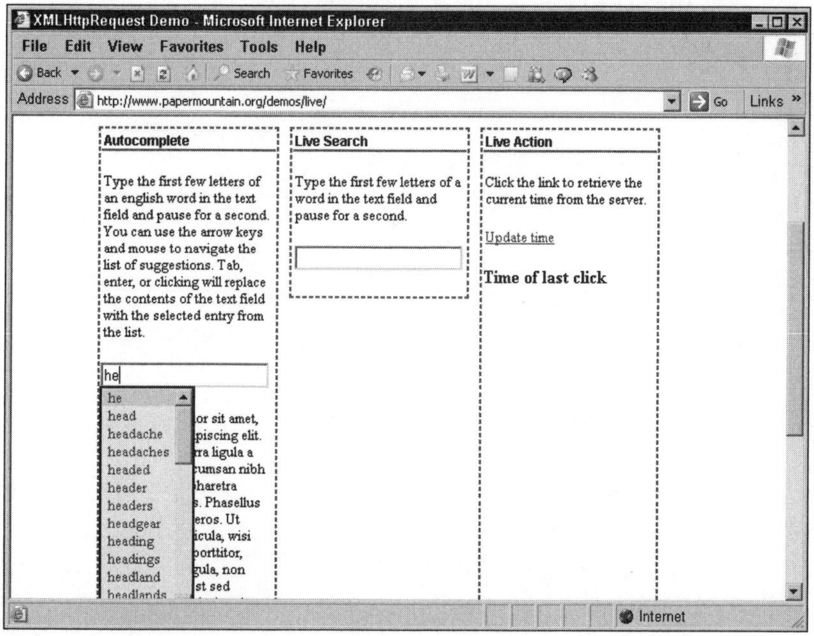

Figure 7-13:
A Ruby on Rails auto-complete example.

Backbase

Another Ajax-enabled framework is Backbase, at `www.backbase.com`. Like WebORB, Backbase specializes in developing rich Internet applications.

Dojo

Dojo is another useful framework, and you can get it at `www.dojotool kit.org`. Dojo calls itself a user-interface toolkit, and it's been updated to include a great deal of Ajax support. It's an open-source package, so you can modify its code if you want to.

Atlas.NET

Frameworks such as Microsoft's ASP.NET (the .NET version of Microsoft's Active Server Pages [ASP] package) are adding more support for Ajax. Microsoft has announced work on the Atlas Client Script Framework, which will integrate Ajax support into ASP.NET and which will work with all modern browsers. Atlas looks like a significant Ajax package, but the details are just starting to emerge. For now, one of the better places to keep tabs on Atlas is `http://beta.asp.net/default.aspx?tabindex=7&tabid=47`, but stay tuned — Atlas is sure to make a splash.

Part IV

In-Depth Ajax Power

The 5th Wave   By Rich Tennant

PROGRAMMING 101

"Before I go on to explain more advanced procedures like the 'Zap-Rowdy-Students-who-Don't-Pay-Attention' function, we'll begin with some basics."

In this part . . .

This part gives you more Ajax power, starting with Chapter 8, which is all about working with XML in JavaScript. When you work with Ajax, the results from the server often are in XML, and knowing how to navigate through that XML and extract the data you want is — in Ajax terms — an invaluable skill. Chapter 9 continues with coverage of cascading style sheets (CSS), which ties in with Ajax by letting you handle realtime displays, such as pop-up menus or drag-and-drop. (*Remember:* Ajax is all about working with the current Web page without reloading that page, and CSS is a big part of that.) Ajax also involves working with code on the server, and Chapter 10 gives you a PHP primer to let you write server-side code. (You don't need to know PHP to read this book, but knowing PHP will help when you start using Ajax yourself, so Chapter 10 is there to give you a foundation for the topic.)

Chapter 8

Handling XML in Ajax Applications

● ●

In This Chapter

▶ Understanding basic XML

▶ Navigating XML documents using JavaScript

▶ Grabbing XML elements *en masse*

▶ Extracting the values of XML attributes

▶ Validating the XML you get from the server

● ●

*"H*m," says the crack Ajax programmer. "I need some help."

"Glad to be of service," you say. "What can I help you with?"

"I've got my XML from the server okay, but now I can't deal with it. How the heck do I navigate from element to element? How do I get the data I need out of this XML?"

"No problem," you say. "Just read this chapter." And you present the surprised Ajax programmer with your bill.

Ajax is all about getting data — often XML data — from the server. How do you handle that XML back in the browser? JavaScript has some strong XML-handling capabilities, as you discover in this chapter. Knowing how to work with XML in JavaScript is essential for any Ajax programmer because the server sends you XML, and you need to know how to extract data from that XML.

Understanding Basic XML

To work with XML in Ajax, you need to understand a few basics about the language and how it works. One key feature of XML is that you're not restricted to a pre-determined set of tags, as in languages like HTML. You can create your own. In addition to tags, you also need to understand what makes an XML document well-formed and valid. I explain what you need to know in the sections that follow.

What's in a tag?

You create your own tags, such as a `<people>` tag, that hold a series of names. Although you make up the tag names yourself, a handful of rules govern what names are legal. Tag names can't start with a number, can't contain spaces, and can't contain a few other illegal characters, such as quotation marks. Here are some illegal tags:

```
<5fish>
<wow that was a big lunch>
<"no way!">
```

Each XML element starts with an opening tag and ends with a closing tag, unless the element is an *empty* element, in which case there's only one tag — no closing tag, and no content of any kind, as you'd usually see between an opening and closing tag. Here's an example of an empty element — note the XML way of closing an empty element, with the markup `/>`:

```
<supervisor />
```

Starting tags can also contain attributes, and the values you assign to those attributes must be quoted text. Also, you must assign a value to each attribute you use. Here are some examples (in the first example, `<witness>` is the tag, `name =` is the attribute, and "`Karen Jones`" is the value):

```
<witness name = "Karen Jones">
<movie title = "Mr. Blandings Builds His Dream House">
<sandwich type = "ham" dressing = "mayo">
```

Even empty elements can contain attributes, as in this example:

```
<language english="yes" />
```

For the full story on XML, take a look at *XML for Dummies,* 4th Edition, by Lucinda Dykes and Ed Tittel. If you want to see the formal XML specification, as published by the World Wide Web Consortium (the people responsible for the XML specs) take a look at `www.w3.org/tr/rec-xml`.

Keeping XML documents well-formed

One criteria for XML documents is that they are *well-formed*. The main rules for a well-formed XML document are that an XML document must

✔ Start with an XML declaration.

✔ Have a document element that contains all the other elements.

✔ Have no *nesting errors* (that is, elements can't overlap, such as `<a><b>This is not good.</a></b>`).

The XML parsers, which read XML in the browsers, won't be able to read XML if it isn't well-formed.

The XML declaration that starts every XML document gives the version of XML you're using. (Currently, only 1.0 and 1.1 are legal values for the version.)

```
<?xml version="1.0"?>
        .
        .
        .
```

Elements can contain other elements in XML, and the document element in an XML document contains all the other elements in the XML document, if there are any. Here's an example of a document element:

```
<?xml version="1.0"?>
<events>
        .
        .
        .
</events>
```

For elements in an XML document to be nested properly, you must nest each child element within its parent. In the following example XML document, `guests.xml`, notice how the guests at a gala ceremony are nested within the `<people>` tag:

```
<?xml version="1.0"?>
<events>
    <event type="informal">
        <event_title>15th award ceremony</event_title>
        <event_number>1207</event_number>
        <subject>gala event</subject>
        <date>7/4/2006</date>
        <people>
            <person attendance="present">
                <first_name>Sam</first_name>
```

```
            <last_name>Edwards</last_name>
        </person>
        <person attendance="absent">
            <first_name>Sally</first_name>
            <last_name>Jackson</last_name>
        </person>
        <person attendance="present">
            <first_name>Cary</first_name>
            <last_name>Grant</last_name>
        </person>
    </people>
  </event>
</events>
```

Making an XML document valid

To make an XML document valid, you have to supply rules for its syntax. For example, should a <person> element always be inside a <people> element? What attributes can an <event> element have?

All the syntax rules can be specified using an XML *document type definition* (DTD, see www.w3.org/tr/rec-xml) or an XML *schema* (see www.w3.org/XML/Schema). How you create DTDs and schema is beyond the scope of this book. But some browsers, such as Internet Explorer, let you validate XML if you supply a DTD or a schema, and you'll see how that works later in this chapter.

Checking to make sure an XML document was created correctly by the server-side software is a useful thing to do in Ajax applications.

Requesting XML Data in Ajax

In this section, you take a look at how Ajax works with XML to pass data. Say that you've stored details about a gala event in an XML document named guests.xml. You want to recover the name of Cary Grant, who was the third guest at the affair, in an Ajax application named guests.html, as you see in Figure 8-1. (Both guests.html and guests.xml are available in the code for this book, which you'll just happen to find available for download at the Web site associated with this book.) When the user clicks the Get the Main Guest button in your Ajax application, the page reads in guests.xml, extracts the third guest's name, and displays it.

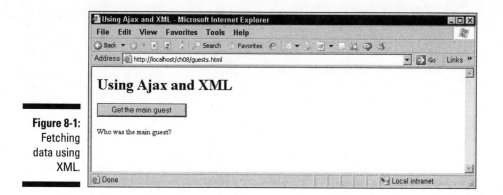

Figure 8-1:
Fetching
data using
XML.

When the user clicks the Get the Main Guest button, what actually happens is
that a function named `getGuest` is called:

```
<body>

  <h1>Using Ajax and XML</h1>

  <form>
    <input type = "button" value = "Get the main guest"
      onclick = "getGuest()">
  </form>

  <div id="targetDiv" width="100" height="100">
    Who was the main guest?
  </div>

</body>
```

The `getGuest` function gets `guests.xml` from the server. The `guests.xml`
file looks like this:

```
<?xml version="1.0"?>
<events>
    <event type="informal">
        <event_title>15th award ceremony</event_title>
        <event_number>1207</event_number>
        <subject>gala event</subject>
        <date>7/4/2006</date>
        <people>
            <person attendance="present">
                <first_name>Sam</first_name>
                <last_name>Edwards</last_name>
            </person>
            <person attendance="absent">
                <first_name>Sally</first_name>
```

```
            <last_name>Jackson</last_name>
        </person>
        <person attendance="present">
            <first_name>Cary</first_name>
            <last_name>Grant</last_name>
        </person>
    </people>
  </event>
</events>
```

The `getGuest` function then passes the XML document in the `XMLHttp Request` objects' `responseXML` property to another function, `display Guest`. (You'll use the `displayGuest` function later to extract the guest's name.)

```
<script language = "javascript">

  function getGuest()
  {
    var XMLHttpRequestObject = false;

    if (window.XMLHttpRequest) {
      XMLHttpRequestObject = new XMLHttpRequest();
      XMLHttpRequestObject.overrideMimeType("text/xml");
    } else if (window.ActiveXObject) {
      XMLHttpRequestObject = new
        ActiveXObject("Microsoft.XMLHTTP");
    }

    if(XMLHttpRequestObject) {
      XMLHttpRequestObject.open("GET", "guests.xml", true);

      XMLHttpRequestObject.onreadystatechange = function()
      {
        if (XMLHttpRequestObject.readyState == 4 &&
          XMLHttpRequestObject.status == 200) {
        var xmlDocument = XMLHttpRequestObject.responseXML;
        displayGuest(xmlDocument);
        }
      }

      XMLHttpRequestObject.send(null);
    }
  }
      .
      .
      .
```

Okay, you've got the XML data. Now you need to extract the third guest's name in the `displayGuest` function in order to display it. There are a couple ways to do this, all useful; I'll take a look at using the node properties like `firstChild` and `lastSibling` here first, followed by accessing elements using methods — instead of properties — next.

Extracting XML Data Using Properties

When you extract data using properties, you use the properties to navigate through the nested tags and locate the data you want to extract. At least that's the simple explanation. In practice, differences in the browsers make the process a bit more complicated. In the following sections, I explain all the details.

Right on the node

To extract Cary Grant's first and last names from your XML file with the help of a little JavaScript, keep in mind that — in JavaScript — XML is treated as a collection of *nodes*. For example, take a look at this simple XML document:

```
<?xml version="1.0" ?>
<document>
    <greeting>
        Hello From XML
    </greeting>
    <message>
        Welcome to the wild and woolly world of XML.
    </message>
</document>
```

Here, the `<document>` node has two subnodes: the `<greeting>` and `<message>` nodes. These subnodes are *child nodes* of the `<document>` node and sibling nodes of each other. Both the `<greeting>` and `<message>` elements themselves have one subnode — a text node that holds character data. Figure 8-2 shows what this document looks like when you look at it as a tree of nodes.

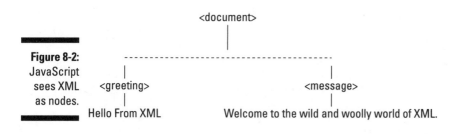

Figure 8-2:
JavaScript
sees XML
as nodes.

Introducing the JavaScript properties

JavaScript has built-in properties you can use to work with the nodes in XML documents, like the one that's returned in the `XMLHttpRequest` object's `responseXML` property. Table 8-1 lists these properties.

Table 8-1	JavaScript Properties for Working in XML
Property	*What It Finds*
attributes	Attributes by this node
childNodes	Array of child nodes
documentElement	The document element
firstChild	First child node
lastChild	Last child node
localName	Local name of the node
name	Name of the node
nextSibling	Next sibling node
nodeName	Name of the node
nodeType	Node type
nodeValue	Value of the node
previousSibling	Previous sibling node

You find out how to use these properties in JavaScript in the next section. Note in particular that the nodeType property holds the type of a node — knowing a node's type is important when you want to extract and work with specific nodes:

- ✔ 1 Element
- ✔ 2 Attribute
- ✔ 3 Text node
- ✔ 4 CDATA (XML character data) section
- ✔ 5 XML entity reference
- ✔ 6 XML entity node
- ✔ 7 XML processing instruction
- ✔ 8 XML comment
- ✔ 9 XML document node
- ✔ 10 XML Document Type Definition (DTD)
- ✔ 11 XML document fragment
- ✔ 12 XML Notation

So how does this work in practice? It's time to start slinging some code.

Navigating an XML document using JavaScript properties

Using the example I introduced in "Requesting XML Data in Ajax," earlier in this chapter, this section explains how you put XML and JavaScript together to extract the third guest, Cary Grant, from `guests.xml`.

To start, the `displayGuest` function is passed to the XML document, `xmldoc`. (This is just the XML from the `XMLHttpRequest` object's `responseXML` property.)

```
function displayGuest (xmldoc)
{
    .
    .
    .
}
```

This XML document has a document element named `<events>`:

```
<?xml version="1.0"?>
<events>
    .
    .
    .
</events>
```

You can get an object corresponding to the document element with the JavaScript `documentElement` property:

```
function displayGuest (xmldoc)
{
    var eventsNode;

    eventsNode = xmldoc.documentElement;
    .
    .
    .
}
```

The `eventsNode` now holds an object corresponding to the `<events>` element — and that document element contains all the other elements. For example, the child element of the `<events>` element is the `<event>` element:

```
<?xml version="1.0"?>
<events>
    <event type="informal">
        .
```

```
         .
         .
    </event>
</events>
```

You can get an object corresponding to the `<event>` element with the `eventsNode` object's `firstChild` property this way:

```
function displayGuest (xmldoc)
{
    var eventsNode, eventNode;

    eventsNode = xmldoc.documentElement;
    eventNode = eventsNode.firstChild;
    .
    .
    .
}
```

Now you have an object corresponding to the `<event>` element. The next step is to get closer to the name of the third guest, which is enclosed in the `<people>` element:

```
<?xml version="1.0"?>
<events>
    <event type="informal">
        <event_title>15th award ceremony</event_title>
        <event_number>1207</event_number>
        <subject>gala event</subject>
        <date>7/4/2006</date>
        <people>
            .
            .
            .
        </people>
    </event>
</events>
```

The `lastChild` property comes to the rescue again, as you use the `event Node` object's `lastChild` property to get an object corresponding to the `<people>` element:

```
function displayGuest (xmldoc)
{
    var eventsNode, eventNode, peopleNode;
    var firstNameNode, lastNameNode, displayText;

    eventsNode = xmldoc.documentElement;
    eventNode = eventsNode.firstChild;
```

```
        peopleNode = eventNode.lastChild;
        .
        .
        .
    }
```

Now you need to get the third, and last, `<person>` element inside the `<people>` node:

```xml
<?xml version="1.0"?>
<events>
    <event type="informal">
        <event_title>15th award ceremony</event_title>
        <event_number>1207</event_number>
        <subject>gala event</subject>
        <date>7/4/2006</date>
        <people>
            <person attendance="present">
                <first_name>Sam</first_name>
                <last_name>Edwards</last_name>
            </person>
            <person attendance="absent">
                <first_name>Sally</first_name>
                <last_name>Jackson</last_name>
            </person>
            <person attendance="present">
                .
                .
                .
            </person>
        </people>
    </event>
</events>
```

The `lastChild` property comes in handy once again to get an object corre-sponding to the correct `<person>` element:

```
function displayGuest (xmldoc)
{
    var eventsNode, eventNode, peopleNode;

    eventsNode = xmldoc.documentElement;
    eventNode = eventsNode.firstChild;
    peopleNode = eventNode.lastChild;
    personNode = peopleNode.lastChild;
    .
    .
    .
}
```

All that's left is to recover the first name and last name of the third guest:

```xml
<?xml version="1.0"?>
<events>
    <event type="informal">
        <event_title>15th award ceremony</event_title>
        <event_number>1207</event_number>
        <subject>gala event</subject>
        <date>7/4/2006</date>
        <people>
            <person attendance="present">
                <first_name>Sam</first_name>
                <last_name>Edwards</last_name>
            </person>
            <person attendance="absent">
                <first_name>Sally</first_name>
                <last_name>Jackson</last_name>
            </person>
            <person attendance="present">
                <first_name>Cary</first_name>
                <last_name>Grant</last_name>
            </person>
        </people>
    </event>
</events>
```

You can get an object corresponding to the `<first_name>` and `<last_name>` elements with the `firstChild` and `nextSibling` properties:

```javascript
function displayGuest (xmldoc)
{
    var eventsNode, eventNode, peopleNode;
    var firstNameNode, lastNameNode;

    eventsNode = xmldoc.documentElement;
    eventNode = eventsNode.firstChild;
    peopleNode = eventNode.lastChild;
    personNode = peopleNode.lastChild;
    firstNameNode = personNode.firstChild;
    lastNameNode = firstNameNode.nextSibling;
        .
        .
        .
}
```

That's great. Now you have JavaScript objects corresponding to the `<first_name>` and `<last_name>` elements. All you have to do now is extract the text in those elements:

```xml
<first_name>Cary</first_name>
<last_name>Grant</last_name>
```

That text is considered a *text node,* and the text node is the first child of the <first_name> and <last_name> elements. That means that in JavaScript, you can recover the text node with the expressions firstNameNode. firstChild and lastNameNode.firstChild.

How do you get the text out of those text nodes once you've gotten them? You can use the text node's nodeValue property.

Extracting with nodeValue

So here's how to get the third guest's first and last names, and display them in a <div> element named targetDiv:

```
function displayGuest (xmldoc)
{
  var eventsNode, eventNode, peopleNode;
  var firstNameNode, lastNameNode, displayText;

  eventsNode = xmldoc.documentElement;
  eventNode = eventsNode.firstChild;
  peopleNode = eventNode.lastChild;
  personNode = peopleNode.lastChild;
  firstNameNode = personNode.firstChild;
  lastNameNode = firstNameNode.nextSibling;

  displayText = "The main guest was " +
    firstNameNode.firstChild.nodeValue + ' '
    + lastNameNode.firstChild.nodeValue;

  var target = document.getElementById("targetDiv");
  target.innerHTML=displayText;
}
```

And that's it — you can see the results in Figure 8-3 in Internet Explorer.

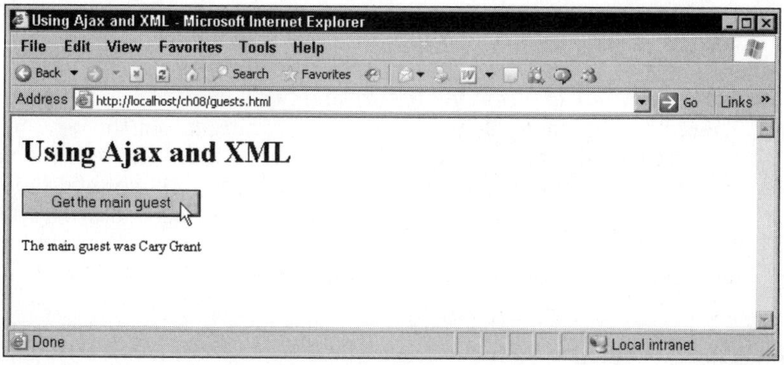

Figure 8-3: Displaying the third guest's name in Internet Explorer.

That looks great, but there's only one problem — this brilliant solution doesn't work in Mozilla-based browsers such as Firefox. The problem is white space, and the sections that follow explain how to create code that works in any browser.

At a total loss as to what specific XML is inside an XMLHttpRequest object's responseXML property? Use the responseXML property's xml property to get the XML as text, which you can take a look at directly. For example, to display the XML in an XMLHttpRequest object in an alert box, you could do this in the Internet Explorer:

```
alert(XMLHttpRequestObject.responseXML.xml);
```

Handling white space in Mozilla and Firefox

Mozilla-based browsers treat all the white space in an XML document (including the spaces used to indent the elements, as you see in our example, guests.xml) as text nodes. Take a look at the guests.xml XML document for this example:

```
<?xml version="1.0"?>
<events>
    <event type="informal">
        <event_title>15th award ceremony</event_title>
        <event_number>1207</event_number>
        <subject>gala event</subject>
        <date>7/4/2006</date>
        .
        .
        .
```

In Internet Explorer, this document is made up of a document element named <events> whose first child is the <event> element. The first child of the <event> element is the <event_title> element, its second child is <event_number>, and so on.

But the story is different in Firefox (and other Mozilla-based browsers). There, the document element is <events> alright, but the <events> element's first child node is the text node that includes the return character after the <events> tag, as well as the indentation space right before the <event> tag. In other words, any white space — tabs, returns, spaces, and so on — between tags is considered a legal text node and as such is not ignored. So in Mozilla terms, this XML looks like:

```
<?xml version="1.0"?>
<events>
[text node]<event type="informal">
```

```
[text node]<event_title>15th award ceremony</event_title>
[text node]<event_number>1207</event_number>
[text node]<subject>gala event</subject>
[text node]<date>7/4/2006</date>
            .
            .
            .
```

So when you access the `firstChild` property of the `<events>` element, you don't get the `<event>` element — you get the white space text node that follows the `<events>` tag. All this means that in Mozilla-based browsers, you have to take the white space into account when navigating XML documents.

So how does that work in code? Here's an example — `guestsmozilla. html` — that shows you how to navigate white space text nodes. For example, to find the name of the third guest, you start at the document element `<events>` in Firefox:

```
<?xml version="1.0"?>
<events>
      .
      .
      .
</events>
```

To get that document element, you use the XML document's `document Element` property, just as you do in Internet Explorer:

```
function displayGuest(xmldoc)
{
  var eventsnode;

  eventsnode = xmldoc.documentElement;
      .
      .
      .
}
```

The next element to get is the `<event>` element:

```
<?xml version="1.0"?>
<events>
    <event type="informal">
          .
          .
          .
    </event>
</events>
```

Although it would be nice to grab that <event> element this way:

```
eventnode = eventsnode.firstChild;
```

That code really just grabs the first child of the <events> element, which in Firefox is the white space text node between the <events> tag and the <event> tag. So you have to skip over the text node and get to the <event> element using the nextSibling property because the <event> element is a sibling of that white space text node to skip over.

```
eventnode = eventsnode.firstChild.nextSibling;
```

The next step is to get an object corresponding to the <people> element:

```
<?xml version="1.0"?>
<events>
    <event type="informal">
        <event_title>15th award ceremony</event_title>
        <event_number>1207</event_number>
        <subject>gala event</subject>
        <date>7/4/2006</date>
        <people>
          .
          .
          .
        </people>
    </event>
</events>
```

It might look like the <people> element is the last child of the <event> element, but that's not true in Firefox. The last child is the text node after the </people> tag and before the </event> tag:

```
<?xml version="1.0"?>
<events>
    <event type="informal">
        <event_title>15th award ceremony</event_title>
        <event_number>1207</event_number>
        <subject>gala event</subject>
        <date>7/4/2006</date>
        <people>
          .
          .
          .
        </people>
[text node]</event>
</events>
```

So instead of using this to get an object corresponding to the `<people>` element:

```
peoplenode = eventnode.lastChild;
```

you have to move backwards one level to skip over the true last child — the white space text node — to get an object corresponding to the `<people>` element. You can do that with the `previousSibling` property:

```
peoplenode = eventnode.lastChild.previousSibling;
```

As you can see, taking into account all those white space text nodes means you have to navigate around them using the `nextSibling` and `previous Sibling` properties. Here's how that works out in code in the example `guestsmozilla.html`:

```
function displayGuest(xmldoc)
{
    var eventsnode, eventnode, peoplenode;
    var firstnamenode, lastnamenode, displaytext;

    eventsnode = xmldoc.documentElement;
    eventnode = eventsnode.firstChild.nextSibling;
    peoplenode = eventnode.lastChild.previousSibling;
    personnode = peoplenode.firstChild.nextSibling
        .nextSibling.nextSibling.nextSibling.nextSibling;
    firstnamenode = personnode.firstChild.nextSibling;
    lastnamenode = firstnamenode.nextSibling.nextSibling;

    displaytext = "The main guest was: " +
        firstnamenode.firstChild.nodeValue + ' '
        + lastnamenode.firstChild.nodeValue;

    var target = document.getElementById("targetDiv");
        target.innerHTML=displaytext;
}
```

This certainly works, but it's annoying. Not only do you have to navigate the XML document while skipping over white space nodes, but you have to use different JavaScript code for Internet Explorer and Firefox. Isn't there some kind of fix that will repair this two-browser problem? There sure is.

Removing white space in Mozilla and Firefox

You can preprocess an XML document in Mozilla-based browsers like Firefox by simply removing all the white space text nodes. After you've done that, you can navigate through XML in Firefox and other Mozilla browsers using the exact same code as you would in Internet Explorer.

For example, you might put together a function named, say, `removeWhite space`, for use in Mozilla-based browsers and pass XML objects such as the one returned in an `XMLHttpRequest` object to this function to remove white space.

Here's a function that strips white space for you. You pass it an XML object and it starts by looping over all the child nodes (which are found with the `childNodes` property, which holds an array of child nodes):

```
function removeWhitespace(xml)
{
  var loopIndex;

  for (loopIndex = 0; loopIndex < xml.childNodes.length;
    loopIndex++) {

    var currentNode = xml.childNodes[loopIndex];
    .
    .
    .
  }
}
```

At this point in the loop, the current child node is stored in the variable named `currentNode`. What kind of a node is the current node? If it's an element node (which means that `currentNode.nodeType` equals 1), perhaps it has its own child nodes that need to have white space stripped out as well. In that case, you can pass the current node to the `removeWhitespace` function again. (Calling the same function from inside the function is called *recursion,* in case you've never heard of it, and it's a handy technique.)

```
function removeWhitespace(xml)
{
  var loopIndex;

  for (loopIndex = 0; loopIndex < xml.childNodes.length;
    loopIndex++) {

    var currentNode = xml.childNodes[loopIndex];

    if (currentNode.nodeType == 1) {
```

```
            removeWhitespace(currentNode);
        }
            .
            .
            .
    }
}
```

On the other hand, if the current node is a text node (which means that
`currentNode.nodeType` equals 3), perhaps it's a white space node, in
which case it should be removed.

How do you check if the current node only contains white space? You can
check the text in the current node, which is `currentNode.nodeValue`,
using a *regular expression* that matches only white space. Regular expressions let you test the content of a text string, and they're supported in
JavaScript. (A full discussion on regular expressions is beyond the scope
of this book; if you want all the details, take a look at `http://perldoc.`
`perl.org/perlre.html`.)

Here's how you can test for white space text nodes and remove them. (Note
in particular the `loopIndex--` expression, which uses the JavaScript `--`
operator to decrement `loopIndex` after the statement containing that
expression is executed, to take into account the removed node.)

```
function removeWhitespace(xml)
{
  var loopIndex;

  for (loopIndex = 0; loopIndex < xml.childNodes.length;
    loopIndex++) {

    var currentNode = xml.childNodes[loopIndex];

    if (currentNode.nodeType == 1) {
      removeWhitespace(currentNode);
    }

    if (((/^\s+$/.test(currentNode.nodeValue))) &&
      (currentNode.nodeType == 3)) {
        xml.removeChild(xml.childNodes[loopIndex--]);
    }
  }
}
```

Now you can call this function to strip white space out of XML documents if
you're working in Mozilla-based browsers like Firefox.

After you strip the white space from documents in Mozilla-based browsers,
you can use the same navigational code as you'd use in Internet Explorer. For
example, Listing 8-1 shows what the final version of `guests.html` (the Web

page that finds the third guest, Cary Grant) looks like, updated to work in both Internet Explorer and Firefox — note how it strips white space out of the XML document in Firefox.

Listing 8-1: Extracting a Guest's Name from an XML Document

```
<html>
  <head>

    <title>Using Ajax and XML</title>

    <script language = "javascript">

      function getGuest()
      {
        var mozillaFlag = false;
        var XMLHttpRequestObject = false;

        if (window.XMLHttpRequest) {
          XMLHttpRequestObject = new XMLHttpRequest();
          XMLHttpRequestObject.overrideMimeType("text/xml");
          mozillaFlag = true;
        } else if (window.ActiveXObject) {
          XMLHttpRequestObject = new
            ActiveXObject("Microsoft.XMLHTTP");
        }

        if(XMLHttpRequestObject) {
          XMLHttpRequestObject.open("GET", "guests.xml", true);

          XMLHttpRequestObject.onreadystatechange = function()
          {
            if (XMLHttpRequestObject.readyState == 4 &&
              XMLHttpRequestObject.status == 200) {
            var xmlDocument = XMLHttpRequestObject.responseXML;
            if(mozillaFlag){
              removeWhitespace(xmlDocument);
            }
            displayGuest(xmlDocument);
            }
          }

          XMLHttpRequestObject.send(null);
        }
      }

      function displayGuest (xmldoc)
      {
        var eventsNode, eventNode, peopleNode;

        var firstNameNode, lastNameNode, displayText;
```

```
            eventsNode = xmldoc.documentElement;
            eventNode = eventsNode.firstChild;
            peopleNode = eventNode.lastChild;
            personNode = peopleNode.lastChild;
            firstNameNode = personNode.firstChild;
            lastNameNode = firstNameNode.nextSibling;

            displayText = "The main guest was " +
              firstNameNode.firstChild.nodeValue + ' '
              + lastNameNode.firstChild.nodeValue;

            var target = document.getElementById("targetDiv");
            target.innerHTML=displayText;
        }

      function removeWhitespace(xml)
      {
        var loopIndex;

        for (loopIndex = 0; loopIndex < xml.childNodes.length;
          loopIndex++) {

          var currentNode = xml.childNodes[loopIndex];

          if (currentNode.nodeType == 1) {
            removeWhitespace(currentNode);
          }

          if ((((/^\s+$/.test(currentNode.nodeValue))) &&
            (currentNode.nodeType == 3)) {
              xml.removeChild(xml.childNodes[loopIndex--]);
          }
        }
      }
    }
  </script>

</head>

<body>

  <h1>Using Ajax and XML</h1>

  <form>
    <input type = "button" value = "Get the main guest"
      onclick = "getGuest()">
  </form>

  <div id="targetDiv" width =100 height=100>
    Who was the main guest?
  </div>

</body>

</html>
```

You can see this page at work in Figure 8-4 in Firefox.

So now you can use the same navigational code to extract data in Internet Explorer and Firefox.

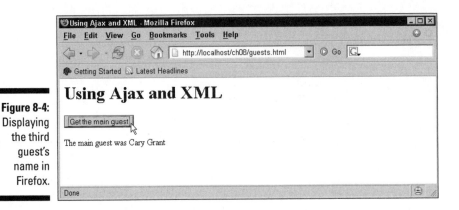

Figure 8-4:
Displaying
the third
guest's
name in
Firefox.

That's fine, but isn't there an easier way? I mean, you have to know all the details about the exact structure of the XML document you're dealing with — which element is a child of what parent element and so on — and it's somewhat awkward to have to navigate step by step throughout a document. Can't you just fetch the data you want?

Accessing XML Elements by Name

You can fetch just the data you want. So far, the code has used properties like `nextSibling` and `nextChild` to navigate XML documents. But you can also get individual elements by searching for them by name using the JavaScript `getElementsByTagName` method. (Note that it's still important to know how to use properties like `firstChild` and `nextSibling` and so on in order to extract the data you want from the elements you retrieve.)

If you're just interested in extracting specific elements from an XML document, `getElementsByTagName` could be your ticket. In the `guests.xml` document, the name of the third guest is enclosed in `<first_name>` and `<last_name>` elements:

```
<?xml version="1.0"?>
<events>
    <event type="informal">
        <event_title>15th award ceremony</event_title>
        <event_number>1207</event_number>
        <subject>gala event</subject>
```

```
        <date>7/4/2006</date>
        <people>
            <person attendance="present">
                <first_name>Sam</first_name>
                <last_name>Edwards</last_name>
            </person>
            <person attendance="absent">
                <first_name>Sally</first_name>
                <last_name>Jackson</last_name>
            </person>
            <person attendance="present">
                <first_name>Cary</first_name>
                <last_name>Grant</last_name>
            </person>
        </people>
    </event>
</events>
```

How can you pick the `<first_name>` and `<last_name>` elements out and extract the text from them? All you need to do is to pass the names of these elements, `"first_name"` and `"last_name"` to the `getElementsByTag Name` method, which will return an array of elements with those names:

```
function displayGuest (xmldoc)
{
    firstnamenodes = xmldoc.getElementsByTagName("first_name");
    lastnamenodes = xmldoc.getElementsByTagName("last_name");
    .
    .
    .
}
```

This example is interested in getting the third guest's first and last name. The first guest's first name would be `firstnamenodes[0]`, the second's `firstnamenodes[1]`, and so on. That means you can extract the first and last names of the third guest this way in a new application, `guests2.html` in the code available for download from the Web site associated with this book.

```
function displayGuest (xmldoc)
{
    firstnamenodes = xmldoc.getElementsByTagName("first_name");
    lastnamenodes = xmldoc.getElementsByTagName("last_name");

    var displayText = "The main guest was: " +
      firstnamenodes[2].firstChild.nodeValue + ' '
      + lastnamenodes[2].firstChild.nodeValue;

    var target = document.getElementById("targetDiv");
    target.innerHTML=displayText;
}
```

You can see this new example, `guests2.html`, in Figure 8-5 in Internet Explorer. Very cool.

That gives you a good handle on working with the XML elements you fetch using JavaScript and Ajax techniques from a server. That's fine for recovering data from XML elements — but what about recovering the values of XML *attributes?*

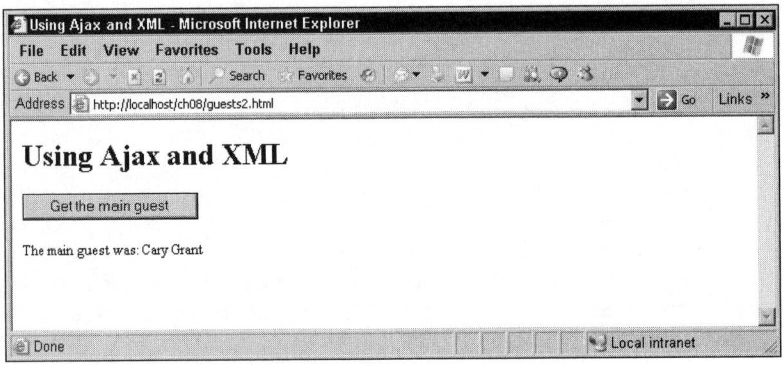

Figure 8-5:
Extracting data from XML elements in Internet Explorer.

Accessing Attribute Values in XML Elements

XML elements can have attributes, of course, and reading the value of XML attributes can be important in Ajax applications because attribute values hold data. The `guests.xml` document contains some attributes, including an attribute named `attendance`:

```
<?xml version="1.0"?>
<events>
    <event type="informal">
        <event_title>15th award ceremony</event_title>
        <event_number>1207</event_number>
        <subject>gala event</subject>
        <date>7/4/2006</date>
        <people>
            <person attendance="present">
                <first_name>Sam</first_name>
                <last_name>Edwards</last_name>
            </person>
            <person attendance="absent">
```

```
            <first_name>Sally</first_name>
            <last_name>Jackson</last_name>
        </person>
        <person attendance="present">
            <first_name>Cary</first_name>
            <last_name>Grant</last_name>
        </person>
      </people>
    </event>
</events>
```

How would you read the value of the `attendance` attribute — specifically, Cary Grant's `attendance` attribute?

Here's how it works in a new example named `attributes.html` in the code for this book. You first navigate through the document to get a JavaScript object corresponding to the elements you're interested in. (You can use `getElementsByTagName` here instead, of course.)

```
function displayGuest (xmldoc)
{
    var eventsNode, eventNode, peopleNode;
    var firstNameNode, lastNameNode;

    eventsNode = xmldoc.documentElement;
    eventNode = eventsNode.firstChild;
    peopleNode = eventNode.lastChild;
    personNode = peopleNode.lastChild;
    firstNameNode = personNode.firstChild;
    lastNameNode = firstNameNode.nextSibling;
    .
    .
    .
}
```

The element that contains the attribute of interest is the `<person>` element. To get the `attendance` attribute from that element, you can use the element node's `attributes` property, which contains a *named node map* of attributes. What the heck is a named node map? It's an object that lets you access items by name, such as when you want to access the `attendance` attribute. How's that work? First, you get the attributes' named node map, which I'll call *attributes*.

```
function displayGuest (xmldoc)
{
    var eventsNode, eventNode, peopleNode;
    var firstNameNode, lastNameNode, displayText;

    eventsNode = xmldoc.documentElement;
```

```
    eventNode = eventsNode.firstChild;
    peopleNode = eventNode.lastChild;
    personNode = peopleNode.lastChild;
    firstNameNode = personNode.firstChild;
    lastNameNode = firstNameNode.nextSibling;
    attributes = personNode.attributes
       .
       .
       .
}
```

Then you can get an `attribute` node corresponding to the `attendance` attribute using the named node map method, `getNamedItem`, this way:

```
function displayGuest (xmldoc)
{
  var eventsNode, eventNode, peopleNode;
  var firstNameNode, lastNameNode, displayText;

  eventsNode = xmldoc.documentElement;
  eventNode = eventsNode.firstChild;
  peopleNode = eventNode.lastChild;
  personNode = peopleNode.lastChild;
  firstNameNode = personNode.firstChild;
  lastNameNode = firstNameNode.nextSibling;
  attributes = personNode.attributes
  attendancePerson = attributes.getNamedItem("attendance");
       .
       .
       .
}
```

Almost there. You've gotten a `node` object corresponding to the `attendance` attribute. To get the value that was assigned to Cary Grant's `attendance` attribute (which is `"present"`), you just need to use that `node` object's `nodeValue` attribute. So here's how this example recovers Cary Grant's name and attendance and displays that data:

```
function displayGuest (xmldoc)
{
  var eventsNode, eventNode, peopleNode;
  var firstNameNode, lastNameNode, displayText;

  eventsNode = xmldoc.documentElement;
  eventNode = eventsNode.firstChild;
  peopleNode = eventNode.lastChild;
  personNode = peopleNode.lastChild;
  firstNameNode = personNode.firstChild;
  lastNameNode = firstNameNode.nextSibling;
```

```
attributes = personNode.attributes
attendancePerson = attributes.getNamedItem("attendance");

var displayText = firstNameNode.firstChild.nodeValue
  + ' ' + lastNameNode.firstChild.nodeValue
  + " was " + attendancePerson.nodeValue;

var target = document.getElementById("targetDiv");
target.innerHTML=displayText;
}
```

You can see the results in Figure 8-6, where this example shows how to extract the value that's been assigned to an attribute in the XML sent back to an Ajax application.

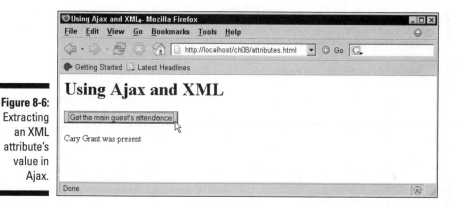

Figure 8-6:
Extracting
an XML
attribute's
value in
Ajax.

Validating XML Documents in Ajax Applications

In major Ajax applications, where you want to make sure you get things right, you may want to check the validity of the XML you receive. As discussed at the beginning of this chapter, XML documents can be both well-formed and valid. *Well-formed* means that the XML document can be read by an XML parser of the type that the major browsers, like Internet Explorer and Firefox, support. If an XML document isn't well-formed, the parser can't read it, and the situation is hopeless. *Valid* is up to you — you can specify the syntax of an XML document and then check if the document adheres to your syntax rules.

What kind of syntax rules can you specify? You can specify which elements are legal in your document and which attributes are legal. You can say which element is a child of which other element. You can say which attributes are legal in which elements. And so on. If your Ajax application is working on important data, it's a good idea to make sure the XML you're working with is valid and that whatever created that data didn't mess it up somehow.

There are two ways to validate XML documents, as already mentioned in this chapter: DTDs and XML schema. DTDs are simpler, but schema give you a lot more power. (You can set, for example, the range of possible numeric values assigned to an attribute when you're using a schema, but not a DTD.) You might want to validate your XML on the server before sending it back to an Ajax application, and many languages (such as Java 1.4 and now 1.5) provide complete support for both DTD and XML schema validation.

Sometimes, however, it's not up to you to generate and then check the XML sent to you — you have to deal with what you get. In these cases, you can validate XML in a browser using JavaScript — if the browser is Internet Explorer.

Here's an example, `validator.html`, that validates XML in Internet Explorer only. (Firefox's XML parser doesn't perform XML validation.) This example adds a DTD to `guests.xml`. (Internet Explorer also validates using XML schema.) Here's what the DTD that specifies the syntax of `guests.xml` looks like in a new document, `guestsdtd.xml`. (For all the details on how DTDs work, see `www.w3.org/tr/rec-xml`.)

```
<?xml version="1.0"?>
<!DOCTYPE events [
<!ELEMENT events (event*)>
<!ELEMENT event (event_title, event_number, subject, date, people*)>
<!ELEMENT event_title (#PCDATA)>
<!ELEMENT event_number (#PCDATA)>
<!ELEMENT subject (#PCDATA)>
<!ELEMENT date (#PCDATA)>
<!ELEMENT first_name (#PCDATA)>
<!ELEMENT last_name (#PCDATA)>
<!ELEMENT people (person*)>
<!ELEMENT person (first_name,last_name)>
<!ATTLIST event
    type CDATA #IMPLIED>
<!ATTLIST person
    attendance CDATA #IMPLIED>
]>
<events>
    <event type="informal">
        <event_title>15th award ceremony</event_title>
        <event_number>1207</event_number>
        <subject>gala event</subject>
        <date1>7/4/2006</date1>
        <people>
```

```
            <person attendance="present">
                <first_name>sam</first_name>
                <last_name>edwards</last_name>
            </person>
            <person attendance="absent">
                <first_name>sally</first_name>
                <last_name>jackson</last_name>
            </person>
            <person attendance="present">
                <first_name>cary</first_name>
                <last_name>grant</last_name>
            </person>
        </people>
    </event>
</events>
```

This document now comes with a DTD, which specifies the syntax for the XML in the document. How can you use this document to test its validity? If you look closely, you'll see that there's an error here: The opening <date> tag actually has been replaced by a <date1> tag.

```
<date1>7/4/2006</date1>
```

To get Internet Explorer to catch this error, you can parse the XML you get from the server to check it. Here's how it works: Create a new Internet Explorer XML parser object, configure it to validate XML, and load in the XML you've received from the server this way in Internet Explorer:

```
function getGuest()
{
  var XMLHttpRequestObject = false;

  XMLHttpRequestObject = new
    ActiveXObject("Microsoft.XMLHTTP");

  if(XMLHttpRequestObject) {
    XMLHttpRequestObject.open("GET", "guestsdtd.xml", true);

    XMLHttpRequestObject.onreadystatechange = function()
    {
      if (XMLHttpRequestObject.readyState == 4 &&
        XMLHttpRequestObject.status == 200) {
        var xmlDocument = XMLHttpRequestObject.responseXML;

        var parser = new ActiveXObject("MSXML2.DOMDocument");
        parser.validateOnParse = true;
        parser.load(XMLHttpRequestObject.responseXML);
        .
        .
        .
}
```

If the `parser` object's `parseError` property is *zero* after it loads the XML, there is no problem. Otherwise, you've got an error, which you can check this way:

```
function getGuest()
{
    .
    .
    .
    XMLHttpRequestObject.onreadystatechange = function()
    {
      if (XMLHttpRequestObject.readyState == 4 &&
        XMLHttpRequestObject.status == 200) {
        var xmlDocument = XMLHttpRequestObject.responseXML;

        var parser = new ActiveXObject("MSXML2.DOMDocument");
        parser.validateOnParse = true;
        parser.load(XMLHttpRequestObject.responseXML);

        if (parser.parseError.errorCode != 0) {
        .
        .
        .
        }
        else {

          displayGuest(xmlDocument);
        }
      }
    }

    XMLHttpRequestObject.send(null);
  }
}
```

If there was an error, this example will use the `error` object in the `parse Error` property to display the details of the error. The `error` object supports these properties: `url` (the name of the file that caused the problem), `line` (the line on which the problem occurred), `linepos` (the position in the line of the problem), `srcText` (text explaining the error), `reason` (the reason for the error), and `errorCode` (the error's numeric code). This example, `validator. html`, uses those properties to display the details of the problem:

```
function getGuest()
{
  var XMLHttpRequestObject = false;

  XMLHttpRequestObject = new
    ActiveXObject("Microsoft.XMLHTTP");

  if(XMLHttpRequestObject) {
    XMLHttpRequestObject.open("GET", "guestsdtd6.xml", true);
```

```
XMLHttpRequestObject.onreadystatechange = function()
{
  if (XMLHttpRequestObject.readyState == 4 &&
    XMLHttpRequestObject.status == 200) {
    var xmlDocument = XMLHttpRequestObject.responseXML;

    var parser = new ActiveXObject("MSXML2.DOMDocument");
    parser.validateOnParse = true;
    parser.load(XMLHttpRequestObject.responseXML);
    var target = document.getElementById("targetDiv");

    if (parser.parseError.errorCode != 0) {
      target.innerText = "Error in " +
      parser.parseError.url +
      " line " + parser.parseError.line +
      " position " + parser.parseError.linepos +
      ".\nError source: " + parser.parseError.srcText +
      "\n" + parser.parseError.reason +
      "\n" + "Error: " +
      parser.parseError.errorCode;
    }
    else {

    displayGuest(xmlDocument);
    }
  }
}

XMLHttpRequestObject.send(null);
  }
}
```

And that's all it takes. You can see the results in Figure 8-7, where Internet Explorer did indeed locate the error, and the application displays the full error details. Not bad.

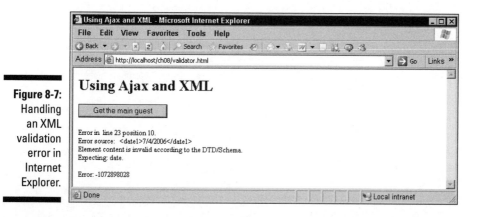

Figure 8-7: Handling an XML validation error in Internet Explorer.

Chapter 9

Working with Cascading Style Sheets in Ajax Applications

"*U*h oh," says the crack Ajax programmer. "This isn't working."

"What's the problem?" you — the highly-paid Ajax consultant — ask.

"I can't get this menu application to work. I can get the data for the menu items from the server using Ajax alright, but I can't make the menus appear and disappear. What gives?"

"What style property are you using to make them appear and disappear?" you ask.

"Style property?" the crack Ajax programmer asks.

"Hoo boy," you say, "better let me take over for a while."

Because Ajax does its thing without page refreshes, Ajax applications are very fond of changing the current page *dynamically*. That is, Ajax applications can't rely on restructuring the page when it next appears — it's already in front of the user. That means that you've got to work your magic right there while the user watches. For this reason, Ajax programmers are very fond of dynamic HTML (DHTML) and cascading style sheets (CSS).

DHTML lets you rewrite the HTML in a page on the fly. You've already seen plenty of examples of using DHTML in this book, as in this line of JavaScript, which rewrites the contents of a `<div>` element to display some text:

```
targetDiv.innerHTML = "You just won a new car.";
```

You can also work with the existing elements in a Web page by working with their *styles*. Using CSS, you can move elements around a page, color them, configure their fonts and borders, make them visible or invisible, set their background images, and more.

That's what this chapter is about — using CSS and Ajax together for maximum effect.

CSS and Ajax are perfect together. You can see them working in unison throughout this book. For example, the drag-and-drop example in Chapter 6 uses CSS to let the user move around the television he's buying. It does that by setting up a `<div>` with the ID `television`:

```
<body>
    <h1>Buy a television by dragging it to the shopping cart</h1>
    <div id="targetDiv"></div>

    <div id="television"
      style="left:200px; top:100px; width:80px; height:80px;"
      onmousedown="handleDown(event);">Television</div>

    <div id="target"
      style="left:300px; top:300px; width:200px; height:100px;">
    Shopping Cart</div>

</body>
```

In a `<style>` element in the Web page's `<head>` section, the `<div>` element's position style property is set to absolute and its z-index property is set to a high number to make sure it will move *over* all other elements in the page, not under them:

```
<html>
  <head>
    <title>Ajax Drag and Drop</title>

    <style type="text/css">
      #television {
        position:absolute;
        z-index:200;
        background: #FF0000;
        color:#0000FF;
```

```
    }
        .
        .
        .
  </style>
```

Style properties such as `position` and `z-index` are what you see in this chapter. Because you set the television `<div>` element's style to `absolute`, you can move it in JavaScript using the `<div>` element's left and top style properties, which let you set the top left position of the `<div>` element. Here's what it looks like in code when the user drags the television:

```
function handleMove(e)
{
  var e = new MouseEvent(e);
  var x = e.x - offsetX;
  e.target.style.left = x + "px";
  var y = e.y - offsetY;
  e.target.style.top = y + "px";
}
    .
    .
    .
```

Being able to work with the elements in a Web page in real time is great for Ajax, especially because you don't get the chance to rearrange things with a page refresh.

For the full, formal details on CSS, see the CSS specification at www.w3.org/tr/css21 and check out *CSS Web Design For Dummies,* by Richard Mansfield (Wiley Publishing, Inc.).

An Ajax-Driven Menu System

One of the most common types of style-intensive Ajax applications around displays a menu system to the user as the user moves the mouse around the page. Take a look at Figure 9-1, which shows an example, menus.html, at work. When the user moves the mouse over one of the images on the page the (such as the *Sandwiches* or *Pizza* image in this example), the application displays a menu with text fetched using Ajax from the server. After the user selects an item, that item is displayed in the Web page, as shown in Figure 9-2.

In the following sections, I show you how to write this application.

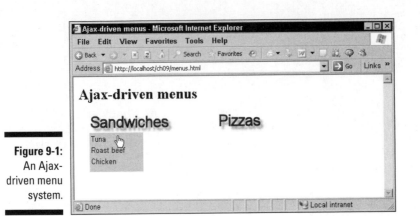

Figure 9-1:
An Ajax-driven menu system.

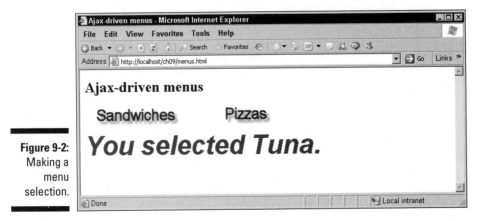

Figure 9-2:
Making a menu selection.

Setting up the styles

The menus.html application gives you a good handle on how styles are used in Ajax applications. Here's how you create the controls in the Web page in this application. (Note the style attribute, which sets the style of each element.)

```
<body onclick = "hide()" onmousemove = "check(event)">

  <H1>Ajax-driven menus</H1>

    <img id = "image1" src="image1.jpg"
      style="left:30; top:50; width:200; height:40;">
    <div id = "menuDiv1" style="left:30; top:100; width:100;
      height: 70; visibility:hidden;"><div></div></div>
    <img id = "image2" style="left:270; top:50; width:200;
```

```
     height:40;" src="image2.jpg">
   <div id = "menuDiv2" style="left:270; top:100; width:100;
     height: 70; visibility:hidden;"><div></div></div>
   <div id = "targetDiv"></div>
</body>
```

Each style pair, such as `visibility:hidden`, makes up a style *rule*. The first part of the pair is the *style* property you're setting, and the second part of the pair is the *value* you're assigning the property. In this case, you're doing the following:

- Giving the `visibility` property the value *hidden* to make the `<div>` elements, which will display the menus hidden to start like this: `visibility:hidden`.

- Using the `left` property (left-edge position of the element) like this: `left:270`.

- Using the `top` property (top position of the element) like this: `top:100`.

- Using the `width` property (width of the element) like this: `width:100`.

- Using the `height` property (height of the element) like this: `height:70`.

When you use the HTML `style` attribute as this code does, you're using *inline* styles. You assign a style property a value in each rule, and separate each rule from the others with a semicolon:

```
<img id = "image1" src="image1.jpg"
   style="left:30; top:50; width:200; height:40;">
```

Besides using inline styles with the `style` attribute, you can also assign styles using a `<style>` element, which is usually placed in the `<head>` section of a page. Such styles are called *embedded styles*. Here, you specify the element you want to set up styles for, and enclose the style rules you want to use — separated by semicolons — inside curly braces. Here's an example that sets the styles for the `<body>` element, setting the foreground (text) color, the background color, and the font to use. (Note that the colors are specified the same way that you specify colors in HTML.)

```
<style>
body {
  color: #000000;
  background-color: #FFFFFF;
  font-family: times;
}
```

You can also specify the *type* of the styles you're using, with the `type` attribute, which you set to `"text/css"` for CSS styles. That's the default, however, so you can omit the `type` attribute:

```
<style type="text/css">
body {
  color: #000000;
  background-color: #FFFFFF;
  font-family: times;
}
```

Some elements, such as the `<a>` anchor element, let you style specific aspects of the element. For example, the `<a>` element lets you style the color of links (you refer to a link as `a:link`), the color of links already visited (`a:visited`), and the color of links when clicked (`a:active`) like this:

```
<style>
    body {background: white; color: black}
    a:link {color: red}
    a:visited {color: blue}
    a:active {color: green}
</style>
```

What if you want to set the styles for multiple `<div>` elements? How can you tell them apart in the `<style>` element? The example here, `menus.html`, contains a number of `<div>` elements that you can supply styles for in a `<style>` element:

```
<body onclick = "hide()" onmousemove = "check(event)">

  <H1>Ajax-driven menus</H1>

    <img id = "image1" src="image1.jpg"
      style="left:30; top:50; width:200; height:40;">
    <div id = "menuDiv1" style="left:30; top:100; width:100;
      height: 70; visibility:hidden;"><div></div></div>
    <img id = "image2" style="left:270; top:50; width:200;
      height:40;" src="image2.jpg">
    <div id = "menuDiv2" style="left:270; top:100; width:100;
      height: 70; visibility:hidden;"><div></div></div>
    <div id = "targetDiv"></div>
</body>
```

Note that each such `<div>` element has a different ID value. To assign a style to a tag with a particular ID, you give that ID preceded by a *sharp sign* (#) like this in the `<style>` element:

```
<html>
 <head>

   <title>Ajax-driven menus</title>
```

```
<style>
#menuDiv1 {
  color: #222222;
  background-color: #77CCFF;
  font-weight: bold;
  font-family: arial;
  position: absolute;
  visibility: hidden;
  cursor: hand;
}

#menuDiv2 {
  color: #222222;
  background-color: #77CCFF;
  font-weight: bold;
  font-family: arial;
  position: absolute;
  visibility: hidden;
  cursor: hand;
}

#targetDiv {
  color: #990000;
  font-size: 36pt;
  font-weight: bold;
  font-family: arial;
  font-style: italic;
}

</style>
```

This styles the two `<div>` elements that will display the menus, `menuDiv1` and `menuDiv2`, this way:

- ✔ Sets a particular text color (the `color` property) this way: `color: #222222`

- ✔ Sets a particular background color (the `background-color` property) this way: `background-color: #77CCFF`

- ✔ Sets bold text (with the `font-weight` property) this way: `font-weight: bold`

- ✔ Sets a specific font type (with the `font-family` property) this way: `font-family: arial`

- ✔ Sets these `<div>` elements at a particular location (by setting the `position` property to `absolute`) this way: `position: absolute`

- ✔ Makes these `<div>` elements hidden by default (with the `visibility` property) this way: `visibility: hidden`

- ✔ Uses a hand icon for the mouse cursor when the mouse is over these menus (this style works in Internet Explorer only) this way: `cursor: hand`

This `<style>` element also styles the target `<div>` element where the result text will be displayed `targetDiv`.

External style sheets

Another way of handling styles (which `menus.html` doesn't use) is to use an *external style sheet.* For example, you could put the style rules from the `<style>` element into an external file named, say, `style.css`, which would have these contents:

```
#menuDiv1 {
    color: #222222;
    background-color: #77CCFF;
    font-weight: bold;
    font-family: arial;
    position: absolute;
    visibility: hidden;
    cursor: hand;
}

#menuDiv2 {
    color: #222222;
    background-color: #77CCFF;
    font-weight: bold;
    font-family: arial;
    position: absolute;
    visibility: hidden;
    cursor: hand;
}
     .
     .
     .
```

You connect an external style sheet to a Web page with the `<link>` element, setting the `rel` attribute to `"stylesheet"` and the `href` attribute to the URL of the style sheet like this:

```
<html>
    <head>
        <title>
            Using An External Style Sheet
        </title>

        <link rel="stylesheet" href="style.css">

    </head>

    <body>

        <center>
            <h1>
                Using An External Style Sheet
            </h1>
```

```
        <P>
            This page uses an external style sheet.
        </center>

    </body>
</html>
```

This code includes the new style sheet, `style.css`, in the page and applies the styles defined in it as appropriate. That's how to set up an external style sheet. (**Remember:** The example `menus.html` sets up its styles using a `<style>` element and inline styles, not an external style sheet.)

Handling mouse events

After you've set up the embedded styles that this example will use, how do you actually use those styles to make this example work? Everything starts with the mouse in this case because when the user moves the mouse over an image, the code is supposed to display a menu of clickable items.

This example works by watching where the mouse is; if it's over an image, the code should display a menu (if that menu isn't already displayed). To track the mouse, the `<body>` tag's `onmousemove` event is connected to a JavaScript function named `check`:

```
<body onclick = "hide()" onmousemove = "check(event)">
```

The `check` function checks to see where the mouse is and starts by creating a browser-independent mouse object (e).

```
function check(evt)
{
    var e = new MouseEvent(evt);
        .
        .
        .
```

That object is created using a JavaScript function named `MouseEvent`, which creates a cross-browser mouse event object (similar to the handling of drag and drop operations in Chapter 6):

```
function MouseEvent(e)
{
    if(e) {
        this.e = e;
    } else {
```

```
      this.e = window.event;
  }

  if(e.pageX) {
    this.x = e.pageX;
  } else {
    this.x = e.clientX;
  }

  if(e.pageY) {
    this.y = e.pageY;
  } else {
    this.y = e.clientY;
  }

  if(e.target) {
    this.target = e.target;
  } else {
    this.target = e.srcElement;
  }
}
```

You can use the new mouse event object to determine where the mouse is currently.

Displaying a menu

If the mouse is inside an image, the code should display a menu. Here's how the code checks to see if the mouse is inside the first image, whose ID equals `image1`:

```
function check(evt)
{
  var e = new MouseEvent(evt);
  var img;

  img = document.getElementById("image1");
  if(e.x > parseInt(img.style.left) && e.y >
    parseInt(img.style.top) &&
    e.x < (parseInt(img.style.left) +
    parseInt(img.style.width))
    && e.y < (parseInt(img.style.top) +
    parseInt (img.style.height))){
    .
    .
    .
  }
    .
    .
    .
```

If the mouse is inside this image, `image1`, the application gets the data for the first menu from the server, which it does by calling a new JavaScript function named `getData` and passing a value of 1 (indicating that it wants the data for the first menu):

```
function check(evt)
{
  var e = new MouseEvent(evt);
  var target = null;
  var img;

  img = document.getElementById("image1");
  if(e.x > parseInt(img.style.left) && e.y >
    parseInt(img.style.top) &&
    e.x < (parseInt(img.style.left) +
    parseInt(img.style.width))
    && e.y < (parseInt(img.style.top) +
    parseInt (img.style.height))){
      getData(1);
  }
  .
  .
  .
```

Similarly, if the mouse is inside the second image, the application should get the data for the second menu:

```
function check(evt)
{
  var e = new MouseEvent(evt);
  var img;
  .
  .
  .
  img = document.getElementById("image2");
  if(e.x > parseInt(img.style.left) && e.y >
    parseInt(img.style.top) &&
    e.x < (parseInt(img.style.left) +
    parseInt(img.style.width))
    && e.y < (parseInt(img.style.top) +
    parseInt(img.style.height))){
      getData(2);
  }
  .
  .
  .
```

Hiding a menu

At this point, the code has checked to see if it should display a menu. But what if the mouse is outside any image and also outside either menu `<div>` element? In that case, you can hide the menus using a JavaScript function named `hide`:

```
function check(evt)
{
  var e = new MouseEvent(evt);
  var target = null;
  var img;
    .
    .
    .
  target = document.getElementById("menuDiv1");
  img = document.getElementById("image1");

  if (target.style.visibility == "visible"){
    if(e.x < parseInt(target.style.left) || e.y <
      parseInt(img.style.top) ||
      e.x > (parseInt(img.style.left) +
      parseInt(img.style.width))
      || e.y > (parseInt(target.style.top) +
      parseInt(target.style.height))){
      hide();
    }
  }

  target = document.getElementById("menuDiv2");
  img = document.getElementById("image2");

  if (target.style.visibility == "visible"){
    if(e.x < parseInt(target.style.left) || e.y <
    parseInt(img.style.top) ||
    e.x > (parseInt(img.style.left) +
    parseInt(img.style.width))
    || e.y > (parseInt(target.style.top) +
    parseInt(target.style.height))){
      hide();
    }
  }
}
```

The `hide` function hides the menus if they're currently visible using the menu `<div>` element's `visibility style` property this way:

```
function hide()
{
  var menuDiv1 = document.getElementById("menuDiv1");

  if(menuDiv1.style.visibility == "visible"){
```

```
    menuDiv1.innerHTML = "<div></div>";
    menuDiv1.style.visibility = "hidden";
  }


  var menuDiv2 = document.getElementById("menuDiv2");
  if(menuDiv2.style.visibility == "visible"){
    menuDiv2.innerHTML = "<div></div>";
    menuDiv2.style.visibility = "hidden";
  }
}
```

Getting a menu's item from the server

The preceding sections handle the mouse and show and hide the menu
<div> elements. Now how about stocking them with some data? In this
example, when the check function calls the getData function, it passes the
number of the menu it wants to get the data for — menu 1 or menu 2. The
menu items for menu 1 are stored in a file named items1.txt:

```
Tuna, Roast beef, Chicken
```

and the items for menu 2 are stored in a file named items2.txt:

```
Pepperoni, Sausage, Olive
```

Here's how the correct menu's text is downloaded in the getData function in
this example:

```
function getData(menu)
{
  var XMLHttpRequestObject = false;

  if (window.XMLHttpRequest) {
    XMLHttpRequestObject = new XMLHttpRequest();
  } else if (window.ActiveXObject) {
    XMLHttpRequestObject = new
      ActiveXObject("Microsoft.XMLHTTP");
  }

  var dataSource = (menu == 1) ? "items1.txt" : "items2.txt";

  if(XMLHttpRequestObject) {
    XMLHttpRequestObject.open("GET", dataSource);

    XMLHttpRequestObject.onreadystatechange = function()
    {
      if (XMLHttpRequestObject.readyState == 4 &&
        XMLHttpRequestObject.status == 200) {
        .
```

```
            .
            .
        }
      }

      XMLHttpRequestObject.send(null);
    }
  }
```

When a menu's text is downloaded and ready to go, this code calls another function (show) to show the actual menu items.

```
XMLHttpRequestObject.onreadystatechange = function()
{
    if (XMLHttpRequestObject.readyState == 4 &&
      XMLHttpRequestObject.status == 200) {
        show(menu, XMLHttpRequestObject.responseText);
    }
}
```

Handling the menu items

The show function is passed the menu number to show and the items that should appear in that menu. This is where the menu items in each menu are constructed. Those items will be placed in an HTML table for easy display in the menu <div> elements.

The show function is passed the number of the menu to work with, and the items appear in that menu in a format like this: "Tuna, Roast beef, Chicken". How can you turn that text into an array that you can use to build the menu itself? Very easily, as it turns out — you can use the built-in JavaScript function, split, which splits a string on the text you pass to this function. So, if you pass a quoted comma to this function, it splits a comma-separated string into substrings automatically:

```
<script language = "javascript">
  var arrayItems;
    .
    .
    .
  function show(menu, items)
  {
    arrayItems = items.split(", ");
      .
      .
      .
```

If you pass this function the string "Tuna, Roast beef, Chicken", after the split function is done, the arrayItems[0] will contain "Tuna", arrayItems[1] will contain "Roast beef", and arrayItems[2] will contain "Chicken". Very handy.

The next step is displaying those items in a menu <div> element, which is done by constructing an HTML table. The code starts constructing that table by looping over the menu items and storing the text for the table in a variable named data:

```
function show(menu, items)
{
  var data = "<table width = '100%'>";
  var loopIndex;
  arrayItems = items.split(",");

  if (arrayItems.length != 0) {
    for (var loopIndex = 0; loopIndex < arrayItems.length;
      loopIndex++) {
      .
      .
      .
    }
  }

  data += "</table>";
  .
  .
  .
}
```

When the user clicks a menu item, the code needs to respond, so it ties the onclick event attribute of each table cell to a function named display, passing that function the index of the item that was clicked:

```
function show(menu, items)
{
  var data = "<table width = '100%'>";
  var loopIndex;
  arrayItems = items.split(",");

  if (arrayItems.length != 0) {
    for (var loopIndex = 0; loopIndex < arrayItems.length;
      loopIndex++) {
      var text = "display(" + loopIndex + ")";
      data += "<tr><td "
        + "onclick='" + text + "'>" +
        arrayItems[loopIndex] +
        "</td></tr>";
    }
  }
```

```
        data += "</table>";
          .
          .
          .
    }
```

Now that the menu items have all been assembled into the HTML table and are ready to go, all that's left is to actually display the menu by setting its `visibility` style to `"visible"` if it's currently hidden. (The code doesn't change the `visibility` style if the menu is already visible — this prevents flickering on the screen.)

```
function show(menu, items)
{
  var data = "<table width = '100%'>";
  var loopIndex;
  arrayItems = items.split(",");
  var target;
    .
    .
    .
  data += "</table>";

  if(menu == "1"){
    target = document.getElementById("menuDiv1");
  }

  if(menu == "2"){
    target = document.getElementById("menuDiv2");
  }

  if(target.style.visibility == "hidden"){
    target.innerHTML = data;
    target.style.visibility = "visible";
  }
}
```

And there you have it. All that's left is to add the `display` function, which is called when the user makes a menu selection. This function is passed the index of the item selected, and displays that item in a styled `<div>` element named `targetDiv` (refer to Figure 9-2). The text for the current menu items is stored in the `arrayItems` array, and the `display` function only needs to fetch the text for the clicked menu item from that array. Here's how it does that:

```
function display(index)
{
  var targetDiv = document.getElementById("targetDiv");

  targetDiv.innerHTML = "You selected "
    + arrayItems[index] + ".";
}
```

And that finishes this application, `menus.html`. This application uses CSS styles to display and hide clickable menus as needed, loading those menus with items fetched from the server using Ajax. When the user moves the mouse over an image, a menu pops up and the user can select menu items; when the user moves the mouse away from the image or menu, the menu closes. Very cool.

Displaying Text That Gets Noticed

Ajax critics sometimes say that a problem with Ajax is that things can change in a Web page without the user noticing. One way to address that is to use CSS styles to make the changes stand out. For example, take a look at Figure 9-3. The fetched text in that figure appears in red for half a second, then changes to black (as it appears in the figure). And when that happens, it's hard not to notice it.

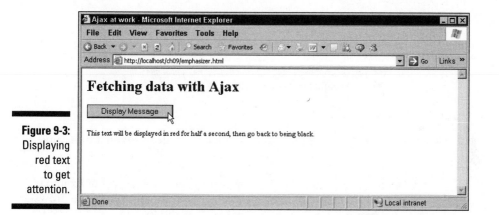

Figure 9-3: Displaying red text to get attention.

You can use styles, along with a little JavaScript, to make this effect happen. JavaScript has a built-in function named `setTimer` that can call your code after a certain amount of time has passed. In this example, the text fetched from the server is displayed in red at first, and then changes back to black. That color change is done using styles, as you might expect. How does this example work? The `setTimer` function is instructed to call another function, `dimmer`, which will change the color of the text to black after half a second:

```javascript
<script language = "javascript">
  function getData(dataSource, divID)
  {
    var XMLHttpRequestObject = false;

    if (window.XMLHttpRequest) {
      XMLHttpRequestObject = new XMLHttpRequest();
```

```
      } else if (window.ActiveXObject) {
        XMLHttpRequestObject = new
          ActiveXObject("Microsoft.XMLHTTP");
      }

      if(XMLHttpRequestObject) {
        var obj = document.getElementById("targetDiv");
        XMLHttpRequestObject.open("GET", dataSource);

        XMLHttpRequestObject.onreadystatechange = function()
        {
          if (XMLHttpRequestObject.readyState == 4 &&
            XMLHttpRequestObject.status == 200) {
              obj.style.color = "#FF0000";
              obj.innerHTML = XMLHttpRequestObject.responseText;
              setTimeout(dimmer, 500);
          }
        }

        XMLHttpRequestObject.send(null);
      }
    }

    function dimmer()
    {
        var obj = document.getElementById("targetDiv");
        obj.style.color = "#000000";
    }
</script>
```

Give this one a try — the fetched text stands out nicely when it first appears
in red.

In fact, the setTimer function is a handy one for many uses. For example,
here's how you can scroll text in the status bar at the bottom of the browser
to catch the user's attention (this won't work in Firefox):

```
<script language="JavaScript">
    var text = "Hello from Ajax! Hello from Ajax! "
    function scroller()
    {
        window.status = text
        text = text.substring(1, text.length) + text.substring(0, 1)
        setTimeout("scroller()", 150)
    }
</script>
```

As you can see, being a master of CSS styles can be very important to Ajax
programmers. But there are so many styles available that it's hard to wade
through all the CSS documentation. For that reason, in the following sections,
I show you some of the most popular style properties for Ajax programmers.

Styling text

Here are some of the popular style properties you can use with text:

✔ font-family: Specifies the actual font, such as Arial or Helvetica. If you want to list alternative fonts in case the target computer is missing your first choice, specify the fonts as a comma-separated list, like this: font-family: Arial, Helvetica.

✔ font-style: Specifies how the text is to be rendered. Set to normal, italic, or oblique.

✔ font-weight: Refers to the boldness or lightness of the glyphs used to render the text, relative to other fonts in the same font family. Set to normal, bold, bolder, lighter, 100, 200, 300, 400, 500, 600, 700, 800, or 900.

✔ line-height: Indicates the height given to each line.

✔ font-size: Refers to the size of the font.

✔ text-decoration: Underlines text. Set to none, underline, overline, line-through, or blink.

✔ text-align: Centers text. Set to left, right, or center.

Here's an example, font.html, putting font properties to work:

```
<html>
    <head>
        <title>
            Setting Font Styles
        </title>
        <style type="text/css">
            body {font-style: italic; font-variant: normal; font-weight: bold;
            font-size: 12pt; line-height: 10pt; font-family: arial, helvetica;
            text-align: center;}
        </style>
    </head>

    <body>
        <h1>Setting Font Styles</h1>
        <br>
        This text has been styled with CSS styles.
    </body>
</html>
```

You can see what font.html looks like in a browser in Figure 9-4.

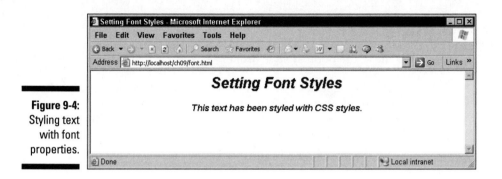

Figure 9-4:
Styling text
with font
properties.

Styling text is one of the most common things to use CSS styles for, but know-ing which style property does what isn't always easy. This next example clears some of the fog by using these text properties:

- ✔ font-style to make text italic
- ✔ font-weight to make text bold
- ✔ font-size to set the font size
- ✔ font-family to set the font face
- ✔ text-decoration to underline the text
- ✔ text-align to center the text

Here's what the example, text.html, looks like:

```
<html>
    <head>
        <title>
            Styling Text
        </title>

        <style>
            p {font-size: 18pt; font-style: italic; font-family:
                Arial, Helvetica; text-align: center;}
        </style>
    </head>

    <body>
        <center>
            <h1>
                Styling Text
            </h1>
        </center>
        <p>
```

```
               This text is in italics. Some of it is
               <span style="font-weight: bold">bold</span>,
               and some is
               <span style="text-decoration: underline">
               underlined</span>.
      </body>
   </html>
```

You can see `text.html` in a browser in Figure 9-5, which displays the text using italics, bold, and underlining. Not bad.

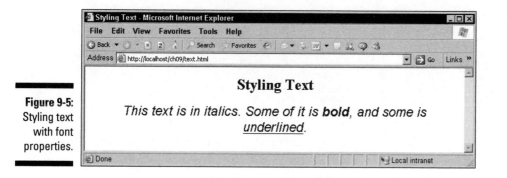

Figure 9-5:
Styling text
with font
properties.

Handling colors and backgrounds

Here are some of the popular style properties that you use to set color and backgrounds:

- ✔ `color`: Sets the foreground color. Set to a color, such as `#FFFFFF`.

- ✔ `background-color`: Sets the background color. Set to a color, such as `#FFFFFF`.

- ✔ `background-image`: Sets the background image. Set to a URL.

- ✔ `background-repeat`: Specifies whether the background image should be tiled. Set to `repeat`, `repeat-x`, `repeat-y`, or `no-repeat`.

- ✔ `background-attachment`: Specifies whether the background scrolls with the rest of the document. Set to `scroll` or `fixed`.

- ✔ `background-position`: Sets the initial position of the background. Set to `top`, `center`, `bottom`, `left`, or `right`.

Here's an example, `colors.html`. In this case, I'm styling both the background and foreground of a document to make some text stand out:

```html
<html>
    <head>
        <title>
            Styling foregrounds and backgrounds
        </title>
    </head>

    <body style="background-color: #AADDDD">

        <div align="left">
            CEO
            <br>
            HTML Styles, Inc.
            <br>
            Oz, North Carolina
        </div>

        <p>
            Dear Leo:
            <div align="center" style="color: #FF0000; background-color:
              #FFFFFF; font-style: italic;">
                Like my new text?
            </div>

            <div align="right">
                <p>
                President
                <br>
                CSS Styles, Inc.
                <br>
                Emerald City, Pennsylvania
            </div>

    </body>
</html>
```

You can see what `colors.html` looks like (in glorious black and white) in Figure 9-6. As you can see in that figure, the text in the middle does indeed stand out (and in real life it stands out even more because it's red).

Want an easy way to set colors? Besides setting colors the usual HTML way (for example, #AAFFAA), you can also use a special function, `rgb`, when setting colors in CSS style sheets. You pass the red, green, and blue values (0–255) you want in your new color to this function — for example, `rgb(255, 0, 0)` would be pure red. Here's an example showing how to set foreground and background colors using `rgb`:

Figure 9-6:
Styling
foregrounds
and back-
grounds.

```
<table border="2" width="400" height="200" style="text-align:center">
    <tr>
        <th style="background-color: rgb(255, 0, 0)">Tic</th>
        <th style="background-color: rgb(255, 0, 0)">Tac</th>
        <th style="background-color: rgb(255, 0, 0)">Toe</th>
    </tr>
    <tr>
        <td style="background-color: rgb(0, 0, 255)">X</td>
        <td style="background-color: rgb(0, 0, 0); color:
            rgb(255, 255, 255)">
            O
        </td>
        <td style="background-color: rgb(0, 255, 0)">X</td>
    </tr>
    <tr>
        <td style="background-color: rgb(0, 0, 0); color:
            rgb(255, 255, 255)">
            O
        </td>
        <td style="background-color: rgb(255, 255, 255)">X</td>
        <td style="background-color: rgb(0, 0, 0); color:
            rgb(255, 255, 255)">
            O
        </td>
    </tr>
    <tr>
        <td style="background-color: rgb(255, 255, 0)">X</td>
        <td style="background-color: rgb(0, 0, 0); color:
            rgb(255, 255, 255)">
            O
        </td>
        <td style="background-color: rgb(0, 255, 255)">X</td>
    </tr>
</table>
```

This example, `colortable.html`, appears in Figure 9-7 — also in glorious black and white. To see what it really looks like, open it up in your browser — there are plenty of colors here.

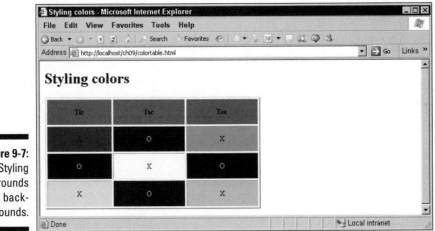

Figure 9-7:
Styling
foregrounds
and back-
grounds.

You can also assign standard colors by name to the `color` and `background-color` properties. For example, you can assign values like `red`, `green`, and even `coral`, `magenta`, and `cyan` to the color properties `color` and `background-color`.

Positioning using styles

Among the favorite CSS styles used by Ajax developers are those that deal with positioning elements in a Web page — good for pop-up menus, drag-and-drop, auto-complete boxes, Google-search boxes, and more. You can find numerous examples of positioning elements throughout this book.

Positioning is commonly used by Ajax programmers when updating a page. Using styles, you can position items in absolute or relative terms. I cover both in the following sections.

Absolute positioning

In *absolute positioning,* you position elements so that the browser measures x and y distances from the upper-left corner of its *client area* (the content display part of the browser, excluding menu bars, status bars, scroll bars, and so on). In other words, the elements are fixed in place in the browser window. Measurements are in pixels by default. Positive x increases to the right, and positive y increases downward. Here are the CSS style properties you use when positioning elements in an absolute way:

✔ position: Set to absolute for absolute positioning.

✔ top: Offset of the top of the element on the screen. By default, this measurement is taken to be in pixels. You can append "px" to the end of this value to make sure the browser interprets the measurement as pixels, as in "50px".

✔ bottom: Offset of the bottom of the element in the browser's client area. By default, this measurement is taken to be in pixels. You can append "px" to the end of this value to make sure the browser interprets the measurement as pixels, as in "50px".

✔ left: Offset of the left edge of the element in the browser's client area. By default, this measurement is taken to be in pixels. You can append "px" to the end of this value to make sure the browser interprets the measurement as pixels, as in "50px".

✔ right: Offset of the right edge of the element in the browser's client area. By default, this measurement is taken to be in pixels. You can append "px" to the end of this value to make sure the browser interprets the measurement as pixels, as in "50px".

✔ z-order: Sets the stacking order of the item with respect to other elements.

Here's an example, absolute.html. In this case, I set position to absolute, and then specified the top and left properties for three <div> elements, each of which holds both an image and text:

```
<html>

    <head>
        <title>
            Absolute Positioning
        </title>
    </head>

    <body>

        <h1 align="center">
            Absolute Positioning
        </h1>

        <div style="position:absolute; left:50; top:60;">
            <img src="image01.jpg" width=205 height=120>
            <br>
            Image 1
        </div>

        <div style="position:absolute; left:200; top:90;">
            <img src="image02.jpg" width=205 height=120>
            <br>
            Image 2
```

```
        </div>

        <div style="position:absolute; left:350; top:120;">
            <img src="image03.jpg" width=205 height=120>
            <br>
            Image 3
        </div>

    </body>

</html>
```

You can see the results in Figure 9-8, where the three images are positioned as they should be.

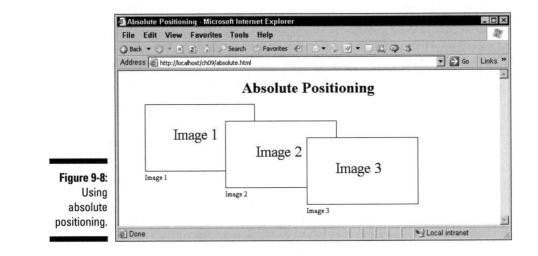

Figure 9-8:
Using
absolute
positioning.

You can also specify how elements in a Web page stack on top of each other using the z-order property. Elements with a higher z-order setting appear on top of elements with a lower z-order setting. For example, say that you set the z-index of the second image to 200, a high value:

```
    <div style="position:absolute; left:200; top:90; z-index:200">
        <img src="image02.jpg" width=205 height=120>
        <br>
        Image 2
    </div>
```

Now Image 2 is on top of the other images in the page, as you can see in Figure 9-9. If you drag that image around, it always rides on top of the other images in the page.

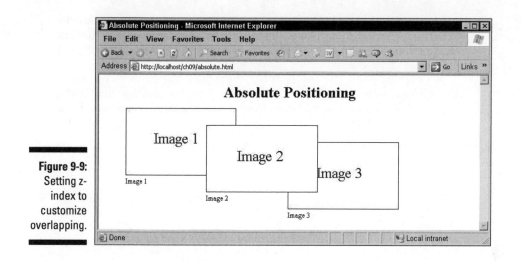

Figure 9-9:
Setting z-
index to
customize
overlapping.

Relative positioning

You can also position elements in a Web page with respect to others, called *relative positioning*. Here are the properties you set to use relative positioning:

✔ position: Set to relative for relative positioning.

✔ top: Offset of the top of the element from where it would otherwise be placed. By default, this measurement is taken to be in pixels. You can append "px" to the end of this value to make sure the browser interprets the measurement as pixels, as in "50px".

✔ bottom: Offset of the bottom of the element from where it would otherwise be placed. By default, this measurement is taken to be in pixels. You can append "px" to the end of this value to make sure the browser interprets the measurement as pixels, as in "50px".

✔ left: Offset of the left edge of the element from where it would otherwise be placed. By default, this measurement is taken to be in pixels. You can append "px" to the end of this value to make sure the browser interprets the measurement as pixels, as in "50px".

✔ right: Offset of the right edge of the element from where it would otherwise be placed. By default, this measurement is taken to be in pixels. You can append "px" to the end of this value to make sure the browser interprets the measurement as pixels, as in "50px".

✔ z-order: Sets the stacking order of the item with respect to other elements.

You use relative positioning in a browser to change the position of an element from where the browser would otherwise normally place it. In other words, relative positioning changes the position of elements with respect to the normal "flow."

Here's an example, `relative.html`. In this case, I'm moving some text up 5 pixels and other text down 5 pixels from the normal position at which the browser would place that text:

```html
<html>

    <head>
        <title>
            Relative Positioning
        </title>
    </head>

    <body>

        <h1 align="center">
            Relative Positioning
        </h1>
        Do you like
        <span style="position: relative; top: -5">roller</span>
        <span style="position: relative; top: 5">coasters</span> as much as I
            do?

    </body>

</html>
```

You can see the results in Figure 9-10. As you see, some of the text is higher by 5 pixels than it would be if placed in the normal flow, and some of the text is lower by 5 pixels.

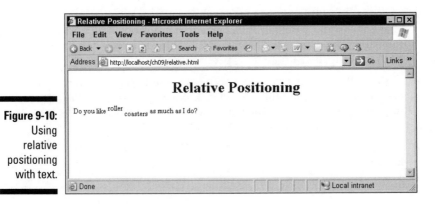

Figure 9-10:
Using
relative
positioning
with text.

Chapter 10

Working with Ajax and PHP

*T*he CEO says, "No, we can't just have static data returned from the server. We need to send data to the server from our Ajax code and have *customized* data returned from the server. How can we do it?"

You, the highly-paid Ajax consultant, step up and say, "No problem. How about using PHP on the server to handle your data interactively?"

"Sounds great," says the CEO. "I hope your rates are reasonable?"

"Nope," you say.

"Darn," says the CEO.

Ajax applications often interact with programming code on the server, and these days, the most frequent choice is PHP. Ajax programmers typically don't need a great deal of in-depth coding on the server, but if you want to write your own PHP scripts, knowing the basics is important — and that's what this chapter gives you: the PHP basics.

Because Ajax involves server-side programming, this chapter focuses on working with PHP on the server. If you can handle JavaScript, you can handle PHP. In fact, much of the syntax is very similar, so you've already got a big leg up.

Note that this chapter is just a PHP primer — I couldn't possibly fit all of PHP in these pages. If you need more than what you see here, check out *PHP 5 For Dummies,* by Janet Valade (Wiley Publishing, Inc.).

Starting with PHP

Technically speaking, you should enclose your PHP scripts, which are stored in files with the extension .php (like checkprice.php) inside <? and ?> like this:

```
<?
        .
        . Your PHP goes here....
        .
?>
```

One of the attractive things about PHP is that you can intersperse HTML and PHP at will. A PHP-enabled server will execute the PHP code inside the <?...?> sections, and just send the HTML on as usual.

Here's an example that runs the built-in PHP function phpinfo, which creates an HTML table that tells you about your PHP installation.

Note that both HTML and PHP are interspersed in this example, phpinfo. php, and note that as in the JavaScript you see throughout this book, you end each PHP statement with a semicolon (;).

```
<html>
    <head>
        <title>
            A first PHP page
        </title>
    </head>

    <body>
        <h1>
            A first PHP page
        </h1>
        <?
            phpinfo();
        ?>
    </body>
</html>
```

What does this look like at work? You can see the results in Figure 10-1. The details will vary according to your PHP installation, but the idea is the same: The phpinfo function displays the table you see in the figure, and the header, A first PHP page, comes from the HTML you've placed in phpinfo.php.

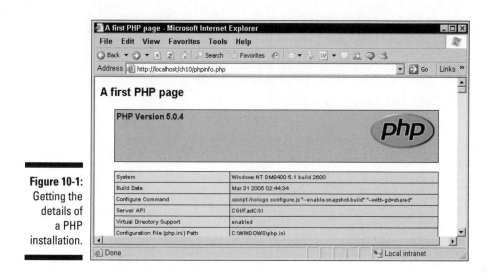

Figure 10-1:
Getting the
details of
a PHP
installation.

What about sending some of your own text back to the browser using PHP?
For that, you can use the PHP `echo` statement. All you do is pass the text you
want to send back to the browser to the `echo` statement as in this example,
`echo.php`:

```
<html>
    <head>
        <title>
            Using the echo statement
        </title>
    </head>

    <body>
        <h1>
            Using the echo statement
        </h1>
        <?
            echo "Hello from PHP.";
        ?>
    </body>
</html>
```

You can see the results in Figure 10-2, where the `echo` statement is doing its
thing and sending text back to the browser, just as planned.

The `echo` statement sends text back to the browser, but sometimes in Ajax you
don't want to send just text — you want to send XML. To make sure that the
text sent back to the browser is treated as XML by the browser, use the PHP
`header` statement and set the HTTP `Content-Type` header to `text/xml`.

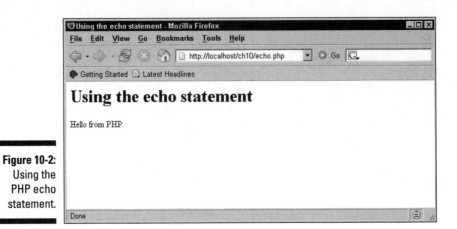

Figure 10-2:
Using the
PHP echo
statement.

Here's an example, `xml.php`, that I show you later in this chapter, in the "Round and round with loops" section, where I cover looping over arrays. This example sends XML back to the browser:

```php
<?
header('Content-Type: text/xml');
$data = array('This', 'is', 'XML.');
echo '<?xml version="1.0" ?>';
echo '<document>';
foreach ($data as $value)
{
  echo '<data>';
  echo $value;
  echo '</data>';
}
echo '</document>';
?>
```

The preceding example sends this XML back to the browser:

```xml
<?xml version="1.0" ?>
<document>
  <data>This</data>
  <data>is</data>
  <data>XML.</data>
</document>
```

Browsers like Internet Explorer display XML in a special way, as you can see in Figure 10-3, where Internet Explorer is indeed convinced that the text in this example, `xml.php`, is bona fide XML.

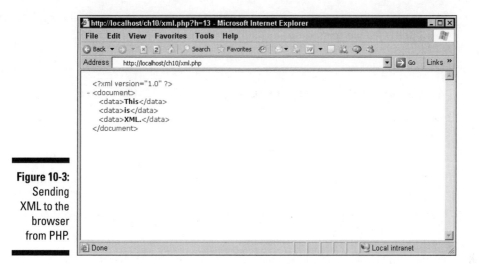

Figure 10-3:
Sending
XML to the
browser
from PHP.

You can also comment your PHP code. There are three types of comments in PHP. The first kind of comment lets you write multi-line comments, beginning with /* and ending with */ like this:

```
<?
/* Start by displaying a
   message to the user */

    echo "Hello from PHP.";
?>
```

The other two types of comments are one-line comments, just as you see in JavaScript, designed to hold text that fits on a single line (the comment ends automatically at the end of the line). To start these comments, you can use either // or #:

```
<?
// Start by displaying a
# message to the user

    echo "Hello from PHP.";
?>
```

Getting a Handle on Variables

How about storing some data in variables? As in JavaScript, variables in PHP can hold numbers, strings, or objects. In PHP, variable names start with a dollar sign ($) character, and you don't have to declare them. For example, to set the variable named $peaches to 1, all you have to do is this:

```
$peaches = 1;
```

You can display the value in this variable this way with the echo statement:

```
echo "Number of peaches: ", $peaches, "<br>";
```

There are two things to note here:

- ✔ You can pass multiple items to the echo statement if you separate the items with commas.
- ✔ You're sending HTML back to the browser, so to skip to the next line, you use HTML like <br>.

Using variables in PHP is much like using them in JavaScript. So here's a PHP example, variables.php, that assigns a value to $peaches and then changes the value in that variable by adding 5 to it:

```
<html>
    <head>
        <title>
            Assigning values to variables
        </title>
    </head>
    <body>
        <h1>
            Assigning values to variables
        </h1>
        <?
            echo "Setting number of peaches to 1.<br>";

            $peaches = 1;

            echo "Number of peaches: ", $peaches, "<br>";

            echo "Adding 5 more peaches.<br>";

            $peaches = $peaches + 5;

            echo "Number of peaches now: ", $peaches, "<br>";
        ?>
    </body>
</html>
```

The results are in Figure 10-4. As you can see, working with variables in PHP is very similar to working with variables in JavaScript.

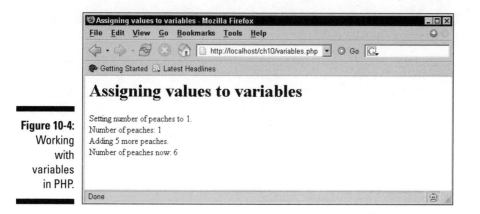

Figure 10-4:
Working
with
variables
in PHP.

Besides assigning numbers to variables, you can also assign text strings, as here:

```
$string = "Hello from PHP.";
```

In JavaScript, you join strings with the + operator, but in PHP, you use the dot (.) operator instead:

```
$string = "Hello " . "from " . "PHP.";
```

PHP also comes with many string functions built in. Here's a sampling:

- ✔ trim: Trims spaces from the beginning and end of a string
- ✔ substr: Extracts substrings from a string
- ✔ strpos: Finds the location of a substring in a string
- ✔ ucfirst: Capitalizes the first character of a string
- ✔ substr_replace: Replaces text in a string
- ✔ strtoupper: Converts a whole string to uppercase

Here's an example that puts these string functions to work:

```
<?
    echo trim("    No problem."), "<br>";
    echo substr("No problem.", 3, 7), "<br>";
    echo "'problem' starts at position ", strpos("No problem.", "problem"),
            "<br>";
    echo ucfirst("no problem."), "<br>";
    echo "'No problem.' is ", strlen("No problem."), " characters long.<br>";
    echo substr_replace("No problem.", "problems.", 3, 8), "<br>";
    echo strtoupper("No problem."), "<br>";
?>
```

Here are the results of this script, line by line (with the "<br>" at the end of each line stripped away):

```
No problem.
problem
'problem' starts at position 3
No problem.
'No problem.' is 11 characters long.
No problems.
ABC
NO PROBLEM.
```

Want to work with arrays? No problem at all. Just use the PHP `array` statement. Here's an example:

```
$data = array(15, 18, 22);
```

And you access any item in an array like this:

```
echo $data[0]; //displays 15
echo $data[1]; //displays 18
echo $data[2]; //displays 22
```

In PHP, you can also refer to items in an array with a text index if you prefer, like this:

```
$data["temperature"] = 81;
echo $data["temperature"]; //displays 81
```

Handling Your Data with Operators

PHP has plenty of operators to handle your data, and most of them are the same as the operators in JavaScript. Here's a sampling of PHP operators:

- new
- [
- ! ~ ++ --
- * / %
- + - .
- == !=
- &
- |
- &&

✔ ||

✔ ? :

✔ = += -= *= /= .= %= &= |= ^= <<= >>=

These operators work as you'd expect. Here's an example, `operators.html`, which puts a few of these operators to work:

```html
<html>
    <head>
        <title>
            Assigning values to variables
        </title>
    </head>
    <body>
        <h1>
            Assigning values to variables
        </h1>
        <?
            echo "2 + 3 = ", 2 + 3, "<br>";

            echo "2 - 3 = ", 2 - 3, "<br>";

            echo "2 * 3 = ", 2 * 3, "<br>";

            echo "2 / 3 = ", 2 / 3, "<br>";

        ?>
    </body>
</html>
```

The results of this example appear in Figure 10-5, where as you can see, the PHP operators have done their thing.

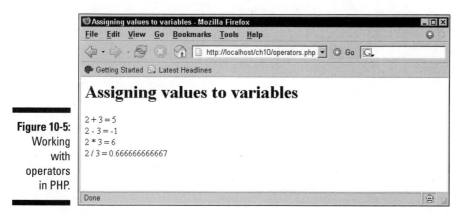

Figure 10-5: Working with operators in PHP.

The list of PHP operators earlier in this section is given in terms of *operator precedence* in PHP, with higher-precedence operators first. Operator precedence indicates which operator will be executed first if there's a conflict. For example, what will the following statement display?

```
echo 2 + 3 * 4;
```

Will the 2 be added to the 3 and then multiplied by 4 to give you 20? Or will the 3 be multiplied by 4 and then added to 2 to give you 14? In PHP, the multiplication operator, *, has higher precedence than the addition operator, +, so the * is executed first. So, 2 + 3 * 4 becomes 2 + 12, which gives you 14.

Making Choices with the if Statement

Just about all high-level programming languages, including PHP, have an if statement. You use if statements to make choices at runtime. Here's an example, if.php, which tests whether the value in a variable named $temperature is less than 80 degrees:

```
<html>
    <head>
        <title>
            Using the if statement
        </title>
    </head>
    <body>
        <h1>
            Using the if statement
        </h1>
        <?
        $temperature = 75;

        if ($temperature < 80) {
         echo "Pleasant weather.";
        }
        ?>
    </body>
</html>
```

In this case, $temperature holds a value of 75, so the statement echo "Pleasant weather."; is executed. The result is shown in Figure 10-6.

Figure 10-6:
Using the if
statement in
PHP.

PHP also has an `else` statement, which works just as it does in JavaScript:

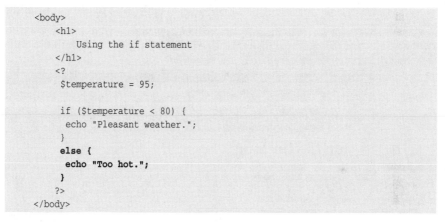

```
<body>
    <h1>
        Using the if statement
    </h1>
    <?
    $temperature = 95;

    if ($temperature < 80) {
     echo "Pleasant weather.";
    }
    else {
     echo "Too hot.";
    }
    ?>
</body>
```

Because the `temperature` variable here contains a value of 95, you're going to see `"Too hot."` from this code.

Round and Round with Loops

PHP also supports several `loop` statements. The `for` loop works just as it does in JavaScript; in fact, the only real difference is that you have to give the loop index variable an initial $, following the PHP way of naming variables. (For more on the `for` loop in JavaScript, see Chapter 2.) Here's an example, `for.php`:

```
<html>
    <head>
        <title>
            Using the for loop
        </title>
    </head>

    <body>
        <h1>
            Using the for loop
        </h1>
        <?
            for ($loopCounter = 0; $loopCounter < 4; $loopCounter++){
                echo "You're going to see this four times.<br>";
            }
        ?>
    </body>
</html>
```

You can see this example do its thing in Figure 10-7.

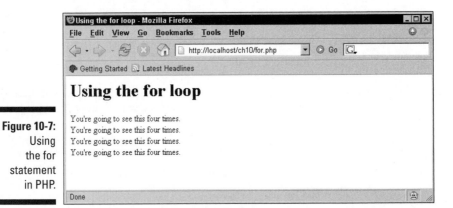

Figure 10-7:
Using
the for
statement
in PHP.

PHP also has a `while` loop that keeps looping while its condition is true. Here's an example that displays the message `You're going to see this four times,` just as the previous `for` loop example did:

```
<html>
    <head>
        <title>
            Using the while loop
        </title>
    </head>

    <body>
        <h1>
```

```
            Using the while loop
        </h1>
        <?
            $loopIndex = 1;

            while ($loopIndex <= 4){
                echo "You're going to see this four times.<br>";
                $loopIndex++;
            }
        ?>
    </body>
</html>
```

PHP also has a `do...while` loop that checks its condition at the end of the loop, not the beginning, which is useful if the condition you want to test isn't even set until the body of the loop is executed. This loop also displays the message four times:

```
        <?
            $loopIndex = 1;

            do {
                echo "You're going to see this four times.<br>";
                $loopIndex++;
            } while ($loopIndex <= 4)
        ?>
```

PHP also has a `foreach` loop, which lets you automatically loop over arrays and other multiple-item objects. This loop is handy because you don't have to explicitly know how many items there are in an array to loop over it — all you have to do is give a name of a variable that will be filled with the current array item each time through the loop. This example, `xml.php`, sends XML back to the server, using a `foreach` loop to create the XML document:

```
<?
header('Content-Type: text/xml');
$data = array('This', 'is', 'XML.');
echo '<?xml version="1.0" ?>';
echo '<document>';
foreach ($data as $value)
{
  echo '<data>';
  echo $value;
  echo '</data>';
}
echo '</document>';
?>
```

Very cool.

Handling HTML Controls

When a Web page is sent to the server, you can extract the data from HTML controls yourself in a PHP script. To send data to the server when a Submit button is clicked, you'll need to set the following attributes of the HTML form containing the text field:

✔ action: This attribute is assigned the URL to which the form data will be sent. You can omit this attribute, in which case its default is the URL of the current PHP document.

✔ method: Specifies the method for sending data to the server. If you set it to GET (the default) this method sends all form name/value pair information in a URL that looks like: *URL?name=value&name=value&name= value*. If you use the POST method, the contents of the form are encoded as with the GET method, but they are sent in hidden environment variables.

For example, this Web page, text.html, asks the user to enter his nickname in a text field named "nickname", and then it posts that data to a PHP script named phptext.php.

```
<html>
    <head>
        <title>
            Sending data in text fields
        </title>
    </head>

    <body>
        <center>

            <h1>
                Sending data in text fields
            </h1>

            <form method="post" action="phptext.php">
                Enter your nickname:

                <input name="nickname" type="text">

                <br>
                <br>

                <input type="submit" value="Submit">
            </form>

        </center>
    </body>
</html>
```

You can see this page at work in Figure 10-8, where it's asking for the user's nickname.

Figure 10-8:
A Web page with a text field asking for the user's nickname.

Getting data from text fields

How do you read the data in an HTML control like you read the `nickname` text field in the preceding PHP example?

✔ **If you sent data to the server by using the GET method,** you can recover that data from the PHP `$_GET` array like this: `$_GET["nickname"]`, where `nickname` is the name you gave to the text field (with the HTML name attribute).

✔ **If you sent the data by using the POST method,** you can access the data in the text field as `$_POST["nickname"]`.

There's another PHP array named `$_REQUEST` that lets you get that data regardless of whether you used the GET method or the POST method. Continuing with the example, here's how to use `$_REQUEST` to recover the text the user entered into the `nickname` text field:

```
<html>
    <head>
        <title>
            Reading data from text fields using PHP
        </title>
    </head>

    <body>
        <center>

            <h1>
                Reading data from text fields using PHP
            </h1>
```

```
        Your nickname is
        <?
            echo $_REQUEST["nickname"];
        ?>
    </center>
  </body>
</html>
```

That's all you need. Now this page, `phptext.php`, can read the text that was entered into the text field, as shown in Figure 10-9.

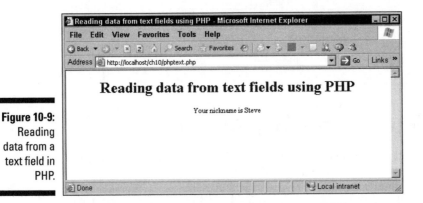

Figure 10-9:
Reading data from a text field in PHP.

Checking out data from check boxes

The technique in the preceding section works for text fields and text areas, but what about check boxes? Here's an example, `checkboxes.html`, which asks the user what toppings she wants on her pizza:

```
<html>
    <head>
        <title>Sending data in checkboxes</title>
    </head>

    <body>
        <center>
        <h1>Sending data in checkboxes</h1>
        <form method="POST" action="checkboxes.php">
            What do you want on your pizza?
            <input name="pepperoni" type="checkbox" value="Pepperoni">
            Pepperoni
            <input name="olives" type="checkbox" value="Olives">
            Olives
            <br>
            <br>
```

```
            <input type="submit" value="Submit">
        </form>
        </center>
    </body>
</html>
```

You can see the two check boxes in a browser in Figure 10-10. The user just selects one or both and then clicks Submit to send her selection to the server.

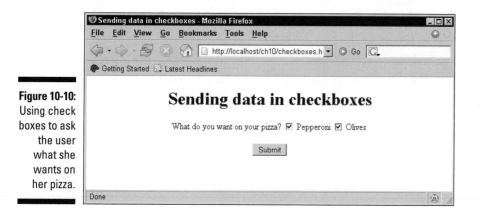

Figure 10-10: Using check boxes to ask the user what she wants on her pizza.

You can determine whether a check box has been checked with the PHP `isset` function, which returns `true` if the parameter corresponding to an HTML control has been set, and `false` otherwise.

If a check box has been checked, you can get the text that has been assigned to the check box's value attribute (that's `"pepperoni"` or `"olives"` in this example) using the `$_GET`, `$_POST`, or `$_REQUEST` arrays. Here's what it looks like in PHP code, `phpcheckboxes.php`, where you can recover the names of the toppings the user requested:

```
<html>
    <head>
        <title>
            Reading data from checkboxes using PHP
        </title>
    </head>

    <body>
        <center>
            <h1>Reading data from checkboxes using PHP</h1>
            You want:<br>
```

```
        <?
            if (isset($_REQUEST["pepperoni"]))
                echo $_REQUEST["pepperoni"], "<br>";
            if (isset($_REQUEST["olives"]))
                echo $_REQUEST["olives"], "<br>";
        ?>
        </center>
    </body>
</html>
```

And as shown in Figure 10-11, this PHP script has indeed been able to determine what the user wants on her pizza. Not bad.

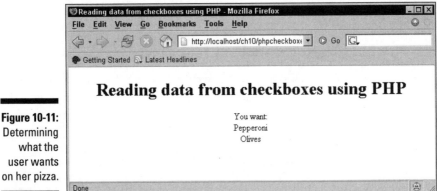

Figure 10-11:
Determining what the user wants on her pizza.

Tuning in data from radio buttons

How do you recover data from radio buttons? Here, you group radio buttons together, so they act as a set, by giving two or more buttons the same name, as you see in `radios.html`. Here, the name given to the radio buttons is `"radios"`:

```
<html>
    <head>
        <title>Sending data in radio buttons</title>
    </head>
    <body>
        <center>
            <h1>Sending data in radio buttons</h1>
            <form method="POST" action="phpradios.php">
                Do you want fries with that?
                <input name="radios" type="RADIO" value="Yes">
```

```
                Yes
                <input name="radios" type="RADIO" value="No">
                No
                <br>
                <br>
                <input type="SUBMIT" value="Submit">
            </form>
        </center>
    </body>
</html>
```

You can see `radios.html` at work in Figure 10-12.

Figure 10-12:
Using radio
buttons.

To recover the radio button that was selected in the radio button group, you use the name of the *group* with $_REQUEST, instead of having to work with each individual control as with check boxes. You can see how this works in `phpradios.php`:

```
<html>
    <head>
        <title>Reading data from radio buttons using PHP</title>
    </head>
    <body>
        <center>
            <h1>Reading data from radio buttons using PHP</h1>
            <?
                echo "You selected: ", $_REQUEST["radios"];
            ?>
        </center>
    </body>
</html>
```

The results appear in Figure 10-13, where the PHP was able to get the user's selection from the radio buttons.

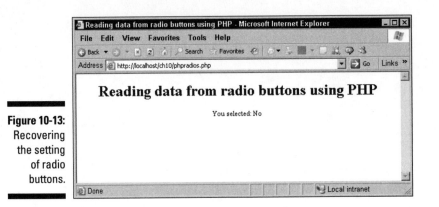

Figure 10-13:
Recovering
the setting
of radio
buttons.

Sending Data to the Server

In Ajax, you don't usually rely on form submission to send data to the server. How do you send data to the server yourself? The usual way is to add your data to the end of the URL and use the GET method (as shown in Chapter 3). In that example, the code encodes the data to send to the server using a parameter named scheme:

```
function getOptions(scheme)
{
  var url = "options2.php?scheme=" + scheme;

  if(XMLHttpRequestObject) {
    XMLHttpRequestObject.open("GET", url, true);

    XMLHttpRequestObject.onreadystatechange = function()
    {
      if (XMLHttpRequestObject.readyState == 4 &&
        XMLHttpRequestObject.status == 200) {
      var xmlDocument = XMLHttpRequestObject.responseXML;
      options = xmlDocument.getElementsByTagName("option");
      listOptions();
      }
    }

    XMLHttpRequestObject.send(null);
  }
}
```

In PHP on the server, you can recover the data in the scheme parameter as $_GET["scheme"]. Here's how options2.php put the recovered value to work in Chapter 3:

```
<?
if(isset($_GET["scheme"])){
header("Content-type: text/xml");
if ($_GET["scheme"] == "1")
  $options = array('red', 'green', 'blue');
if ($_GET["scheme"] == "2")
  $options = array('black', 'white', 'orange');
echo '<?xml version="1.0"?>';
echo '<options>';
foreach ($options as $value)
{
  echo '<option>';
  echo $value;
  echo '</option>';
}
echo '</options>';
}
?>
```

Using the GET method this way makes sending data to the server easy.

Reading Files

PHP lets you work with files on the server, and that's a big help to save data —
everything from guest books to current lawn mower prices. To read from a
file, you can use the PHP fopen function to open that file on the server. Here's
how you typically use this function:

```
fopen (filename, mode)
```

Here, *filename* is the name of the file you're opening, and *mode* indicates
how you want to open the file:

- ✔ 'r': Open the file for reading only.

- ✔ 'r+': Open the file for reading and writing.

- ✔ 'w': Open the file for writing only and truncate the file to zero length. If
  the file does not exist, PHP will attempt to create it.

- ✔ 'w+': Open the file for reading and writing and truncate the file to zero
  length. If the file does not exist, PHP will attempt to create it.

- ✔ 'a': Open the file for appending only. If the file does not exist, PHP will
  attempt to create it.

- ✔ 'a+': Open the file for reading and writing, starting at the end of the file.
  If the file does not exist, PHP will attempt to create it.

✔ 'x': Create and open the file for writing only. If the file already exists, the fopen call will not create the file and will return FALSE.

✔ 'x+': Create and open the file for reading and writing. If the file already exists, the fopen call will not create the file and will return FALSE.

The fopen function returns a *file handle,* which stands for the file from then on in your code. You pass this file handle to various functions to read from the file, or write to it, and so on. For example, there are a variety of ways to read data from a file using PHP functions such as fgets, which reads a line of text from a file. To read a line of text, you pass it a file's handle. Say you have a file, file.txt, on the server that has these contents:

```
This
text
comes
from
the
server.
```

How would you read this text? You can open file.txt with fopen and read successive lines with fgets in a loop. You can determine when you've reached the end of the file with the feof function, which returns true when you're at the end of the file. Here's how the text in file.txt can be read and displayed by PHP in phpreadfile.php.

```
<html>
    <head>
        <title>
            Reading text from a file using PHP
        </title>
    </head>
    <body>
        <h1>
            Reading text from a file using PHP
        </h1>
        <?
        $handle = fopen("file.txt", "r");
        while (!feof($handle)){
            $text = fgets($handle);
            echo $text, "<br>";
        }
        fclose($handle);
        ?>
    </body>
</html>
```

Note the expression !feof($handle). This expression uses the PHP "not" operator, !, which reverses true to false and false to true. So !feof($handle) is true while you haven't reached the end of the file yet.

Note also the use of `fclose` at the end of the code to *close* the file. When you're done with a file, you should close it with `fclose`. (Closing a file is the complementary operation to opening it.) You can see `phpreadfile.php` at work in Figure 10-14.

Figure 10-14: Reading a file on the server.

This example uses `fgets` to read strings of text from a file on the server. PHP offers other ways to do that as well, such as `fgetc` (which reads individual characters) and `fread` (which reads data byte by byte).

Writing Files

You can also write to a file on the server using PHP and the `fwrite` function. For example, say that you wanted to create the file `file.txt` on the server, with the same content I use in the previous sections. You can start by putting the text that you want in this file in a variable named `$text`.

```
$text = "This\ntext\ncomes\nfrom\nthe\nserver.";
```

Note the `\n` codes here: Each such code stands for a newline character that breaks the text up into separate lines, just as the original text for this file.

To be able to write files on the server, you first have to make sure you have permission to do so. If you aren't authorized to write to files, you can't use examples like this one.

To write to `file.txt`, you just have to open that file for writing (passing a mode of `"w"` to `fopen`), and then use `fwrite` to write to the file the text you want. The `fwrite` function returns `true` if it is successful and `FALSE` otherwise. Here's what creating the file looks like in `phpfilewrite.php`:

```
<html>
    <head>
        <title>
            Writing a file using PHP
        </title>
    </head>
    <body>
        <center>
            <h1>
                Writing a file using PHP
            </h1>

            <?
            $handle = fopen("file.txt", "w");

            $text = "This\ntext\ncomes\nfrom\nthe\server.";

            if (fwrite($handle, $text) == FALSE) {
                echo "Could not create file.txt.";
            }
            else {
                echo "Created file.txt OK.";
            }
            fclose($handle);
            ?>
        </center>
    </body>
</html>
```

Opening a file with `"w"` truncates it to zero length first (before you start writing) so the current contents are lost. In addition to creating files this way, you can also open them for appending, using `fopen` mode `"a"`, which means anything you add to the file will be added to the end of the file.

Working with Databases

PHP excels at connections to various database systems, which can be good for Ajax programmers who want to retrieve data from the server.

PHP has many built-in functions to work with various database systems; one popular choice is MySQL (`www.mysql.com`). PHP comes with built-in functions like `mysql_connect` (to connect to a MySQL database server), mysql_select_db (to select a database to work with), mysql_query (to send an SQL query to the database), mysql_fetch_array (to convert the results of a query to an array), and so on.

Although a full treatment of working with PHP and databases is beyond the scope of this book, here's an example to get you started. Say you have a database named products, and a table inside that database named pencils, which lists the type and number of pencils you have in stock.

Here's how you can fetch the products database and the pencils table inside it, displaying the values in the type and number fields in the table's rows in an HTML table:

```
<?
    $connection = mysql_connect("localhost","root","");
    $db = mysql_select_db("products", $connection);

    $query = "SELECT * FROM pencils";
    $result = mysql_query($query);

    echo "<table border='1'>";
    echo "<tr>";
    echo "<th>Type</th><th>Number</th>";
    echo "</tr>";

    while ($row = mysql_fetch_array($result))
    {
        echo "<tr>";
        echo "<td>", $row['name'], "</td><td>", $row['number'],
            "</td>";
        echo "</tr>";
    }

    echo "</table>";

    mysql_close($connection);
?>
```

If you're interested in finding out more about working with databases in PHP, check out *PHP 5 For Dummies,* by Janet Valade (Wiley Publishing, Inc.).

Part V
The Part of Tens

The 5th Wave   By Rich Tennant

"What I'm looking for are dynamic Web applications and content, not Web innvendoes and intent."

In this part . . .

No *For Dummies* book would be a *For Dummies* book without a few Part of Tens chapters. Here, Chapters 11 and 12 give you useful Ajax info in a handy top-ten-list format. Chapter 11 lists Ajax design issues that you'll encounter sooner or later, and what to do about them. Chapter 12 takes another route by providing you with a list of ten essential Ajax resources online, from the seminal Ajax sites to Google Ajax groups to Ajax blogs. If you've got a problem with your Ajax coding, these are the sites to go to. Take a look — I think you'll discover that the Ajax online community is a pretty friendly place.

Chapter 11

Ten Ajax Design Issues You Should Know About

In This Chapter

▶ Handling the Back button

▶ Thinking about security

▶ Storing search terms in Ajax pages

▶ Watching out for caching

Ajax is a new ball of wax when it comes to Web applications, and as such, new rules about how the interface should and shouldn't work are emerging. Those rules have not been formalized yet, but the Ajax community is discussing them. Before launching into creating your own Ajax applications, thinking about the design issues I explain in this chapter is a good idea.

You can also find more information on the best practices for Ajax programming (also called Ajax *patterns*) at `http://ajaxpatterns.org`. Chapter 12 introduces the Ajax patterns site in more detail, along with several other helpful Ajax resources.

Breaking the Back Button and Bookmarks

When you have control over what's going on in a Web page and you're using JavaScript to make things turn on and off in a page — or even to alter the page's entire appearance — the browser's Back button won't work anymore. The Back button works from the browser's history object, which stores the successive pages that have been loaded into the browser. But if you aren't loading new pages — which is what Ajax is all about — the history object doesn't know about them.

This is one to keep in mind as you design your Ajax applications. If necessary, provide your own local Back button using JavaScript. If you want to let the user move backwards to previous window states, you have to keep track of what's been going on and let the user navigate as they want to.

There have been attempts at fixing this problem, although they're usually pretty complex to implement. One of the best is Mike Stenhouse's effort at www.contentwithstyle.co.uk/articles/38, which works by playing around with URLs to make the browser store pages in its history object.

Giving Visual Cues

Ajax works mostly behind the scenes, and that can be hard on the user. If you're loading a lot of data, for example, or waiting for the server, a visual cue, such as a rotating hourglass image, is a good idea because a cue helps users understand they need to be patient and their connections are in fact working. You can display animated images using small .gif files and use dynamic styles to make those images appear or disappear in JavaScript:

```
document.getElementById("image1").style.visibility= "visible";
document.getElementById("image1").style.visibility= "hidden";
```

The user might expect some visual cues in the normal way of browsers, such as a control that shows a blue line slowly creeping from left to right, or anything you can come up with that will help the user match expectations.

Leaving the User in Control

Ajax applications can seem to take on a life of their own because they operate behind the scenes. And they can communicate with the server even when the user doesn't want them to — as when the user makes a typing error. You can imagine how you'd feel if you'd just entered a typo and it was immediately stored in a database by an application that didn't ask you if you wanted to store anything.

So, to give your applications a good feel, here are a few tips for putting users in control:

✔ Don't whisk data away for storage until the user really wants to store it.

✔ Remember that, ideally, your application is supposed to respond to events caused only by the user. Users can find too much server-side validation disconcerting because it creates the impression that you're correcting them at every keystroke. Don't forget that one of the design principles of graphical user interfaces (GUIs) is that the user should be in control, that they should direct the action.

✔ And don't forget to offer the user a way of undoing errors.

Remembering All the Different Browsers

As with any Web application, it's worthwhile to keep in mind that there are many different browsers around, and your Ajax application should be tested in the ones you want to support.

As of this writing, Internet Explorer and Firefox make up about 96 percent of browser use, and the rest (Opera, Safari, and so on) are each in the 1 percent or less category.

And don't forget that not all browser will support JavaScript, or will have JavaScript turned on — and for those users, you should have a backup plan.

Showing Users When Text Changes

A powerful Ajax technique is to change the data displayed in a page using <div>, <span>, or other HTML elements or by using HTML controls like text fields. Ajax applications can change the data in a page after consulting with the server — but *without* consulting with the *user*. For example, you may have altered the data in a table of data when the data on the server has changed.

That means that the user might not notice that the data has changed. So be careful about how much you change in a Web page and where because the user might miss it.

Once again, visual cues can help here — if you've changed some text, you might give it, or the control it appears in, a different background color. For example, here's how to turn the text in a <div> element red using the color style property:

```
document.getElementById("targetDiv").style.color = "red";
```

Want to change the background color instead? Use the background-color style property instead:

```
document.getElementById("targetDiv").style.background-color = "red";
```

Avoiding a Sluggish Browser

Ajax applications can be large, and when they start using up resources like memory and CPU speed, you've got to be careful. A large application can use up a huge amount of memory, especially if you're not careful about getting rid of large objects that have been created.

Sometimes, developers use Ajax just because it's a new thing. Be careful about that tendency, too. Ajax solves many problems, but if you don't have to use it, there's no reason to. And also, don't forget that your Ajax applications might not work in all browsers — such as those where JavaScript has been turned off. You should provide some kind of backup plan in that case.

Handling Sensitive Data

With Ajax, it's easy to send data without the user knowing what's going on. In fact, that's part of the whole client/server connection thing that makes Ajax so popular. But it's also true that the user may not want to send the data you're sending.

It's best to be careful about sensitive data. The Internet is not necessarily a secure place for sensitive data, after all, and if you start sending social security numbers or credit card numbers without the user's permission, you could wind up in trouble. So give the users the benefit of the doubt — ask before you send sensitive data.

Creating a Backup Plan

Ajax relies on being connected to a server but don't forget that not everyone is online all the time. And your own server may go down, so your users may be working from cached pages. If you can't connect to a page online, you should have some kind of backup. And that goes for users who have browsers that don't support JavaScript, too.

Showing Up in Search Engines

Google searches billions of Web pages for the text that its users search for — but if the text you display is loaded into a page based on user actions, not on browser refreshes, Google isn't able to see that text. So bear in mind that if you want to make your page searchable on search engines like Google, you've got to give your page the search terms they need. (You can store your keywords in a `<meta>` tag in the browser's `<head>` section, for example, which is where search engines expect to find them. See `www.searchenginewatch.com/webmasters/meta.html` for more information on that.)

Sidestepping a Browser's Cache

Okay, enough with the things to be careful about. How about getting some programming going on here?

Browsers such as Internet Explorer *cache* Web pages. That means that if someone accesses a URL using Ajax more than once, the browser may give them a copy of the page from its cache, as opposed to actually going back to the server and getting a new copy of the page. And that can be a problem if the data on the server has changed.

If you change the data on the server but still see the same data as before in your Ajax application, you may be a victim of caching.

If you want your Ajax applications to avoid caching, you can try setting various headers when you send data back from the server; that would look like this in PHP:

```
header("Cache-Control", "no-cache");
header("Pragma", "no-cache");
header("Expires", "-1");
```

However, this method turns out to be unreliable with Internet Explorer. One practical way to help your applications avoid caching is to alter the URL the application is requesting from the server. For example, you might append a meaningless value named `t` — which your server-side program ignores — to the end of the URL like this:

```
var myUrl = "data.php?name=steve" + "&t=" + new Date().getTime();
```

This appends the current time, measured in milliseconds, to the end of the URL. Because this URL has never been accessed before, it hasn't been cached, and you can be sure that your application is getting the latest data from the server.

One of the Ajax frameworks that lets you turn caching on and off like this is `request.js`, which you can pick up at `http://adamv.com/dev/javascript/http_request`. See Part III for more on Ajax frameworks.

Chapter 12

Ten Super-Useful Ajax Resources

*T*here's plenty of Ajax help on the Internet, ready to give you all sorts of information and advice. You can find a good list of Ajax resources in this chapter, including the Web address for the original article by Jesse James Garrett of Adaptive Path that started the whole Ajax juggernaut going. You can also get wrapped up in any of the Ajax blogs and discussion groups that I introduce here.

Don't forget, this being the Internet, that URLs can change without notice. And also keep in mind that the Ajax phenomenon is still exploding — more sites, frameworks, and discussions are appearing all the time. Keep in touch with the Ajax community online — there are great days ahead.

The Original Ajax Page

`www.adaptivepath.com/publications/essays/archives/000385.php`

Yep, this is the big one, the original Ajax page where Jesse James Garrett coined the term *Ajax*. This article, named "Ajax: A New Approach to Web Applications," even includes a nice picture of Jesse. Although some people have noted that all the technologies involved in Ajax were in use before this article came out, the article, nevertheless, focused vast amounts of attention on Ajax and what it could do.

Adaptive Path says, "Since we first published Jesse's essay, we've received an enormous amount of correspondence from readers with questions about Ajax." You can find a question and answer section at the end of the page where Jesse answers some of those questions.

The Ajax Patterns Page

```
http://ajaxpatterns.org
```

The Ajax Patterns page is a great Ajax resource. *Patterns* refers to best programming practices, and there's a lot of discussion on this site about the topic.

In addition, this site has a great page of links to Ajax examples (`http://ajaxpatterns.org/Ajax_Examples`) and to the various Ajax frameworks available (`http://ajaxpatterns.org/Ajax_Frameworks`). In Part III, I explain many ways in which you put these frameworks to use.

In my view, the interactive discussion and huge number of resources help make this the best Ajax site available anywhere, bar none. Take a look!

The Wikipedia Ajax Page

```
http://en.wikipedia.org/wiki/AJAX
```

Wikipedia's Ajax page is also a great resource. Wikipedia is a free, online encyclopedia, and this page has an in-depth discussion with many links on what Ajax is (and isn't).

This page has one of the best all-around Ajax overviews you're going to find anywhere, including not only a discussion of what Ajax is good for, but a discussion of problems — in other words, both the pros and cons.

And you can also find many links to Ajax resources of all kinds, from Ajax examples to Ajax frameworks.

Ajax Matters

```
www.ajaxmatters.com/r/welcome
```

Ajax Matters is another power-packed Ajax site, currently updated all the time, on all things about Ajax. It's great for all-around Ajax topics of any kind. Here's a quick list of what you can find:

- ✔ Headlines on new product releases
- ✔ Links to books, example sites that use Ajax, and resources that Ajax developers need, such as JavaScript references
- ✔ Frameworks
- ✔ Articles
- ✔ Discussions

XMLHttpRequest Object References

Where are the official references showing how to use XMLHttpRequest objects in the various browsers? You can find the official references for each browser, listing object methods and properties at the following sites:

- ✔ **Internet Explorer:** `http://msdn.microsoft.com/library/ default.asp?url=/library/en-us/xmlsdk/html/ 7924f6be-c035-411f-acd2-79de7a711b38.asp`
- ✔ **Mozilla (including Firefox) and Apple Safari:** `http://developer. apple.com/internet/webcontent/xmlhttpreq.html`

Ajax Blogs

A handful of Ajax blogs out there have a lot of great Ajax commentary. Here's a list of some of the better ones:

- ✔ `http://ajaxblog.com`
- ✔ `www.ajaxian.com`
- ✔ `http://weblogs.asp.net/mschwarz/archive/2005/11.aspx`
- ✔ `www.robsanheim.com/category/software/ajax`

Ajax Examples

Sometimes, nothing helps more than seeing what you want to do already done in an example. And there are plenty of examples available for you. For instance, a very simple example showing how to get started with Ajax is available at

```
www.openajax.net/wordpress/simple-ajax
```

You can find two of the best lists of Ajax examples at these URLs:

- ✔ The fiftyfoureleven.com list of Ajax examples is at

```
www.fiftyfoureleven.com/resources/programming/xmlhttprequest/examples
```

- ✔ Ajax Pattern's list of examples is at

```
http://ajaxpatterns.org/Ajax_Examples
```

Ajax Tutorials

There are a number of Ajax tutorials available on the Internet, but most of them deal with using specific Ajax-enabled frameworks, such as Ruby on Rails. Here are some good general-purpose Ajax tutorials not tied to a specific framework:

- ✔ A "30-second" Ajax tutorial

```
http://marc.theaimsgroup.com/?l=php-general&m=112198633625636&w=2
```

- ✔ This tutorial uses PHP:

```
www.phpbuilder.com/columns/kassemi20050606.php3
```

- ✔ This tutorial builds a tree of nodes, whose text is downloaded as needed:

```
http://www.codeproject.com/aspnet/ajax_treeview.asp
```

Ajax Discussion Group

```
http://groups.google.com/group/ajax-world
```

If you're looking for interactive Ajax help, check out the active Google group discussion on Ajax.

This group is a good place to go to ask questions and receive answers about Ajax. No matter how complex the question, there's probably someone on this group that can offer a few suggestions.

More Depth on XMLHttpRequest

http://jibbering.com/2002/4/httprequest.html

Here's a site that has more information on how to use XMLHttpRequest objects and goes into more depth than the usual Ajax page.

You can find many sites that give you the Ajax basics, but sites like this one, which go deeper into the topic, are very useful when you're ready to move on from the preliminary discussions. This site includes how to use Head requests and much more.

Index

● **F** ●

Notes

Notes

Notes

Notes

Notes

Grant Writing

0-7645-5307-0

Home Buying 2nd Edition

0-7645-5331-3 *†

Also available:
- Accounting For Dummies †
  0-7645-5314-3
- Business Plans Kit For Dummies †
  0-7645-5365-8
- Cover Letters For Dummies
  0-7645-5224-4
- Frugal Living For Dummies
  0-7645-5403-4
- Leadership For Dummies
  0-7645-5176-0
- Managing For Dummies
  0-7645-1771-6

- Marketing For Dummies
  0-7645-5600-2
- Personal Finance For Dummies *
  0-7645-2590-5
- Project Management For Dummies
  0-7645-5283-X
- Resumes For Dummies †
  0-7645-5471-9
- Selling For Dummies
  0-7645-5363-1
- Small Business Kit For Dummies *†
  0-7645-5093-4

Windows XP

0-7645-4074-2

Microsoft Office Excel 2003 ALL-IN-ONE DESK REFERENCE

0-7645-3758-X

Also available:
- ACT! 6 For Dummies
  0-7645-2645-6
- iLife '04 All-in-One Desk Reference
  For Dummies
  0-7645-7347-0
- iPAQ For Dummies
  0-7645-6769-1
- Mac OS X Panther Timesaving
  Techniques For Dummies
  0-7645-5812-9
- Macs For Dummies
  0-7645-5656-8

- Microsoft Money 2004 For Dummies
  0-7645-4195-1
- Office 2003 All-in-One Desk Reference
  For Dummies
  0-7645-3883-7
- Outlook 2003 For Dummies
  0-7645-3759-8
- PCs For Dummies
  0-7645-4074-2
- TiVo For Dummies
  0-7645-6923-6
- Upgrading and Fixing PCs For Dummies
  0-7645-1665-5
- Windows XP Timesaving Techniques
  For Dummies
  0-7645-3748-2

Feng Shui

0-7645-5295-3

Poker

0-7645-5232-5

Also available:
- Bass Guitar For Dummies
  0-7645-2487-9
- Diabetes Cookbook For Dummies
  0-7645-5230-9
- Gardening For Dummies *
  0-7645-5130-2
- Guitar For Dummies
  0-7645-5106-X
- Holiday Decorating For Dummies
  0-7645-2570-0
- Home Improvement All-in-One
  For Dummies
  0-7645-5680-0

- Knitting For Dummies
  0-7645-5395-X
- Piano For Dummies
  0-7645-5105-1
- Puppies For Dummies
  0-7645-5255-4
- Scrapbooking For Dummies
  0-7645-7208-3
- Senior Dogs For Dummies
  0-7645-5818-8
- Singing For Dummies
  0-7645-2475-5
- 30-Minute Meals For Dummies
  0-7645-2589-1

Digital Photography

0-7645-1664-7

Starting an eBay Business 2nd Edition

0-7645-6924-4

Also available:
- 2005 Online Shopping Directory
  For Dummies
  0-7645-7495-7
- CD & DVD Recording For Dummies
  0-7645-5956-7
- eBay For Dummies
  0-7645-5654-1
- Fighting Spam For Dummies
  0-7645-5965-6
- Genealogy Online For Dummies
  0-7645-5964-8
- Google For Dummies
  0-7645-4420-9

- Home Recording For Musicians
  For Dummies
  0-7645-1634-5
- The Internet For Dummies
  0-7645-4173-0
- iPod & iTunes For Dummies
  0-7645-7772-7
- Preventing Identity Theft For Dummies
  0-7645-7336-5
- Pro Tools All-in-One Desk Reference
  For Dummies
  0-7645-5714-9
- Roxio Easy Media Creator For Dummies
  0-7645-7131-1

SPORTS, FITNESS, PARENTING, RELIGION & SPIRITUALITY

0-7645-5146-9

0-7645-5418-2

Also available:
- Adoption For Dummies
  0-7645-5488-3
- Basketball For Dummies
  0-7645-5248-1
- The Bible For Dummies
  0-7645-5296-1
- Buddhism For Dummies
  0-7645-5359-3
- Catholicism For Dummies
  0-7645-5391-7
- Hockey For Dummies
  0-7645-5228-7

- Judaism For Dummies
  0-7645-5299-6
- Martial Arts For Dummies
  0-7645-5358-5
- Pilates For Dummies
  0-7645-5397-6
- Religion For Dummies
  0-7645-5264-3
- Teaching Kids to Read For Dummies
  0-7645-4043-2
- Weight Training For Dummies
  0-7645-5168-X
- Yoga For Dummies
  0-7645-5117-5

TRAVEL

0-7645-5438-7

0-7645-5453-0

Also available:
- Alaska For Dummies
  0-7645-1761-9
- Arizona For Dummies
  0-7645-6938-4
- Cancún and the Yucatán For Dummies
  0-7645-2437-2
- Cruise Vacations For Dummies
  0-7645-6941-4
- Europe For Dummies
  0-7645-5456-5
- Ireland For Dummies
  0-7645-5455-7

- Las Vegas For Dummies
  0-7645-5448-4
- London For Dummies
  0-7645-4277-X
- New York City For Dummies
  0-7645-6945-7
- Paris For Dummies
  0-7645-5494-8
- RV Vacations For Dummies
  0-7645-5443-3
- Walt Disney World & Orlando For Dummies
  0-7645-6943-0

GRAPHICS, DESIGN & WEB DEVELOPMENT

0-7645-4345-8

0-7645-5589-8

Also available:
- Adobe Acrobat 6 PDF For Dummies
  0-7645-3760-1
- Building a Web Site For Dummies
  0-7645-7144-3
- Dreamweaver MX 2004 For Dummies
  0-7645-4342-3
- FrontPage 2003 For Dummies
  0-7645-3882-9
- HTML 4 For Dummies
  0-7645-1995-6
- Illustrator CS For Dummies
  0-7645-4084-X

- Macromedia Flash MX 2004 For Dummies
  0-7645-4358-X
- Photoshop 7 All-in-One Desk Reference For Dummies
  0-7645-1667-1
- Photoshop CS Timesaving Techniques For Dummies
  0-7645-6782-9
- PHP 5 For Dummies
  0-7645-4166-8
- PowerPoint 2003 For Dummies
  0-7645-3908-6
- QuarkXPress 6 For Dummies
  0-7645-2593-X

NETWORKING, SECURITY, PROGRAMMING & DATABASES

0-7645-6852-3

0-7645-5784-X

Also available:
- A+ Certification For Dummies
  0-7645-4187-0
- Access 2003 All-in-One Desk Reference For Dummies
  0-7645-3988-4
- Beginning Programming For Dummies
  0-7645-4997-9
- C For Dummies
  0-7645-7068-4
- Firewalls For Dummies
  0-7645-4048-3
- Home Networking For Dummies
  0-7645-42796

- Network Security For Dummies
  0-7645-1679-5
- Networking For Dummies
  0-7645-1677-9
- TCP/IP For Dummies
  0-7645-1760-0
- VBA For Dummies
  0-7645-3989-2
- Wireless All In-One Desk Reference For Dummies
  0-7645-7496-5
- Wireless Home Networking For Dummies
  0-7645-3910-8

0-7645-6820-5 *†   0-7645-2566-2

Also available:
- Alzheimer's For Dummies
  0-7645-3899-3
- Asthma For Dummies
  0-7645-4233-8
- Controlling Cholesterol For Dummies
  0-7645-5440-9
- Depression For Dummies
  0-7645-3900-0
- Dieting For Dummies
  0-7645-4149-8
- Fertility For Dummies
  0-7645-2549-2

- Fibromyalgia For Dummies
  0-7645-5441-7
- Improving Your Memory For Dummies
  0-7645-5435-2
- Pregnancy For Dummies †
  0-7645-4483-7
- Quitting Smoking For Dummies
  0-7645-2629-4
- Relationships For Dummies
  0-7645-5384-4
- Thyroid For Dummies
  0-7645-5385-2

UCATION, HISTORY, REFERENCE & TEST PREPARATION

0-7645-5194-9   0-7645-4186-2

Also available:
- Algebra For Dummies
  0-7645-5325-9
- British History For Dummies
  0-7645-7021-8
- Calculus For Dummies
  0-7645-2498-4
- English Grammar For Dummies
  0-7645-5322-4
- Forensics For Dummies
  0-7645-5580-4
- The GMAT For Dummies
  0-7645-5251-1
- Inglés Para Dummies
  0-7645-5427-1

- Italian For Dummies
  0-7645-5196-5
- Latin For Dummies
  0-7645-5431-X
- Lewis & Clark For Dummies
  0-7645-2545-X
- Research Papers For Dummies
  0-7645-5426-3
- The SAT I For Dummies
  0-7645-7193-1
- Science Fair Projects For Dummies
  0-7645-5460-3
- U.S. History For Dummies
  0-7645-5249-X

Get smart @ dummies.com®

- **Find a full list of Dummies titles**
- **Look into loads of FREE on-site articles**
- **Sign up for FREE eTips e-mailed to you weekly**
- **See what other products carry the Dummies name**
- **Shop directly from the Dummies bookstore**
- **Enter to win new prizes every month!**

parate Canadian edition also available
parate U.K. edition also available

able wherever books are sold. For more information or to order direct: U.S. customers visit www.dummies.com or call 1-877-762-2974.
customers visit www.wileyeurope.com or call 0800 243407. Canadian customers visit www.wiley.ca or call 1-800-567-4797.